THE FIRE THIS TIME

EDITED BY VIVIEN LABATON AND DAWN LUNDY MARTIN

Vivien Labaton is a third-year law student at New York University School of Law. She was the founding director of the Third Wave Foundation, the only national young feminist organization in the country, and currently serves on the boards of Third Wave, Political Research Associates, and the Women's Funding Network. She lives in Brooklyn, New York.

Dawn Lundy Martin is one of the four cofounders of the Third Wave Foundation. She has a long history of activism in antiwar, queer rights, and environmental justice movements. A Ph.D. candidate in English at the University of Massachusetts in Amherst, she is also an award-winning poet and author of the chapbook *The Morning Hour*. She lives in Northampton, Massachusetts.

THE FIRE THIS TIME

THE FIRE THIS TIME

YOUNG ACTIVISTS AND THE NEW FEMINISM

Edited by

Vivien Labaton and Dawn Lundy Martin

Foreword by Rebecca Walker

Coda by Wilma Mankiller

ANCHOR BOOKS

A Division of Random House, Inc.

New York

AN ANCHOR BOOKS ORIGINAL, MAY 2004

Copyright © 2004 by Vivien Labaton and Dawn Lundy Martin

All rights reserved under International and Pan-American
Copyright Conventions. Published in the United States by Anchor Books,
a division of Random House, Inc., New York, and
simultaneously in Canada by Random House of
Canada Limited, Toronto.

Anchor Books and colophon are registered trademarks
of Random House, Inc.

Library of Congress Cataloging-in-Publication Data
The fire this time : young feminists and the new activism / edited by Vivien Labaton
and Dawn Lundy Martin ; foreword by Rebecca Walker.
p. cm.
Includes bibliographical references.
ISBN 0-385-72102-1 (trade pbk.)
1. Feminism.   2. Feminist theory.   3. Women political activists.
I. Labaton, Vivien.   II. Martin, Dawn Lundy.
HQ1111.F47 2004
305.42—dc22   2003063675

Book design by JoAnne Metsch

www.anchorbooks.com

Printed in the United States of America
10 9 8 7 6 5 4 3 2 1

To the activists

CONTENTS

Foreword: We Are Using This Power to Resist   xi
REBECCA WALKER

Introduction: Making What Will Become   xxi
VIVIEN LABATON AND DAWN LUNDY MARTIN

PART I CHANGING MINDS AND EYES: MEDIA
AND CULTURE

Claiming Jezebel: Black Female Subjectivity and Sexual   3
Expression in Hip-Hop
AYANA BYRD

An Independent Media Center of One's Own: 19
A Feminist Alternative to Corporate Media
JOSHUA BREITBART AND ANA NOGUEIRA

Cut-and-Paste Revolution: Notes from the Girl   42
Zine Explosion
JENNIFER BLEYER

Can You Rock It Like This? Theater for a New Century   61
HOLLY BASS

The New Girls Network: Women, Technology,   84
and Feminism
SHIREEN LEE

PART II NEW ACTIVISM IN THE GLOBAL CITY

Exporting Violence: The School of the Americas,   107
U.S. Intervention in Latin America, and Resistance
KATHRYN TEMPLE

Domestic Workers Organize in the Global City   150
AI-JEN POO AND ERIC TANG

A Baptism by Fire: Vieques, Puerto Rico   166
ELISHA MARÍA MIRANDA

When Transgendered People Sue and Win: Feminist   181
Reflections on Strategy, Activism, and the Legal Process
ANNA KIRKLAND

Bearing the Blame: Gender, Immigration,   220
Reproduction, and the Environment
SYD LINDSLEY

She Who Believes in Freedom: Young Women Defy   254
the Prison Industrial Complex
ROBIN TEMPLETON

Afterword   279
Looking Ahead: Building a Feminist Future
VIVIEN LABATON AND DAWN LUNDY MARTIN

Coda   291
WILMA MANKILLER

Recommended Organizations   295
Notes   315
Acknowledgments   345

FOREWORD: WE ARE USING THIS POWER TO RESIST

Rebecca Walker

> Life is plurality, death is uniformity.
> —*Octavio Paz*

I

I have been waiting twelve years for this book.

Imagine. It's 1992, and I am a graduating senior at Yale University, the school my mother warned me about. I have spent much of my time there protesting: the university's investment in South Africa under apartheid, the paucity of students and faculty of color, the racist-sexist-classist-homophobic characterization and content of my courses. I have attended speakouts against date rape and sexual harassment and for the creation of a teachers' union, and sat on the founding board of the first paper to bring together voices from the Asian and Asian-American, African and African-American, Native American, Puerto Rican, and Mexican-American communities under the controversial new term "people of color." For two years I have been directing a documentary on these same "people of color," looking at socioeconomic and ideological diversity among allegedly monolithic communities. When I am not reading queer theorists like Judith Butler (fluidity and performative aspects of gender and sexuality) and cultural critics like Michel Foucault (hegemony and the language of power), or studying with bell hooks (the white supremacist capitalist patriarchy), I am waiting in line to hear the Dalai Lama. When I am not reading Paolo Freire (*Pedagogy of the Oppressed*) and Thich Nhat Hanh (*Peace Is Every Step*), I am being dismissed from lecture halls for asking world-renowned professors why their classes are called The History of Art and not The History of White Western Male Art, and why African women are viciously murdered in so many "postcolonial" texts. When I am not reading Audre Lorde (*Sister Outsider*) and Trinh T. Minh-ha (*Woman, Native, Other*), I am talking with brilliant young black female poets who speak of suicide, and soulful Lebanese philosophers who speak angrily and with great longing of Beirut before the invasion.

Outside my ivory tower, rampant police brutality has been captured on home video (LAPD versus Rodney King), Bush I has signed legislation which continues to erode access to reproductive choice to all but the well-heeled and urban (the gag rule, twenty-four-hour notification, and parental consent laws), AIDS deaths mount while the acronym never crosses the administration's lips, and environmental racism perpetuates the dumping of runoff toxins from power plants and factories into poor urban and rural communities around the country. Though it is pre-NAFTA, pre-GATT, and pre-WTO, there are still plenty of international abominations in play—

the invasion and interminable bombing of Iraq, for example, and the burgeoning number of women laboring under intolerable conditions at the *maquiladoras,* for another.

Even though almost everyone I know is involved in some form of social change work, from teaching after-school programs for disadvantaged kids to building houses for poor people in inner cities and starting "cheap art" revolutions à la the Guerrilla Girls, the media scream incessantly that ours is the most apathetic and least politicized of any known generation. Feminism is dead, the civil rights movement is not happening, communism is taking its last gasp, and educated twenty-somethings, traditionally the most radical of all demographics, are apparently content to sit back and reap the benefits of our parents' world-changing labor. While some young activists are able to use this distinction to their advantage, incorporating the need to contradict the media into their mission statements, the public hears that the racist, capitalist status quo is acceptable: even the youth have acquiesced.

While my community includes queer-fabulous Chicanos and ACT UP–affiliated lipstick lesbians, budding black revolutionaries and brilliant baby art stars, neo-utopian Marxist bohemians and well-meaning trust-fund recluses, sensuously defiant womanists and politicized Muslim academics, it seems a rare event to see any of these individuals breaking rank and communicating meaningfully with one another. I certainly never see this happening within the walls of the campus Women's Center, and it's not because I haven't looked. I enter this cramped home of Feminism on the Old Campus once as a freshman and once again as a sophomore, both times looking for resonance and both times finding only the now-too-often cited group of well-off white women, organizing Take Back the Night marches and lectures on eating disorders, neither of which, in the face of all that is going on, manages to capture my imagination.

I am not alone in my assessment that capital *F* Feminism needs an overhaul. By 1992 Feminism has been roundly critiqued by the majority of the world's women, including but not limited to indigenous women, Third World women, American women of color, and working-class women. Even among the privileged and/or converted, there is a resistance to identifying with its rebel yell. Sure, there are those "I am not a feminist but . . . " girls who don't have a clue, but then there are the rest of us, who are feminist but not Feminists. We came to our radical consciousness in the heady postmodern matrix of womanist texts, queer culture, postcolonialist discourse, Buddhism, direct action, sex positivity, and so much more. We are intimate with racist feminists, sexist postcolonialists, and theorists who are so far removed from the street they can't organize their own wallets, let alone a rally. We find that the nexuses of power and identity are constantly shifting, and so are we. We find that labels which seek to categorize and define are historical constructs often used as tools of oppression. We find that many of our potential allies in resistance movements do feminism but do not, intuitively, embrace Feminism.

In the context of all this, to call oneself a Feminist without a major disclaimer seems not only reductive but counterproductive. While this complexity makes for meetings full of fervor and supreme sensitivity to differences of all kinds, it also leaves many of us at the forefront of a movement with no name.

II

Shannon Liss, a young organizer of the Anita Hill conference in New York City, reads an article I have written in *Ms.* magazine titled "Becoming the Third Wave" and telephones me in New Haven to ask if I might be interested in doing something together. In fact, I have been trying to figure out how to organize the two hundred or so young women from around the country who have written me passionate letters echoing my sentiments that "I am not a post-feminism feminist, I am the third wave." To what organization can I refer them? What books can I suggest they read? The book that you are holding in your hands did not exist. There are no articles in *Ms.* magazine about young women doing brave new things. There is not yet a W.E.R.I.S.E., a Black Grrrl Movement, a Shakti, a Third Wave Foundation, an Active Element Foundation. There has not been a "Just do it" Nike campaign for women, an Urban Outfitters chain catering to the earthy, funky DIY young woman, and no WTO protests flying in the face of both. There has been no twenty-something-year-old Julia Butterfly Hill living in a tree for a year to protect it from loggers and then writing a best-selling memoir about the experience. There is no WNBA. Politicians are not trying to win our vote on MTV. There is bell hooks, Queen Latifah, Susie Bright, and the Indigo Girls, but there is no Erykah Badu, no India.Arie, no Ani DiFranco, no asha bandele, no La Bruja on Def Jam Poetry Slam.

In our first of many marathon conversations, Shannon brings her organizing acumen and knowledge of the "Gen X" activism she sees in New York and contextualizes the article and its response within something larger. I bring all of my frustration with identity politics, all of my desires to do social change work that is vibrant and creative and not prone to divisive infighting. Three or four estrogen-packed, burrito-and-margarita-filled meetings later, we decide to found a direct action organization devoted to cultivating young women's leadership and activism in order to bring the power of young women to bear on politics as usual. We want to flex the muscle of young women's might, to make it visible not just to the media and the progressive left but also to the older female activists whose lives have so profoundly shaped our own.

From our first conversation we know that Third Wave Direct Action Corporation will be multiracial, multicultural and multi-issue. It will consist of people of varying abilities and sexual preferences. It will include men. We hope it will be international. While we have strong opinions about what issues we want to begin to work around, we believe strongly that young women and men will articulate their own concerns, and that it is not our job to decide which are worthy of being included. Our job is to support young activists in whatever ways we can, by connecting them to resources, tools, or most important, one another. The young woman who wants to organize against sweatshop labor or homophobia or toxic dumping in her backyard can call and be connected to other young women with similar foci; groups of young women and men can start chapters (independently acting cells), which can be mobilized for a product boycott, an action, a support group. Because we believe that change is also internal, we plan to initiate projects that bring people of different backgrounds and perspectives together; participants will unite around a common agenda, work-ing interpersonally through issues of difference in the process and learning how to build communities based on mutual respect and understanding.

We pride ourselves on being utopic but also pragmatic. We want to extend the parameters of the "feminist" community and include even those who do not identify with Feminism, and so we make a conscious decision to avoid the use of the word in our mission statement, press releases, and other organizing materi-als, choosing instead to use "young women's empowerment." We want to be linked with our foremothers and centuries of women's movement, but we also want to make space for young women to create their own, different brand of revolt, and so we choose the name Third Wave. We don't want to be exploited in the name of social change, and so we vow to factor salaries for ourselves into our budgets and call ourselves a corporation. We do not want to be marginalized as we have seen so many activist groups become, and so we vow, too, to be unafraid of both large sums of money and the media, and aggressively seek both out, determined to market our empowerment message.

I speak of marketing social change, and actually feel hope-ful when young advertising executives show up at my talks armed with yellow legal pads. They peer at my seemingly incongruous work boots and short dresses, my suit jackets and long dreadlocks, and ask me questions about how young women want to see themselves in the media. I am young and naïve enough to believe that these smart and fresh-faced white women are only on our side, and that by marketing us to our-selves they will help young woman–power of all kinds to grow.

III

What I don't know then, and what I would have known if this book had come out in 1992 and not 2004, is that even though there is no Us and Them, and we need to move beyond binarism and labels and to have compassion for all, including the heads of heinous multinational corporations and the executives at the IMF, the truth is that there is a clear line in the sand. That line is global hypercapitalism, that line is greed, that line is human exploitation, that line is the utter disregard for the delicate balance of the earth. Either you believe that the system that assures 50 percent of the world's resources for 6 percent of its population by any and all means necessary is leading us to annihilation one cancer case at a time, or you do not. Whether or not you are able to act in opposition to this reality in every instance is beside the point. Do you see it?

What I don't understand in 1992 and what I would have if this book had existed is that it is this line that separates a system designed to colonize and homogenize from one that seeks to honor and cultivate the diversity that is our birthright as human beings. Those of us who dare, toil not to force our way upon others but simply to make a space in which all are honored: capitalism and communalism, the patriarch and the matriarch, the exiled settler and the indigenous nomad, and so on. It is this imperative for true pluralism that runs through and connects, however tenuously, all of our different activisms, all of our different feminisms. It is this place where we all may rest that snakes through our dreams. We can barely imagine now what this world fueled by real right to self-determination will look like, and yet we know it must be born. As we belong to it, this planet must belong to all of us.

While I believe that Shannon and I were right about some things—decentralized, multifront, multilingual, and multi-aesthetic movement for one, and working with men and families for another—we were wrong about some other things, like the very real risk of our own complacency, our own tendency to get more cynical and pessimistic with age, more removed from the cultural and political work there is to be done instead of more radical. I think that we were right about pushing our sensibility and ideas into the marketplace of the mainstream but we were shortsighted in that we did not anticipate that young women and men would think buying books or magazines, or supporting films and fashion that reflected their diverse beauty and beliefs, could replace the many important struggles still to be waged against an unjust system. And finally, while we were right to found an organization, we had no idea just how much effort and endurance was necessary to build an institution, let alone a movement.

Third Wave Direct Action had a fairly successful run spearheading projects, building a national network, and raising awareness about the existence of some incredible young women. Ultimately, however, then-Chairwoman of the Board Amy Richards and I decided to reenvision its original scope and with the cofounders Catherine Gund and Dawn Lundy Martin, one of the editors of this book, to throw ourselves into the Third Wave Foundation, the only national, activist, philanthropic organization serving women aged fifteen to thirty. In other words, we realized we had to get out of the business of direct action and into the business of redistributing wealth, of moving it from one side of the line to the other. We had to get real about what was essential and what we, a group of privileged, educated women born and raised in the United States, could provide.

And yet, I cannot adequately describe here the tremendous pride and gratitude I feel in the knowledge that our dreams for revitalized, multipronged movement are being realized. Whether the work described in these pages is called third wave, young feminism, hip-hop womanism, humanist global activism, or anything else matters very little. What matters is that this work is being done by women and men from various communities who slowly, step by step, find themselves working alongside those who previously may have been seen only as Other. The editors and writers here have done an excellent job refocusing our attention, reframing the debate, and forging even more space for the potential coming together of our ever-widening revolutionary community.

I have been waiting for this book for twelve years because, finally, it articulates what I have known and believed all along: there is a fire this time, burning, and it cannot, will not, go out, because that would mean the end of life as we know it. And we, those of us who love this planet and one another, are not yet ready to let that happen.

Berkeley, California

INTRODUCTION: MAKING WHAT WILL BECOME

Vivien Labaton
and Dawn Lundy Martin

What Wave?

During the course of our work with the Third Wave Foundation—a national organization that supports young feminists who are doing progressive activism around the country—we are frequently asked by the media, older activists, philanthropic organizations, and others where the next generation of feminist movers and shakers is, what we care about, and whether or not we embody the Generation X myth of apathetic, apolitical slackers that was created for us to live up (or down) to. People wonder who is carrying on the legacy of the women's movement, and they look to the same old haunts to find the answers. The problem is, they are looking in the wrong places.

Young feminists in large numbers—both women and men—are doing social justice work all over the country. They are moved to action by social and economic injustice, the growing divide between rich and poor, contemporary manifestations of colonialism, the rapid growth of the prison industrial complex, and the deterioration of democracy. They are protesting free trade at meetings of the World Bank, the World Trade Organization, and the International Monetary Fund, in Genoa, Washington, D.C., Quebec City, and other cities all over the world. They are creating independent media that reach people on almost every continent with fresh, corporation-free news. They are creating youth-run organizations that address issues as far-ranging but interconnected as immigration, welfare, education, and queer rights.[1] Growing pockets of young feminist activism across the country (and the world) are building steam with renewed vigor and a broadened vision.

In 1996, though, the landscape of feminist activism looked very different. Both of us felt uncertain about whether we were relevant to any sort of feminist activity; we weren't sure if the feminist movement wanted us, or if we wanted it. As Dawn remembers that time:

When I was twenty-five I felt cast out of feminism. Back then, feminism seemed like a physical place, a destination—as in: Last year, I went to feminism, and then I left. My perception was that it was a place for a certain kind of professionalized older activist whom I couldn't relate to. A young, queer, African-American woman, I hunkered down in the progressive feminist-lesbian organization where I worked, and dreamed of something better. Ironically, I was, I believe now, at the very height of my political idealism— more ready than ever to get sweaty for a cause. Yet I didn't feel like an activist at all. I felt mostly like a paper pusher, a utilitarian arm in a vast but indifferent machine. I had friends just like me. They had taken "assistant" or "associate" positions at traditional feminist organizations but felt, in the end, that the movement, whose philosophies had literally changed their lives, neither wanted nor needed them.

Vivien had just graduated from college and was looking for a job. She recalls:

I was looking for a job that reflected my political perspectives and the range of issues that I was passionate about. What I found instead was that I was forced to pick. I could work at an organization that dealt with abortion rights or I could work at an organization that dealt with racial and economic justice, but I could not do both. Yet I found it impossible to think about abortion rights without thinking about racial and economic justice. It was like being forced to think about my index finger without thinking about my thumb, or my whole hand. I began to believe that we needed a more comprehensive feminism.

Then Dawn and three other young activists—filmmaker Catherine Gund and writers Amy Richards and Rebecca Walker—decided to create an organization that reflected our feminist sensibilities, the Third Wave Foundation. For us, "third wave" feminism simply meant young women and men doing social justice work while using a gender lens. We didn't have any complicated theories about how the third wave differed from previous feminist uprisings. Yet we were aware of the impact we might have on reinventing feminism for future generations of young people who, like us, had at times been burdened by popular misconceptions about the feminist movement.

This reinvention would be both cosmetic and substantive. We wanted to put new faces on the feminist movement. We wanted to make it hot, sexy, and newly revolutionary. No more women's symbol with a fist through the circle, no more recycled-looking mauve paper, and no more images of women who looked nothing like us. Feminism needed an elective surgery—a face-lift, a remodeling—but it also needed an ideological expansion so that it could be more pertinent to contemporary realities and attractive to younger activists. Yes, we were interested in helping to obliterate media-constructed perceptions of feminism (a militant, irrelevant sect of man-hating dykes), but most of all, we wanted a movement that addressed our races, sexualities, genders, and classes. It would be untrue to suggest that we have achieved all of our lofty goals (few would describe feminism as "sexy"), but we did succeed in carving out a space for a diverse group of younger feminists. They have joined the ongoing dialogue about gender equality and are beginning to revise our definitions of what it means to be a feminist. Is this what it means to be "third wave"?

There have been several efforts to describe what third wave feminism is. Rebecca Walker's 1995 collection of essays *To Be Real: Telling the Truth and Changing the Face of Feminism* "wanted to explore the ways that choices or actions seemingly at odds with mainstream ideas of feminism push us to new definitions and understandings of female empowerment and social change."[2] *Listen Up: Voices from the Next Feminist Generation* (1995), edited by Barbara Findlen, focuses on events of our time and place and how they have shaped young feminist perceptions. The academic collection edited by Leslie Heywood and Jennifer Drake, *Third Wave Agenda* (1997), stakes out a different territory, presenting a "generational per-spective, gathering voices of young activists struggling to come to terms with the historical specificity of our feminisms and with the times in which we came of age (the late 1970s through the late 1980s)."[3] Most recently, *Manifesta,* by Jennifer Baumgardner and Amy Richards, attempts to communicate to a new generation of young women the power and possibility of feminism while simultaneously critiquing the old guard's inability to involve young women in the movement. All of these works suggest what it might mean to have another wave of feminism sweep through and *shake shit up,* this one built by that generation of feminist activists born after 1965.

For the most part, however, third wave feminism has been articulated as a generational difference—a reaction against perceptions about feminists that have permeated society, not the movement itself. Many young women's reservations about belonging to the feminist movement are due not to ideologi-cal differences but to misconceptions about feminists—that they are separatists, that they are unfashionable, that they burn bras and have lots of cats. Some progressive political young women even shun the term *feminist* as a way to describe their belief systems. Young feminists have shed the media-espoused propaganda about feminists but have taken to heart the criticism from women of color that the second wave was not racially or sexually inclusive enough. The addition of the *third wave* in front of the term *feminism,* for them, is a recla-mation—a way to be feminist with a notable difference.

One of the luxuries that our generation has enjoyed is that we've reaped the benefits of all the social justice movements that have come before us; we have come of age in a world that has been shaped by feminism, queer liberation movements, antiracist movements, labor movements, and others. Consequently, many young women and men not only have an understanding of the interconnection of social justice issues but also see them as inextricable from one another.

In 1990 the legal scholar Angela P. Harris wrote, "As feminists begin to attack racism and classism and homophobia, feminism will change from being only about 'women as women' . . . to being about all kinds of oppressions based on seemingly inherent and unalterable characteristics. We need not wait for a unified theory of oppression; that theory can be feminism."[4] Now, in 2004, feminist practices are fulfilling this prediction. By blowing open the idea that class, race, sexuality, and gender are singular entities that exist independently of one another, *The Fire This Time* provides a framework for looking at various tendencies toward domination. In this context, feminism offers a central belief system that helps interpret how power imbalances affect our lives. To demand that people focus on one area of concern without recognizing the interconnection of multiple issues would be to demand a level of self-abnegation that does not mirror the way these issues are experienced in our daily lives.

Indeed, young women and men are doing multi-issue work that embodies and reflects the many complications of our global world. If we want to build a feminist world, we must look not only at reproductive rights and equal pay for equal work, but also at the working conditions of women who labor in sweatshops; we must battle sex trafficking as well as the global economic policies that have made sex trafficking a thriving industry and a normative part of the move toward a borderless economy. The feminism that emerges in *The Fire This Time* shows that there are few issues beyond the movement's reach. It may not be possible to identify a third wave, but we do know that feminist women and men, most thirty-five and under, are making feminism do more work.

Breaking Ranks

Those issues that have traditionally been associated with the feminist movement—reproductive rights, domestic violence, date rape, and equal pay for equal work—are not the only issues that should define it. This is not to suggest, however, that a new set of feminist issues is supplanting the old. Sweatshop labor and police brutality are not new, and the defense of reproductive rights is certainly as necessary as ever. Archetypal feminist issues have been important to women worldwide— and essential to the lives of many of the writers included in this collection. They continue to require our devotion. But we should not become so distracted by the core issues that we neglect other social justice concerns. The borders of feminism need to be split open, both so that we are freed from ideological rigidity and so that other identity claims of race, sexuality, class, nationality, and geography can move beyond being simply "tolerated" or "included."

Our feminism has roots in past feminist work. Revolutionary writers like Gloria Anzaldúa, Audre Lorde, Cherríe Moraga, Barbara Smith, and other United States Third World feminists have described the intersection of race, sexuality, and gender, and the many ways that these multiple and overlapping identities interact. Similarly, the plan of action that came out of the landmark 1977 Houston Women's Conference, which convened to develop a national agenda for women, focused on many issues, including immigrant rights, Native American rights, lesbian rights, health care, and employment.

Yet the prevailing understanding of feminism has placed a select few issues at the center of what is thought of as feminist activism, neglecting the full range of experiences that inform women's lives. Indeed, one of the major criticisms of mainstream second wave feminism was its inattentiveness to racial, cultural, sexual, and national differences. In this view, feminism found its strength in putting the concerns of First World white women first and framing them as universal, often at the expense of people of color. As Kum-Kum Bhavnani points out, "The 'sisterhood is global' discourse denied [women of color] the space to assert our differences from white women and masked the power inequalities present within women's movements."[5]

In 1979, when Audre Lorde gave her seminal paper "The Master's Tools Will Never Dismantle the Master's House," at the Second Sex Conference, she chastised organizers for ignoring "Black and Third World women and lesbians." She asked bitingly, "What does it mean when the tools of a racist patriarchy are used to examine the fruits of that same patriarchy?"[6] From their position of marginality, second wave feminists of color and queer feminists formed a critique of the movement and forced the women's movement to include women of color and lesbians in their ranks.

That there is a diversity of women sitting around the decision-making table is progress, but if there is little modification in the selection of issues worthy of feminist concern, then the fact of diversity is moot. *Diversity* has become a popular word, a word so tacitly politically correct that it has lost much of its meaning. It often closes off possibilities rather than opening them up. "We need to diversify our office" means we don't have enough "women," "people of color," "gays and lesbians," "differently-abled," et cetera. Inclusion in this light barely challenges the racist, sexist, homophobic, ability-centric, societal norms. Instead, it reiterates them. Hiring a black or gay worker is something that helps organizations and businesses legitimize their commitment to our friend diversity. Organizations can broaden their appeal [read: get more donations], and businesses can better market their products to the "increasing numbers of Latina/os" and the "growing black middle class." This is not to say that even this kind of diversity should end, but as a culture we must move beyond superficial inclusions.

The feminism of younger activists goes beyond the rhetoric of inclusion. The most significant lesson that we have learned from the second wave's faux pas is that a feminist movement cannot succeed if it does not challenge power structures of wealth and race. If the model within which one works centralizes whiteness and/or wealth, the poorest and most victimized women in the world will be overlooked. This concentration on "traditional" women's rights often obscures the importance of the complex network of gendered injustices that we bring to the foreground in *The Fire This Time*. In other words, we see a new movement evolving from one in which there is a dialogue *about* feminism and race to a feminist movement whose conversation *is* race, gender, and globalization.

No Labels, Just Work

Although increasingly young feminists are carving out their own spaces for action (like the Center for Young Women's Development in San Francisco), creating their own organizations (like Sista II Sista in Brooklyn, New York), and defining feminism in their own ways, often our work takes place in organizations that allow broader social justice work to be contextualized as feminist. To notice the next wave of feminism (or however one chooses to label it), one has to look far beyond the National Organization for Women (NOW), the Feminist Majority, or the National Abortion Rights Action League (NARAL). Feminists in their twenties and thirties can also be found at the CAAAV: Organizing Asian Communities, Critical Resistance, and the Center for Third World Organizing; at Internet start-ups and in magazine and book publishing; at bachelorette parties, Gay Pride parades, and vacationing in the Hamptons; in rap music, in independent media, working at fast-food restaurants and on college campuses. From these sites and many more, cutting-edge feminist critiques, analyses, and activisms are expanding the depth and breadth of today's movement.

The essays in *The Fire This Time* show how a generation of activists is developing feminist responses to contemporary social and political problems. Some of us boldly claim the term *feminist;* some of us embrace Alice Walker's term *womanist,* which "is to feminist as purple is to lavender";[7] and the not-so-secret truth is, some of us choose not to claim any term at all. And although the narrative we've constructed here is not about what a feminist looks like or what credentials a feminist needs to have, it *is* about pressing hard on the surface of the movement so that a kind of fracture erupts, allowing more young women and men to claim feminism as a framework not just for activism but for living. What some may see as a detrimental fragmentation within the feminist movement, we understand to be a place of power.

If we were to build a feminist movement made up primarily of "feminists" between the ages of eighteen and thirty-five, we would find no single ideological framework from which their activisms emerge. In fact, if we asked ten young feminists what feminism meant to them, we'd likely get ten different answers. We would find, instead, *linked* ideas that incorporate certain second wave feminist tenets: a movement that, like the collected voices in this book, is situated in discrete and multiple sites. Unlike second wave feminism, which has operated from a monolithic center, multiplicity offers the power of existing insidiously and simultaneously everywhere. "Woman" as a primary identity category has ceased to be the entry point for much young activist work. Instead, it has become one of the many investigatory means used to affect an indefinite number of issues and cultural analyses. But this is only part of the story.

The real story takes place at the ground level, where young women and men are getting down and dirty on the front lines of the struggle for equality and justice. In the first section of this collection, media and popular culture activists use a feminist lens to unearth different truths about hip-hop music, corporate media, girl zines, new theater forms, and new technologies. In "Claiming Jezebel: Black Female Subjectivity and

Sexual Expression in Hip-Hop," Ayana Byrd provides a powerful critique of the female rap artist Lil' Kim's lyrics and persona, which reiterate mainstream assumptions about what it means to be a black woman. The question at the heart of this essay is whether Lil' Kim's use of stereotypical black female sexuality in performance is dangerous. Or is she playing with those long-held perceptions of black women in order to call attention to their falsity? Byrd complicates these issues by looking at them through her own consumption of hip-hop music. She wonders what it means that she is increasingly unable to engage in a "feminist" critique of how women are portrayed (and how women choose to portray themselves) in hip-hop culture. Because Lil' Kim asserts that she is indeed a feminist, this analysis raises critical questions about the fluid definitions of feminism in contemporary America.

Joshua Breitbart and Ana Nogueira, in "An Independent Media Center of One's Own: A Feminist Alternative to Corporate Media," show just how unbalanced reporting by the mainstream media can be. They argue that mainstream media hide behind First Amendment rights, which guarantee free speech, in order to be able to present biased versions of the truth. Often this truth favors the powerful and makes villains of the less so. Independent Media Centers, which have popped up all over the world, are do-it-yourself media outlets "for the people" where media-making is multivoiced and uninfluenced by corporate structures. Breitbart and Nogueira assert that these centers are powerful feminist models for media that is more representative of the populations whose issues get ignored by the mainstream media.

Yet Indymedia is certainly not the first (or the last) group of activists to speak to what can seem like a monolithic representation of what's going on in the world. Girl zines emerged in the United States during the 1980s to provide young women with a space to articulate their concerns. In part a response to women's magazines like *Vogue* and *Elle,* which circulate an unreachable ideal of the thin, big-busted woman, girl zines took advantage of new computer technologies and inexpensive photocopies to speak to young women who were uncomfortable with these stereotypes. As Jennifer Bleyer writes in her essay "Cut-and-Paste Revolution: Notes from the Girl Zine Explosion," these zines were "free speech on demand without apology." Like the Independent Media Centers that followed, girl zines were not just about selling magazines but were individual utterances within "a vast participatory conversation which everyone was expected to join."

Holly Bass, in "Can You Rock It Like This? Theater for a New Century," offers a critique of the male-dominated world of a new art form—hip-hop theater—that brings together spoken word, hip-hop culture, and traditional theater for audiences who might not otherwise find themselves experiencing the black box. Bass argues that hip-hop theater, like its predecessor, hip-hop music, portrays women in misogynistic ways just to "keep it real." Even in plays that are woman-directed and woman-produced, Bass notes, "the main protagonists are often male." For the gatekeepers of this burgeoning art form, even hip-hop theater stars such as Sarah Jones are not hip-hop enough because their sensibilities reflect the hard edge of urban life in a different way. Bass redefines notions of racial and gender authenticity in her essay and makes a case for broadening hip-hop theater's sometimes stifling categories.

In all of these essays, technological advances contribute to new discussions of media and popular culture that are particular to our historical moment. Shireen Lee's "The New Girls Network: Women, Technology, and Feminism" considers what it means to imagine a technological future. How technology is used is not the issue. Lee investigates the creation of technology itself as an opportunity of privilege. Although there are a few women who are innovators in technological fields, Lee reveals that the barriers to women's participation are more than exceptional; they are institutional. Feminist interventions in the high-tech sector, however, move beyond making money. Women in high tech are developing mentoring networks and creating socially conscious alternatives to the old boy networks.

In these investigations, we hope to show that a feminist future is not "either this or that" but "this *and* that." Although there are some stunning and unforeseen overlaps of concern, many contradictions emerge. This book is very much like the movement that Nogueira and Breitbart describe in their essay—instead of presenting our readers with our singular vision of what we think the future of feminism is, we present multiple (and sometimes opposing) voices that together constitute a new feminist possibility.

In the second section, "New Activism in the Global City," feminist concerns reach farther into uncharted territories. Kathryn Temple's "Crossing the Line: The School of the Americas, Globalization, and Resistance" exposes the military training camp for the terrorist breeding ground that it is. Although part of the stated mission of the School of the Americas (SOA) is to "promote democratic values and respect for human rights; and foster cooperation among multinational military forces," during the 1980s and '90s its graduates maimed, raped, and killed thousands of people in Latin America. Temple's provocative and moving piece portrays the workings of the SOA and its relationship to Latin American countries as analogous to domestic abuse. Looking through the lens of her experience as an activist, she demonstrates that American military and economic policy abroad is a central concern for feminist activism.

Similarly, "Domestic Workers Organize in the Global City" by Ai-jen Poo and Eric Tang shows how rapid globalization has driven Third World women from their home countries into the dangerous and underpaid field of domestic work. They call for a progressive feminist agenda that "takes into consideration race, gender, class, and sexuality." The global economy, particularly through free trade agreements, positions domestic workers as commodities, shipable across borders like so many cheap goods. Domestic workers in the United States fight their legislative and judicial disenfranchisement, the authors say, by "script[ing] different forms of citizenship and political participation." Poo and Tang's analysis gets to the root of the problem of disenfranchised domestic workers—primarily immigrant women—by uncovering a network of global economic strategies that place undue burdens on the Third World marketplace.

Economic globalization has been described as "a compression of the world through advances in technology and increased intensification of economic activities that are eroding the autonomy of states."[8] This contemporary imperialism is directly linked, in our view, to other invasive impulses, such as the U.S. military occupation of Vieques, Puerto Rico. In her autobiographical-critical interpretation "A Baptism by Fire: Vieques, Puerto Rico," Elisha María Miranda draws a precise parallel between the appropriation of Puerto Rican land and the occupation of the Puerto Rican female body. Miranda also shows how the contemporary fight to end the military occupation succeeded in gaining the support of American lawmakers, which has influenced the government's decision to end the bombing in Vieques. Her question now is: What will happen to the people of Vieques in the wake of decades of bombing and occupation?

Anna Kirkland explores the world of American jurisprudence as it pertains to transsexual claims for civil rights. In "When Transgendered People Sue and Win: Feminist Reflections on Strategy, Activism, and the Legal Process," Kirkland explains that transsexuals must enact gender "authentically" in order to succeed in their legal claims. Those who don't act like stereotypical women or men pay a heavy price in court for their transgressions. Using a range of cases as evidence, Kirkland carefully reveals how certain apparent legal victories are important for feminists because, although they result in seemingly benign reiterations of gender categories, they contribute to gender regulation in the rest of society.

Syd Lindsley's essay "Bearing the Blame: Gender, Immigration, Reproduction, and the Environment" explores the relationship between immigration policy and mainstream environmental groups who advocate zero population growth. Those who see people of color as a threat to their own wealth and well-being scapegoat immigrants of color for environmental problems,

Lindsley says. At the heart of their effort to preserve racial dominance is the desire to control immigrant women's reproduction. The equation is simple: if immigrants of color don't have children, there will be fewer of them. Lindsley suggests that such thinking is behind population regulation that makes women's bodies the primary site of control. Her compelling evidence makes it impossible not to wonder what is behind the holier-than-thou images of some environmental groups.

Finally, "She Who Believes in Freedom: Young Women Defy the Prison Industrial Complex," by Robin Templeton, takes on the archaic and repressive prison system in America. Equating the system with slavery, Templeton shows how young women are "coming to leadership in the twin struggles against police abuse and prison expansion." In particular, poor women and women of color are confronting the prison industry because of its daily impact on their lives. In the past two decades the number of people incarcerated in the United States has quadrupled, and Templeton's profound critique of the prison system is timely and important.

Younger feminist activists have a keen sense of the interconnectedness of issues based on identities, and how the ugly realities beneath economic globalization interfere with the liberation of a whole class of women across the planet. The battle for a feminist future, of course, is several-headed. We must look in many directions at once. The fire this time will burn in our own backyards and in the yards of neighbors. A match will be struck here, and its sulfur will be smelled elsewhere. In these pages, new feminist voices chart a fresh path for feminism— one that lifts the feminist work that has previously been shadowed into the light.

PART I

CHANGING MINDS

AND EYES: MEDIA AND CULTURE

CLAIMING JEZEBEL: BLACK FEMALE SUBJECTIVITY AND SEXUAL EXPRESSION IN HIP-HOP

Ayana Byrd

Ayana Byrd is a writer and editor living in Brooklyn, New York. She is an entertainment journalist whose work has appeared in Vibe, Rolling Stone, Honey, TV Guide, *and* Paper *magazines. She is the coauthor of* Hair Story: Untangling the Roots of Black Hair in America.

All it used to take was one "bitch" reference in a song, one gratuitous ass shake in a video and I was on a roll, criticizing the sexism of black men, denouncing the misogynistic societal structures set up by white men who supported it from their music industry corner offices, lamenting the misrepresented ways that black female bodies were on display. It didn't take much to get me back on my soapbox. But that, apparently, was a long time ago. Because today, allowed a receptive audience and the opportunity to wax passionately and even philosophically about the state of women in hip-hop—the art form that I once believed most defined me—I draw a big blank, barely able to muster up a halfhearted "You won't believe what I just heard . . ."

What happened since my rankled ire over Snoop Doggy

Dogg's 1993 *Doggystyle* album cover of a black female behind wiggling, naked, out of a doghouse? Things haven't gotten any better. The "feminist rapper" Queen Latifah now uses the once taboo B word in her lyrics. Alongside Chaka Khan, who sings the hook for "It's All Good," the onetime "conscious" group De La Soul had a video complete with a Jacuzzi overflowing with near-naked women. Since the debut of rap videos, outfits in videos are skimpier, the sexual references lewder, and the complicity by women in their own exploitation more widespread. Yet all I generally feel is an apathy.

I can now listen to a song with the hook "Hoes/I've got hoes/in different area codes" and instead of cringing at thoughts of debasement, chuckle at the artist Ludacris's witty delivery. Maybe it's that I've defined my own sexuality and know for sure what I only suspected in the past—that these men aren't talking about me. The problem is, *they* don't know they're not talking about me. Further, a lot of women, particularly girls and young adults, aren't sure that they don't want to be talked about in this way. These songs, and the videos that illustrate them, offer the most broadly distributed examples of seemingly independent black women that many young and sexually pubescent girls see. And unfortunately few girls transitioning into womanhood understand that the representation of female bodies in rap videos is not an empowering power-of-the-pussy but a fleeting one.

Because I grew up in the 1970s and '80s, I find it easy to list all the people who looked like me that were on television. There was Penny on *Good Times,* Tootie from *The Facts of Life,* and the occasional appearance of Charlene on *Diff'rent Strokes.* In the mid-eighties, there were as well the wholesome Huxtable daughters of *The Cosby Show.* Those of us who came of age then had a near void of images upon which to draw for representations of black women our age, negative or positive. It was a decade devoted both to saving and to condemning the "Endangered Black Male." But teen pregnancy was skyrocketing, and often the predominant young black female faces on television were in public service spots against babies having babies. Yet there were few policies or social organizations that were addressing their need to be saved or uplifted.

As the eighties progressed, things didn't get much better. In film as well as television, portrayals of black women were at either extreme of the sexual spectrum. In Spike Lee's *She's Gotta Have It,* which has been raked over the coals by feminists since its release, the lead, Nola Darling, was, among other atrocities, raped by one of her lovers (the supposed nice one) and got back together with him for a short time. On *The Cosby Show,* the television program that perhaps came closest to engaging and entertaining an entire generation of black kids, the female characters were completely desexed. On one episode we learn that Denise, the "wild child" of the family, was a virgin until her wedding night. Though their cousin Pam and her friend Charmaine both flirt with the idea of "giving it up" to their boyfriends, they seem less interested in actually having sex than in keeping their mates happy.

As popular culture weighed in on young black female sexuality, there were also deeply embedded societal stereotypes with which to contend. The lingering effects of the Moynihan Report, the controversial paper by Daniel Patrick Moynihan, who would later become a U.S. Senator, were still being felt. It asserted that black social immobility was caused by a crisis in the black family, and that Black Superwomen had emasculated black men, causing a fissure in the normal family setting.[1] President Reagan had effectively constructed the idea of the Welfare Mother: a black woman who refused to get a job and be a normal contributor to society but instead sat at home all day (most likely in the projects), maybe hitting the crack pipe, having babies by a host of men, living off welfare checks that came out of the pockets of decent, hardworking (white) Americans. Outside of academic conferences, few observers pointed out that the majority of women in the country on welfare were white, and that most women stayed on public assistance for two years or less.

By the early nineties there were other messages in which black women were made into villains. While the media highlighted the Tawana Brawley case, in which the fifteen-year-old black girl alleged a racist attack by white police officers but was found by a grand jury to be lying,[2] they virtually ignored the 1990 case of five white student athletes who were charged with sodomy and sexual abuse for repeatedly sexually assaulting a Jamaican woman in a fraternity house at St. John's University. In the latter case, there was more than enough evidence to convict, but according to one juror, the acquittal was based on the jury's desire to save the boys' lives from "ruin." Together the cases colluded in delegitimizing claims of rape by black women. There was also Mike Tyson's 1991 conviction for raping Desiree Washington. As vehemently as the white press sought to turn Tyson into a beast, many blacks cried foul to the champ's imprisonment. "What was she doing in his room anyway?" "That bitch set him up!" "How was she laughing and smiling at the show if just the night before he had raped her?"

There was often more talk about how he had been framed than about the fact that Tyson had a history of physical abuse toward women. Around the same time, Clarence Thomas's self-declared "high-tech lynching" was played out on television screens across the nation, although it was women—Anita Hill and black women in particular—who were left feeling like the ones hanging from the tree of political, if not necessarily public, opinion.

So what does any of this have to do with hip-hop? It is telling that the women—whether they're the rappers topping the charts or the dancers in the videos—formed their own identities at a time when black female sexuality in the cultural marketplace was not at all positive. The way black women experience and interpret the world has indeed been determined by our having to wage constant battles in order to determine our subjectivity—to say that we are not whores à la Desiree Washington, tricksters and liars à la Tawana Brawley, or disgruntled spinsters à la Anita Hill. In *Black Looks* the cultural theorist bell hooks writes, "The extent to which Black women feel devalued, objectified, dehumanized in this society determines the scope and texture of their looking relations. Those Black women whose identities were constructed in resistance, by practices that oppose the dominant order, were most inclined to develop an oppositional gaze."[3] Yet those women whose identities were instead constructed in compliance with the status quo were most inclined to absorb these images and make these representations and stereotypes of heterosexual black female sexuality their own.

Today, through the music video, there are so many black female bodies on view on any given day of watching television that it is impossible to list them. In many ways that is probably the point. Through the constant barrage of hypersexualized images, the young, black female has ceased to be an anomaly in the marketplace and is now back in the slave era position of anonymous chattel. Hooks sums it up in *Black Looks* when she writes, "Just as nineteenth-century representations of Black female bodies were constructed to emphasize that these bodies were expendable, contemporary images (even those created in black cultural production) give a similar message."[4] The hip-hop video has taken rap music to a level never imagined during its roots in the house parties of the 1970s Bronx. Early rap videos were overwhelmingly low-budget affairs. But in the late 1980s, *Video Music Box*—now the longest-running hip-hop video show in New York City—debuted from Miami and collided with the national explosion of that same city's 2 Live Crew, forever changing hip-hop video.

Before Luther Campbell and his 2 Live Crew, there were countless images of scantily clad women in music videos. Bands like Van Halen and Mötley Crüe had perfected the art of the gratuitous bikini shot long before rappers. The difference was that these women were white. And they were not being depicted in a genre proclaiming itself to be politically charged and revolutionary. As the rap historian Tricia Rose explains in her seminal work *Black Noise,* "Rap music is a black cultural expression that prioritizes black voices from the margins of urban America."[5] During the Reagan and Bush administrations, as prisons went up as rapidly as homelessness and drug use, and police brutality spread across the country, hip-hop became the medium for the disenfranchised citizens of the inner city to state their rage, vent their concerns, educate themselves about political issues, and fight back against government propaganda. Public Enemy, whose lyrics advised the disenfranchised to "fight the power," or spoke to controversial urban realities ("I don't wanna be called yo nigga"), were by far the most visible political rappers, but they were hardly the only ones.

By the time of the "Me So Horny"s and "Baby Got Back"s of the rap world, there were legions of hip-hop tunes that were not deep or meaningful in their lyrical content. But the accompanying videos, with images of women with DD cups washing soapy car windows with their breasts, were groundbreaking. "The visualization of music has far-reaching effects on musical culture and popular culture generally, not the least of which is the increase in visual interpretations of sexist power relationships,"[6] Rose wrote. In short, it became as easy as the click of the cable remote to see images of black women as so sexually licentious, so insatiably horny that Van Halen's "Hot for Teacher" looked almost tame.

In the early days of the booty video, the depiction of women in the music was overwhelmingly cut-and-dried. With a few notable exceptions, they were portrayed as gold-digging vixens. Hip-hop music extended the idea with videos that showed women dressed in G-strings, bikinis, and stripper outfits, oftentimes in situations that had nothing to do with the beach or a strip club. It was a time when many feminists and other interested onlookers noted that, as misconstrued and narrow as the representation of black women in rap music was, it would most likely be balanced once more women became viable, popular rappers. The idea was that, given the space to define themselves, female rappers would construct an image of black womanhood which encompassed a more realistic scope of sexuality, not to mention give voice to the day-to-day struggles of women living in the urban arenas that were typically the focus of hip-hop music.

The meteoric rise of Lil' Kim's career was the likely starting point for the muddying of the waters that has taken place for me and many others who once felt that there were only two sides in the sexual war of hip-hop. She is arguably the female rapper closest to achieving iconic status. And although she has attracted many fans based on interest in her music, Kim's real infamy stems from the public way she has lived her life. Nothing has been deemed too private for the diminutive rapper from Brooklyn. She's admitted that she never had her dad's acceptance and that as a teen she used sex and her body to survive. After the Notorious B.I.G., the man who had been her mentor as well as her married lover, died, she told *People* magazine how she kissed his urn each morning. On her sophomore album, *Notorious KIM,* she revealed how she aborted a pregnancy from her rap Svengali. We have watched Kim publicly wrestle with weight, undergo two breast enlargements, a nose job, blond hair, and blue contact lenses.

In 1995 Kim and her then-friend Foxy Brown opened the door for the public's acceptance of sexual female rappers. Before them, those relatively few women who were sexually brazen in hip-hop—groups like Hoes with Attitudes and Bytches Wit Problems are good examples—were often dismissed by cultural critics and feminists as willing participants in their own dehumanization. Instead, there was a perceived transgressiveness in Kim's and Foxy's acts of asserting desire and sexual wants in a culture where female sexuality is not typically linked with the pursuit of pleasure.

Yet while these two performers challenged notions of what it meant to be a woman in hip-hop, it could be argued that they were simultaneously supporting an image of black female sexuality that the white patriarchy had been trying to sell us since slavery. During the whole of the nineteenth century, for example, depictions of black female bodies were often sexualized in ways that white women's never were.[7] The black female was a licentious counterpart to the white woman's virtue, in fact making that virtue possible. The supposed sexuality of black women was the thing that white women could set themselves against. One of the most emblematic (and bizarre) representations of black female sexuality was the Hottentot Venus, whose "grossly overdeveloped labia," "enlarged clitoris," and large buttocks were seen as evidence of the "primitive sexuality of African women."[8] Like the African Hottentot, the black female body not only had a divergent sexual physiology made up of more pronounced sexual organs but a divergent sexual psychology that dictated uncontrollable "primitive" sexual desire. Although the Hottentot Venus was a medical myth, it was presented to the public as pure fact. Such fictions, whether they pertain to the hypersexual Hottentot or her diametrical opposite, the sexless archmother mammy, are all too powerful images. Contemporary black women are forced to negotiate the traces left by these contaminated constructions of black female sexuality.

Many black women who have always felt a need to strive for respectability in a culture that hypersexualizes them almost from birth see in Lil' Kim the freedom of "acting out" their sexuality. She not only refuses to shy away from the male gaze by desexing herself but openly preens for the male gaze while returning it. As bell hooks would say, she looks back. Some like to assert that rappers like Kim are intimidating men, shaking the very foundations of male sexuality by demanding that female sexual urgency and female pleasure be taken into account. Yet alongside demanding that they be sexually pleased, many female rappers convey a parallel overriding message in their lyrics: that the men who sexually satisfy them should also provide money, cash, and clothes.

By comparing the majority of female rappers in the entertainment marketplace with the undisputed queen of commercialized female sexual agency, Madonna, it becomes clearer how precariously drawn the line is between self-determination and coconspiring in one's own exploitation. "Madonna provides a perfect example of the postmodern, feminist heroine, selling the virtues of political indeterminacy in her insistent play with sexual expression," wrote Roseann M. Mandzuik in her essay "Feminist Politics and Postmodern Seductions." "Yet in her discourse as a postmodern icon, [there is] something [very] familiar in her transformation of politics into pleasure: Madonna sounds the same old cultural message that a woman's place is to be sensual, stylish and self-involved."[9] Underscoring this point and bringing it back to female rappers is Lil' Kim's video "How Many Licks," in which she turns herself into a doll with replaceable parts, a move so infused with self-objectification that it seems almost laughable in its obviousness. The question must be asked: What kind of transgressiveness is Kim enacting when she performs a femininity that mimics misogynistic patriarchal desires? In another song, she denounces her previous fear of fellatio: "Now I throw lips to the shit/Handle it like a real bitch." Can sexual empowerment be articulated by making oneself a powerful agent in the familiar pornographic images of sexual acts?

It would be easy to state that had these women, had all of us, been privy to more realistic images of black women in popular culture as we were growing up, things would be different today. But it's not that simple. There is a market impetus behind these images. "The artistry takes a backseat to the image," said Faith Newman, vice president of A&R at Jive Records, in the hip-hop publication *Blaze*. "Men control [these] women's careers, and it seems like if [the women] aren't looking like sluts or some hardcore dykes—excuse the expression—they aren't going to get the necessary push."[10] The commodification of blackness in the entertainment industry rewards black women much more readily for reactionary or regressive thinking about gender and sexuality. Both Foxy Brown and Lil' Kim, who were molded by older, already popular male rappers, have stated repeatedly that in the beginning of their careers they were pretty much told what their image would be and how they needed to play it up to sell records, whether this was how they chose to be depicted or not. "At sixteen I was just so happy to have a nice car and a nice home that I didn't complain about [my image]," Foxy said in *Essence* magazine. "I had all the influences around me, and I wasn't always strong enough to come back like, 'No. I don't want to do that.'"[11]

Back in 1999, when my soapbox preaching had harshly turned on female rappers as the real problem, I wrote a review of Foxy Brown's second album, *Chyna Doll*. I declared that if we were supposed to believe Foxy was any kind of doll at all, it was of the blow-up variety, willing and ready at all times to be the receptacle for a man's sexual pleasures. While it was hardly a nuanced, subtle statement, it seemed, at the time, fitting to explain what appeared to be going on. Rappers like Trina, Hurricane G, and Charli Baltimore (another mistress of the Notorious B.I.G.), alongside Foxy and Kim, were reveling in the narrow confines of this Pussy Free-For-All. Because while, yes, these assertions of female sexual agency were a direct challenge to the notion that black male sexuality within hip-hop exists as a conquering force over women, it was, to put it in blunt vernacular, getting tired. While these female rappers were perhaps providing a voice for those who had been silent sexual objects in male hip-hop, the rules had not been overturned in how they were being read by the rest of the society. So though it may at first be shocking or new to assert that you, a woman, want sex *and* oral sex *and* a man who can last for a long time, after a few similarly themed songs, the shock has worn off and what is left is confirmation of something that many men of all races and quite a few non-black women had always suspected: black women are whores.

The near-total lack of media images depicting the real lives of working class, inner city black girls in the 1980s left a void, and that space was filled with male-centered constructs of the licentious black female. What will be the effect on a young black girl today as she is bombarded with images of black female asses, breasts, and dirty talk? A group of teen black girls at the mall dressed as if they had just finished taping a video could arguably be not much different from white girls in the eighties donning see-through lace getups and scaring their parents with recitations of "Like a Virgin." But it could also be said that more is at stake: the very grim realities of sexually transmitted diseases, AIDS, teen pregnancy, and sexual assault and abuse. Just as important, mainstream American culture interprets black cultural articulations of misogyny, sexism, and unbridled female sexuality differently from their white counterparts. In the 1990s, during the fiercest criticisms of teen pop star Britney Spears for sporting bare midriffs and see-through pants, she professed to be a virgin. When Foxy Brown came onto the scene, at age fifteen, she was featured on a song called "Ain't No Nigga," rhyming, "Ain't no nigga like the one I got/sleeps around but he gives me a lot," and very few people expressed disgust, or even shock, at her age. And with white suburban youth being one of the biggest consumer bases for rap music, it is safe to say that while some of the kids buying the CDs may have never met a black woman, they've all seen at least one (probably quite a few) wrap her legs around a pole and dance to a hip-hop tune during an afternoon spent watching BET, MTV, or the Box.

Of course, black women aren't the only ones being sexualized in the new millennium. Magazines like *Maxim* and *Rolling Stone* enjoy massive sales due in large part to the soft porn shots of white celebrities that grace their covers. Within all levels and substrata of society, women are dabbling with a hypersexual, yet decidedly pro-woman persona, epitomized by the characters on the popular HBO show *Sex and the City*. (Incidentally, the show's stylist, Patricia Fields, has admitted that Lil' Kim is a major influence for the wardrobe of Carrie, the Upper East Side, fashion-fabulous protagonist.)

And, of course, not all women rappers are playing out triple

X–rated fantasies, just as not every video contains a bevy of near-naked ladies. Lauryn Hill has earned fans, respect, critical acclaim and awards with her mix of earthy sensuality and political and social awareness. Her themes run the gamut from love, motherhood, and simple reminiscing to the current state of gender relations. In "Lost Ones," Hill rhymes, "Don't be a hardrock when you really are a gem/Baby girl, respect is just the minimum," as she encourages women to seek their true selves and demand respect at the very least. The rapper Eve does not hesitate to admit that for a short time before her rap career she was a stripper. Yet it is told not as a way to entice but simply as a fact, and Eve seems to be very much in control of her current image, which is part pop star sass, part round-the-way-girl tough, and part sexy plaything.

So now, as I find myself humming along to a catchy "ho" anthem, I'm curious about what happened to my once-rankled ire. A few months ago, when I began thinking about this essay, I would probably have argued that my apathy was proof that while sexism and self-objectification still existed, there was a balance that allowed me to breathe easier. That maybe it was because women rappers have come into the industry, and while it's not the utopia of sexual equality I had hoped for, at the very least we are there, pushing the envelope, being recognized. Or that there's a likely chance the next song on the radio could be, if not redeeming, at least inoffensive to women. That for every thug love ode like the one by Bonnie Shyne, there's a "my beautiful queen" song by a "conscious" rapper like Common.

But now I can say that it's nothing like that. More likely I have calmed down because the powers that be—the programming executives, the music industry bigwigs, the video casting agents—have achieved a major goal. Through a saturation of the market with tramplike black women, I, too, have fallen victim to the normalizing effects of visual and lyrical hoochie overkill.

In order to see if that was the case, I took time off from being a pop culture consumer—I turned off the cable television and never listened to the radio unless I needed a weather update. I wanted to test whether I'd climb back up on the soapbox, newly charged with disgust and anger once I'd stopped being so used to all the ass. During my hiatus, Puffy became P. Diddy and made a public statement of apology to any Asian women he may have unintentionally offended with one line from his song "Diddy," yet offered nothing to the black women he's been insulting throughout his career. *Vibe* magazine printed an article on the current state of hip-hop for its 2001 year-end issue, and a full-page photo accompanying the piece was of a black woman's behind, even though the story never made any reference to it.

Two nights ago I found myself at a party for the rapper Jay Z's clothing line, Rocawear, where my time-out officially came to an end. The models, mostly men, were positioned inside cases meant to look like store window displays. And each black woman who was featured was wearing too-small shorts that let a portion of butt cheek peek out as she danced around a pole in front of excessively dressed men (coats, baggy pants, boots, hats) who offered her dollars. I looked around at the crowd and saw that few looked irritated or even seemed to question the ludicrousness of the setup. At the very least I hoped that some would find it passé. Just as I began searching for my car keys, more than aware that it was time for me to leave, the dee-jay put on the song that started all of this: "I've got hoes/I've got hoes/in different area codes." I didn't sing along, nor did I applaud Ludacris's linguistic wit. Instead I walked through the dancing bodies and headed out the door, wishing for a space in hip-hop where sex could be sexy and not insulting and women could be Smart and Interesting as well as Sexy. On that cold February night, it seemed like a goal that would be a long time coming.

AN INDEPENDENT MEDIA CENTER OF ONE'S OWN:

A FEMINIST ALTERNATIVE TO CORPORATE MEDIA

Joshua Breitbart and
Ana Nogueira

Ana Nogueira is a writer and organizer within the Indymedia network. She is a founder of the New York City Independent Media Center and The Indypendent, *Indymedia's longest-running newspaper. Fluent in Spanish, Portuguese, and English, she has also helped start and build Independent Media Centers throughout South America. Her writing on Indymedia and the global justice movement has appeared in magazines such as* Punk Planet, New Internationalist, Washington Peace Letter, Left Turn, Zmag, *and* The Indypendent, *as well as in the anthology* From ACT UP to the WTO. *She is also a producer of the radio program* Democracy Now.

Joshua Breitbart is a writer and organizer within the Indymedia network. He is a founding board member of Allied Media Projects, a nonprofit organization that supports participatory media like Clamor Magazine, *where he is a consulting editor, and* Rooftop Films, *which he helped found. A native of Brooklyn, he is a member of the New York City*

Independent Media Center, contributing frequently to its monthly print publication, The Indypendent. *He is also a director of the Lela Breitbart Memorial Fund, named for his sister, which supports reproductive health and young women's activism.*

At George W. Bush's inauguration, protesters filled entire sections of the parade route and the streets beyond the perimeter, making it clear that the country was not unified behind the new president. "Feminists will be out in full force at the Inauguration on January 20, 2001, reminding Bush, Cheney and the Cabinet nominees that we won't tolerate a roll-back of our rights," promised National Organization of Women President Patricia Ireland.[1] And they were, along with anarchists, black nationalists, civil rights activists, democrats, environmentalists, anticapitalists, and a host of other groups. Considering the pure quantity of media coverage—live broadcasts on all the networks, banner headlines on major papers the next day—the American public should have been very aware of the country's lack of unity. But the mainstream media outlets had a different story to tell.

Instead of presenting the wide range of activists converging on the nation's capital in protest, many in the mainstream media colored the view, making demonstrators appear arbitrary, frivolous, or virtually nonexistent. "The demonstrators want to be heard and some of them simply want to do damage," Peter Jennings explained. "Some people have just come for the sake of demonstrating."[2] *The New York Times* bore the headline "Bush, Taking Office, Calls for Civility, Compassion and 'Nation of Character'; Unity Is a Theme" but mentioned only once, and as an aside, the thousands of protesters who represented so many disenchanted Americans. In the second-to-last paragraph of the two-thousand-word article, the protesters were finally acknowledged: "After the ceremony was the parade, and once the car transporting the new president and first lady down Pennsylvania Avenue had passed most of the protesters, the couple climbed out of the vehicle to walk only the end of route." In fairness, the *Los Angeles Times's* front-page article on the inauguration spoke more accurately to the events surrounding Bush's speech. The headline "Protests, Tight Security Line Bush Parade Route; Inaugural: Outnumbering Observers in Some Places, Demonstrators Turn the Event from a Symbol of National Unity into a Display of Political Dissent," documented not only the quantity of protesters but the significance of a "display of political dissent not seen in nearly thirty years." But if the nation's trusted network news anchors and its "paper of record," *The New York Times,* say it happened one way, that is likely to be how people remember it if they were not there.

This is precisely the power of journalism: to write history, to silence some, and to promote others. Judging from the way many mainstream media outlets covered the inauguration, we can see the type of community they were trying to create: one that excludes dissenting voices in favor of a false unanimity. "The tension of those protesters is completely evaporated, at least on the television screen," said Jennings once Bush's motorcade had made it to the final section of the parade route, reserved for fifty-dollar ticket holders. "That's right," replied ABC News Correspondent Terry Moran. "The only thing I see are cowboy hats."

In order to pursue our feminist vision of a world in which difference is celebrated as essential to society, we need to build alternative media that are open to all and that value multiple perspectives from many contributors—media that weave together seemingly disparate issues and encourage horizontal relations of community rather than hierarchical relations of ownership and exclusivity. We need multiple voices recording their perspectives on the same event instead of a few loud voices arrogantly supposing that they speak for us all.

Thousands of people around the world acting individually, in small collectives, and in global networks are creating just that. Hundreds of them were in Washington, D.C., for the inauguration. Working out of the ad hoc newsrooms of the DC Independent Media Center, we presented different pictures of the day's events and helped to disseminate that collage to others over the Internet, in print, and through video.[3] Our view of the inauguration came not from an anchor, a pundit, or a press release but from hundreds of participants posting their own reports to www.indymedia.org, a site composed of independent newsmakers. Thanks to a technological innovation called open publishing, any visitor to the website can publish a text report, picture, audio recording, or video clip; and all contributions are subject to commentary from readers. Dozens took advantage of the open publishing function each hour, providing hundreds of reports over the course of the day, each inspiring many responses.

One person using the site described herself as "a middle-class, getting to be middle-aged female American—first time ever demonstrating—there to participate with my legal, constitutionally guaranteed right to free speech (so I thought until that day)."[4] As part of the Voter March, which was promoting voters' rights and had joined forces with the NOW marchers, she and thousands of others arrived at the intersection of Fourteenth and L. There the police had boxed in a few hundred protesters—most of whom were members of the anarchist Black Bloc group—and were preparing to make mass arrests. "I never thought I'd be happy to see people with Gore-Lieberman signs!" said one Black Bloc member.[5] The appearance of such a large number of supporters on the scene, many also middle-class and middle-aged, rattled the police. They tried to hold their line and keep the groups separate. "I was so scared I didn't know what to do," the woman wrote. "I was looking at the various police, trying to find a face that might be approachable—there were none!" The police began to push the NOW–Voter March group back, but the Black Bloc began to chant, "Don't sell us out!" and the march surged, breaking the police line and allowing the anarchists to escape into their midst. This image of mainstream feminists and reform-oriented voters' rights advocates coming to the rescue of a batch of anarchists "was nowhere to be found on television or in corporate news accounts," according to the independent journalist L.A. Kauffman. "You had to be there or read about it on Indymedia."[6]

". . . 'masculinity' is also a bottom line."

As people working for social change pick their battles, they frequently forget the role the media play in all of them. Even when attacking corporations, people go for the advertisers rather than the advertising medium itself. "When we think of the rapacious corporations of industrial capitalism we tend to picture big oil companies opening up wells and driving indigenous peoples from their lands, giant fruit multinationals controlling vast, pesticide-filled plantations, steelworks, mines, roads across pristine wilderness," says Katherine Ainger, an editor at *New Internationalist* magazine. "But the globalizing conquistadors of the twenty-first century are the media giants of cultural capitalism—Disney, AOL Time Warner, Sony, Bertelsmann, News Corporation, Viacom, Vivendi Universal."[7] Subcomandante Marcos, spokesperson of the indigenous Zapatista rebels of Mexico, agreed when he said that the global media "present a virtual world, created in the image of what the globalization process requires."[8]

The concentration of information outlets in the hands of a few corporations narrows the range of voices that can reach a mass audience, and it encourages those audiences to accept the status quo and become uniform and complacent. According to a former chairman of the Federal Communications Commission, "It is generally understood that the rise of media monopolies led to a shift in editorial content, city by city, to a far-less confrontational, far-less controversial, far-less skeptical and challenging press."[9] Dependent on advertising and focused on the bottom line, the media monopolies are concerned primarily with what women (and men) want insofar as they are consumers, not citizens or advocates. And they avoid anything that might cost them a substantial share of the audience.

Driving the growth and consolidation of media conglomerates over the past twenty years has been the desire for access to every marketable moment of people's lives—from dusk to dawn. "Our reach is unmatched around the world. We're reaching people from the moment they wake up to the moment they fall asleep," says Rupert Murdoch;[10] and from cradle to grave: "You can literally pick an advertiser's needs and market that advertiser across all the demographic profiles, from Nickelodeon with the youngest consumers to CBS with some of the oldest consumers," says MTV Chief Tom Freston.[11]

Seeing people as consumers rather than as an interested citizenry makes it all but impossible for these corporations to participate responsibly in the free exchange of information.[12] Not only are news outlets increasingly used as cross-promotion platforms for their owners' other products but the news they do deliver is intended to ensure an audience for advertisers of other companies' goods and services. Since poor people are considered a less desirable demographic for that purpose, news about poverty treats them as objects rather than subjects who have agency. And female consumers are addressed very narrowly. Take America Online (AOL), for example. "'AOL is a bread and butter family service and we offer content in many areas traditionally handled by women,' says Katherine Borsecnik, president of AOL Brand Programming. 'Who makes purchasing decisions? Who does research on education and health issues? It tends to be the female in the house.'"[13] Women are seen as caring for stereotypically women's issues—education and health—and are valued for the purchasing decisions they make in those areas.

This confinement can be so rigid as to persist even when it affects the bottom line, as Gloria Steinem tells us in her account of *Ms.* magazine's relationship with advertisers. *Ms.* was founded in 1972 to provide an alternative to women's magazines that contain little more than fluff aimed at telling women what to consume and that present beauty and fitness, marriage and motherhood as the complete range of women's issues. It also provided a feminist alternative to large, mainstream publications like *Time* and *Newsweek*. At its peak it was circulating 700,000 copies a month, with top-notch editorial content, though many of these copies were circulated for free in an attempt to attract advertisers. *Ms.* had an audience of concerned, intelligent women, but advertisers treated it like another *Cosmopolitan*, *Good Housekeeping,* or *Vogue,* demanding complimentary copy for beauty and cooking merchandise and refusing to purchase ads for anything other than "women's products."

Even after *Ms.* provided market research showing its readers to be as interested as men are in products such as cars and electronics, the advertisers refused to purchase space. "When I was just a writer, I thought the point of business was to make money," Steinem says. "That was before credit cards, electronics, and other companies taught me that 'masculinity' is also a bottom line. Now, I think if you can get them to want to make money, you've won a battle."[14] In 1990 *Ms.* decided to stop selling advertisements altogether and raised the cover price to $5.95 per issue in the United States. But it was not able to sustain itself and it is now published by the Feminist Majority Foundation with a loyal readership of around 100,000.[15]

Women continue to be disempowered in other media decision-making processes. According to a study by the Annenberg Public Policy Center, women make up only 9 percent of the boards of directors of media, telecom, and e-companies. In the wider category of people in positions with real "clout," women constitute a mere 3 percent.[16] Parity is also lacking at the front lines. Women account for 41 percent of all journalists, but the percentages vary greatly when categorized by issue. Women report slightly more frequently but still less than men on the environment (47 percent), health (46 percent), and education (42 percent), and considerably less frequently on politics (26 percent), war (25 percent), and international crises (19 percent).[17] These figures translate into consistently and quantifiably skewed reporting. As research by the Global Media Monitoring Project 2000 shows, a sample day of the world's media production revealed that only 18 percent of all people interviewed were women. When the interviewee has a specified occupation, such as scientist, politician, or athlete, the percentages drop to 12, 10, and 9 respectively.[18] This underrepresentation may be affected by imbalances in societies at large, but it also seems to reflect a bias among editors and reporters about who the experts are. In other words, to the extent that individual reporters can make choices about how to report the news, they usually choose to report it from a male perspective. The numbers also suggest that subjects such as the environment, health, and education are considered women's issues, while politics and war are not. But even a "women's issue" is presented at least as often by a man.

Even when issues of particular significance to women—such as child care or abortion, at least in a society that still equates being female with being a mother—are addressed, reporters can misrepresent. "When [media] cover welfare in the corporate press, they cover it generally as it will relate to politicians," says Jennifer Pozner, founder and executive director of Women In Media News (WIMN). Coverage is largely limited to "how passing welfare reform makes Al Gore look to women," for example, or "how passing the global gag rule will affect Bush's image as a uniter-not-a-divider." Rarely is welfare reform policy framed by how it is "affecting women and children who are being kicked out of shelters now because there aren't enough beds for them, or how the global gag rule might affect poor women in developing countries—from Albania to Peru to Zimbabwe."[19]

With a system of media so biased against women, it makes sense to consider efforts to reform it along feminist lines. And it is hard to see how someone could consider himself or herself feminist without wanting an alternative to corporate media. Furthermore, a gendered critique of media is necessarily a simultaneous condemnation of the way mainstream media address sexual orientation, ethnicity, immigrant status, political orientation, age, and race. Because whole classes of people are effectively excluded from the corporate media, it is almost impossible for that system to present events as they are actually experienced. And, as Gloria Steinem suggests, media conglomerates do not use their oligopoly of information simply to accumulate dollars, they use it to consolidate power.

"We are about something much different . . ."

Since November 1999, when hundreds of people with cameras, pens, computer skills, or just a desire to tell their stories joined together in one newsroom during the protests against the World Trade Organization in Seattle, more and more alternative media makers around the world have been linking to a news network called Indymedia. "Imperfect, insurgent, sleepless, and beautiful, we directly experienced the success of the first Independent Media Center (IMC) in Seattle and saw that the common dream of 'a world in which many worlds fit' is possible—step by step, piece by piece, space by space, photo by photo, word by word, over the Net, on pirate broadcast, in the streets, streaming live, and most importantly: face to face," says Greg Ruggiero, editor of Seven Stories Press. "Fanned by the real shutdown of the WTO and our capacity to bypass corporate media, the IMC brushfire spread."[20]

The Seattle Independent Media Center received over 1.5 million hits in its first week, remarkable since it had prepared little publicity. Now the network receives over 400,000 hits a day, still without buying any advertising. "The showdown between traditional media and the new media in Seattle also provided a glimpse of what lies ahead for journalism in the new century. It is a message that older media ignore at their own peril," said Tom Regan of *The Christian Science Monitor*.[21]

Born out of frustration with the way the mainstream media ignores or sensationalizes the almost daily antiglobalization protests occurring around the world, Indymedia has become a powerful amplifier for the voices of millions of people who otherwise can only take to the streets to share knowledge about issues that affect them. Autonomous local media centers now dot the globe, collaborating through the Internet and regional gatherings. This network of Independent Media Centers is an experiment in global, democratic media production and information-sharing. Although it faces many challenges, Indymedia is a promising model for a feminist media system.

Now Independent Media Centers around the world are signing on to the principles of participatory media. As of January

2002, there were close to one hundred IMCs (not all with web-sites)[22] spanning forty countries on six continents. Using anarchist principles of decentralized decision-making combined with scrupulous attention to process, Indymedia is trying to build an institutional structure to accommodate our diverse political world. "We are the next generation and we're building a media institution that is revolutionary," says Sheri Herndon, a Seattle IMC volunteer. "We have a huge responsibility, by default. We've got huge hurdles ahead of us. We live in an oppressive, authoritarian, patriarchal system that likes discipline and punishment as the primary modus operandi for teaching us how to learn and grow. We are about something much different."[23]

Thus far, the results have been encouraging. Independent Media Center sites tallied as many as 1.5 million page views over the two-day period in April 2001 that coincided with the protests around the Free Trade Area of the Americas meeting in Quebec City,[24] and over 5 million page views over the five days of the July 2001 Group of Eight meeting in Italy.[25] And the coverage is deep as well as broad. As *The Christian Science Monitor* noted, "While big broadcasters like CNN and Fox focused almost exclusively on the confrontation between protestors and police in Seattle—especially the first couple of days—the independent sites provided in-depth papers and research about the WTO, not to mention some fascinating discussion areas where people from both sides of the trade issue argued back and forth for days."[26]

The global trade issues that inspire so much debate on the Web and protest in the streets have united diverse communities from all over the world in the search for alternatives. Corporate globalization does not affect everyone equally: a system that prioritizes the monetary value of life and labor benefits (in the short term) people who have money, while harming poor people and women, who do the bulk of the world's unpaid labor. But it is affecting everyone everywhere. A news source that allows people to analyze and share their experiences with globalization will obviously have a global audience and, more important, an infinite wealth of firsthand content. Indymedia, utilizing the type of peer-to-peer sharing that the Internet makes possible, is such a news source. And that audience has seized it. One server that hosts fifty separate IMC websites now records 180,000 posts to the newswires each month.

Its growing prominence leads people to want to characterize the whole network uniformly. This is difficult because Indymedia combines a global reach with local autonomy. It is one network that connects many smaller networks. For example, there are IMCs in Nigeria, Madrid, Montreal, Boston, Chiapas, Uruguay, and Sydney, but each is independent of the others and has its own mission statement, its own finances, and its own decision-making process. What the individual centers share is a commitment to grassroots, democratic, noncorporate coverage of happenings around the world. Beyond the collaborative, antiauthoritarian spirit of the people involved, the very structure of IMCs encourages openness and inclusion, and fosters connections among groups and issues. Indymedia lets people tell their own stories in their own words and asserts that each person is an expert on her or his own life and the issues he or she faces. In this way, it reinforces democracy and undermines the ability of the corporate press to tell us what to think.

". . . listen to our story."

In New York City we see a photo from Chiapas. In it, a round-faced young Indian woman with a bandanna tied over her face stares into the camera. She holds out a microphone to interview another masked Zapatista. They are in a simple wooden room somewhere in rural Mexico. Behind the woman, three compañeras play back a minidisc recorder. They are making media.[27] They are documenting the violence and war that are part of everyday life, the kind the corporate media will not report. They are using their Independent Media Center to report on acts of rape and torture by paramilitary soldiers, the negotiations in parliament over the rights of indigenous people to their land, and visions for and actions taken toward a better and more feminist society.[28]

One such post, from Reynalda Pablo Cruz, chronicles the violent events in Marques de Comillas on July 27, 2001:

The police followed other men, women, and children in helicopters when they were running away. They landed the helicopter in the stables and grabbed them all. All of us who got away slept, frightened, in the mountains. Other women went to the other ejido [communal farm], and they're still scattered. At night we heard them firing again. We didn't know where, but we heard it. Saturday morning, a group of women had returned to the community. A helicopter passed overhead. They teargassed a woman who was watching through her door, and she fell down, unconscious, with her baby.

Cruz concludes with a simple but universal call: "We hope that you listen to our story. We wait for your presence in our community. And that's all I can say."[29]

". . . amplifying voices within a critical context."

Distinguishing women-owned media from the mainstream, primarily male-owned media, Donna Allen, founder of the Women's Institute for Freedom of the Press, summarized some of the characteristics of women's journalism: "Women's journalism reports its news in the first person, allowing the newsmakers to speak for themselves." She quoted from the mission statements of women-owned publications and claimed they focus on "harmony and interconnection" with the goal of "effective use of media as an instrument of change," rather than on conflict and violence with the alleged goal of objectivity. As for structure, "Women-owned media are nearly all non-hierarchical," emphasizing cooperation, internally and with other organizations, and valuing diversity, in both participation and subject matter.[30]

These may sound like wishful ideals, but Allen culled her information from over seven hundred women-owned periodicals or other media and fifteen years of publishing *Media Report to Women,* which provides information on all types of media—network and cable television, magazines, newspapers, Internet, and other emerging media—and the way they depict women and issues of interest to women.[31] These characteristics are not inherent in all women reporters, of course, but we can accept them as a description of feminist alternative media, actually and ideally. The IMC network, for the most part, fits these characteristics in practice, albeit often in the faltering way one might expect from a still-nascent organization. It combines technological innovations with feminist organizational principles in an attempt to open the media-making process up to multiple progressive voices.

On every IMC site, for example, the material posted through the open publishing function appears at the top of the newswire section on the front page just as quickly as the computers can connect, without being edited, approved, or otherwise filtered. On the NYC Indymedia website, a writer is just a few clicks away from publishing an article. Under "Newswire" the reporter can click on "How do I publish?/What do I publish?" which leads to a page that describes the methods for posting articles, photos, video, and audio. A click on the link "Publish Your News" allows the user to fill out a form that includes space for article text and multimedia file uploading. This function encourages direct participation, allowing newsmakers to speak for themselves. Readers of any post can add comments, so each story can inspire discussion, potentially connecting many different points of view. This process also eliminates the need for an omnipotent editor, revising or eliminating whatever she or he thinks needs to be. False statements can be refuted, factual errors corrected, and inflammatory or chauvinist remarks dismissed without relying on traditional editorial controls.

The version of an event or issue presented through IMC newswires is not the monolithic truth but an assembly of many people's views. Open publishing works best when many people are posting their versions of the same event, as with the opening example of the inauguration. Instead of relying on one person's supposedly objective assessment, users can build their own understanding of an event or issue.

Open publishing can also be a way for news production to become an organic part of many people's lives, instead of just the profession of a few. It can flatten the hierarchy that exists whenever specialized news producers are separated from their passive audience. Alternative media that rely on the distinction of "professional" journalists reproduce this hierarchy even when they publish feminist content.

Not surprisingly, open publishing on IMC sites is utilized by some to post items that are derogatory or trivial, or that suggest illegal acts. So, just as with other information sources, the user should question their reliability. Independent Media Centers do not claim that content on their newswires is always accurate. But that accessibility means that, as a practice, open publishing puts the burden on the reader to make decisions about what to believe. Those of us who get our news from mainstream sources too often allow others to relieve us of that burden. Tools including categorization of the newswire, rating systems, and "skins," a programming code that allows individuals to design and determine their own personal newswires so that unwanted topics are filtered out, are intended to increase the editorial power of the reader.

The original idea of the IMC newswire was simply to provide a space that alternative media organizations could access to share content. But the programming was clunky and relied on privately owned technology, which limits access to people who own the specific software. An Australian programmer named Mathew Arnison met one of the IMC organizers just before the protests in Seattle and offered the code he had helped develop. The program, called Active, is open source, which means it is publicly available, modifiable, and transmittable. Because anyone in the world with a computer and know-how can use open source and offer refinements and innovations, it works much better than technology developed by a single company, especially if you want to collaborate across the Internet. The Active code was installed shortly before the protests in Seattle began.

Over 150 firsthand accounts of the actions were published on each of the first five days of the website's existence, providing up-to-the-minute coverage of the protests alongside contextual discussion of the issues. "The unexpected thing that came through was all the stories we got from individuals who'd been to the protests, been to the lockdowns and stuff, and who'd come back home, checked out the website and written up their story. It's *still* making me tingle just thinking about it. . . . To plug in was amazing," said Arnison, who was back in Australia during the action.[32] In addition, hundreds of volunteer journalists worked together to produce a daily documentary that aired on Free Speech TV, a daily newspaper passed out to people in Seattle, and hundreds of hours of audio and video material, all archived as history-in-the-making on the newswire. The corporate media could not compete.

"It's easy enough for TV cameras to videotape scenes of vandalism in a shopping district," says the media critic Norman Solomon. "A far more difficult task would be to cover the institutionalized violence that is a quiet part of everyday life. When Western banks collect interest on loans to poor countries, the suffering—and the links between wealth and poverty—go largely unreported. That's how 20,000 children worldwide die each day from preventable diseases."[33]

Today's media activists are fighting for the human right to communicate not because it is more important than other struggles for social justice but because it is a necessary component of all those struggles. As Michael Eisenmenger, member of the Paper Tiger TV nonprofit video collective, has said, "We do this work because we feel these are important, historical moments that if not documented and allowed to be told, will simply be treated as if they never occurred, like much of the rest of our history. As a tactic, we view our work as potentially a key part of a larger struggle or mobilization. Neither a mouthpiece for someone's movement, nor an arrogant self-appointed voice of a movement, but hopefully as a means of amplifying voices within a critical context. All of our efforts have reached more people as a result."[34]

There are many communities that Indymedia cannot yet link together. This limitation was made very clear in the fall of 2001. On September 11, 2001, traffic to the main Indymedia server doubled. As CNN and Fox News replayed images of the attacks on the World Trade Center and the Pentagon, people were tuning in to Indymedia to dialogue and debate, express sorrow and outrage, advocate peace and justice. The history and context of issues ranging from U.S. foreign policy and Islamic fundamentalism to the Israel-Palestine conflict were dynamically debated through the interactive medium of the Internet. In New York City, independent journalists made it down to ground zero to photograph and film the devastation. Most, however, were more interested in covering the crowds of people gathered in Union Square, debating in dozens of small pockets and in big town-square-type meetings for hours on end about why anyone would be motivated to kill in this way and how we should respond.

Seeing that the corporate media were framing the disaster with hate-filled calls for vengeance, dozens of independent journalists came out to get the response from the street. Besides maintaining the website, the NYC IMC produced two newspapers that week, a total of 25,000 copies, printed with money that came from community donations as well as our own pockets. It also produced a video documentary, called *9.11,* which has been widely distributed and seen by millions all over the world via the Internet and public video screenings, eclipsing the demand for any other IMC documentary to date. However, since there was no local IMC in Afghanistan, we did not get a similar human perspective from there as American and British planes began to attack.

This is one of Indymedia's current structural shortcomings: its development mirrors the path of global development. Wealthy regions are more likely to have IMCs than poor regions. A progressive community is more likely than a reactionary one to have an IMC of its own. Even on a more local level, the people using Indymedia often have college educations and their own equipment. Although it has amplified the call to correct the global imbalance of wealth, Indymedia has not yet been able to transfer resources effectively from those who have them to those who do not. As communities in the global South and less privileged communities in developed countries launch IMCs and the connections among IMCs strengthen, communication should increase. While IMCs are intended to be open organizations where people are encouraged to work together, it is important for participants to feel comfortable among their colleagues, have a sense of shared ownership of the project, and be able to retain control over their media. The network structure can connect these autonomous groups. This is the significance of having an Independent Media Center of one's own.

". . . all of us who speak and listen."

Around the world, local IMC reporters are joining the ranks of professional journalists who have been risking their lives for decades to document war, economic oppression, and widespread corporate violence. As the companies that once employed these journalists become less inclined to take risks or to report honestly on situations where they may have a financial stake, on-the-ground, independent, community-based media will become an indispensable source of "unofficial" information on the world's most repressive governments and criminal corporations.[35]

As Independent Media Centers spread to economically impoverished countries and women there find a forum for raising their voices of opposition and having them heard, we will slowly begin to see the full strength of our community. From the ability to show the world how people on the street actually shut down the meeting of the World Trade Organization and sent its partners running behind police lines, to the coverage of massive peace rallies after September 11 that gave evidence of a desire for justice rather than vengeance, Indymedia's successes tell us that we have a shot at taking control of our public lives.

Together, we are realizing the vision of the Zapatistas, expressed by Subcomandante Marcos in his statement to the 1996 Zapatista Encuentro in Chiapas:

> We will make a network of communications among all our struggles and resistances. An intercontinental network of alternative communication against neoliberalism . . . [and] for humanity. This intercontinental network of alternative communication will search to weave the channels so that words may travel all the paths that resist. . . . [It] will be the medium by which distinct resistances communicate with one another. This intercontinental network of alternative communication is not an organizing structure, nor has a central head or decision maker, nor does it have a central command or hierarchies. We are the network, all of us who speak and listen.[36]

Now the construction of alternative networks of communication has come full circle: Chiapas has an IMC of its own. Launched by Zapatistas participating in the caravan to Mexico City and the National Indigenous Congress in March 2001, today it is a perpetual place for Reynalda Pablo Cruz and the people of southern Mexico to speak and a resource for listeners around the world. Facing huge disparities in access to technology and other resources when compared with the United States and other Western nations, the Chiapas IMC is nonetheless one of the most active. It is passion and the connection between those with passion that makes Indymedia possible.

"This is the essence of Zapatismo, and explains much of its appeal: a global call to revolution that tells you not to wait for the revolution, only to stand where you stand, to fight with your own weapon," says the author Naomi Klein. "It could be a video camera, words, ideas, 'hope'—all of these, Marcos has written, 'are also weapons.' It's a revolution in miniature that says, 'Yes, you can try this at home.'"[37]

CUT-AND-PASTE REVOLUTION:

NOTES FROM THE GIRL ZINE EXPLOSION

Jennifer Bleyer

Jennifer Bleyer was an original member of Riot Grrrl in the early 1990s and published the zines Roar, Gogglebox, *and* Mazeltov Cocktail, *the last two both named "Editor's Choice" by* Factsheet 5. *She has since produced a radio program on WBAI-Pacifica Radio, worked at* Harper's Magazine, *and founded* Heeb Magazine.

Death to all fucker punk boys who refuse to acknowledge the girl punk revolution. We are real and we are important and what we are doing is so beyond their comprehension. What this is is so big we can't even see it but we can feel it, it's coming.

—*Riot Grrrl Fanzine,*
Spring 1992

When they started publishing *Cupsize* in 1994, most of the other zines that Sasha Cagen and Tara Emelye Needham had seen were "creepy things by boys who hung out in the East Village." The two friends had clicked with each other as disgruntled first-years at Amherst College in Massachusetts, and when circumstances and school transfers found them reunited in New York City a few years later, they knew that making a zine as sassy and smart as themselves was exactly the way to cement their friendship. Cagen was working, ironically, at a major women's glossy—the kind of magazine that runs stories like "Drop Twenty Pounds in Two Weeks!" and "Moves That Will Make Him Beg for Mercy!"—and thus had unlimited access to office equipment and supplies. Late at night Needham would come to Cagen's midtown office building, and the two would ride to the twenty-first floor and take over the corporate suite. Writing, cutting, gluing, and drawing, they would laugh riotously into the wee hours, looking out over the twinkling Manhattan skyline.

Cupsize was the conduit through which their inner censors were silenced and their deepest voices unearthed. They wrote weighty personal tomes about bisexuality and analyzed the virtues of public and private education. At the same time, they wrote jokey stories about excessive eyebrow tweezing and memoirs of their first visit to a porn shop. On the cover, they would photocopy a swatch from a favorite article of clothing that one of them owned, a final wink to this very personal collage. Cagen would surreptitiously make hundreds of copies of the zine at her office over the course of a month. People—especially teenage women, who ordered copies in droves—loved *Cupsize,* and Cagen and Needham loved making it. "I think one of our impulses was political, but on the deepest level it was creative," Cagen recalls, almost five years after the final issue came out. "Tara and I had a fabulous chemistry between us that was really unique. It was just this absolute freedom that we believed in each other and could put whatever we wanted on the page. It was such a unique time in our lives, not having to worry about meeting professional obligations or standards." Cagen, who is now thirty and publishes the magazine *To-Do List* in San Francisco, wistfully remembers the zine heyday as a sort of literary Wild West, in which the utter lack of rules could yield extraordinary results. "You wound up with some really sloppy stuff," she says, "but you also ended up with these beautiful unpolished gems like *Cupsize* that would never make it in a commercial context."

Cagen and Needham were not alone. From the late eighties to the mid-nineties, thousands of zines sprouted up like resilient weeds inside the cracks of the mainstream media's concrete. Like those of most underground phenomena, their origin is fuzzy and debatable. Some trace it to the political broadsheets of the anti–Vietnam War movement; others link it to the raunchy, edgy comix of the seventies and eighties. One thing is certain, however: after Xerox machines became widely accessible and before the explosion of the Internet, there was a brief moment during which people realized that they could make their own rudimentary publications on copy paper, fasten them with staples, and send them out along the zine distribution thoroughfares that coursed across the country, without any permission or guidance whatsoever. There were gay zines, travel zines, country music zines, and film noir zines. There were socialist zines, stripper zines, bicycle zines, and radical environmental zines. As Sasha Cagen explains it, the homemade publications were not bound by any particular standards of quality—sophomoric writing, lunatic ravings, and bizarre obsessions were more common than not—yet there was something beautifully democratic about letting readers sift through it all on their own, instead of having an armada of elite publishers, editors, and critics do it for them. In many ways zines predicted what would soon happen on the Web, and although the comparison is akin to that between a firecracker pop and a nuclear bomb, they helped pave the way for a culture that would allow anyone with anything to say, to say it. Zines demonstrated what by the end of the twentieth century became a credo: Free speech on demand and without apology.

The zine world, as it turned out, was as susceptible to sexism as the larger society from which its niche was carved. Sarah Dyer was the only woman in a collective of male friends working on a music zine in the late eighties, and she was constantly aggravated that people calling about the zine would instinctually ask to speak with someone else when she answered the phone. Even when she branched off to start her own zine, *Mad Planet,* Dyer realized that many people couldn't quite accept that a woman could be doing this on her own. "It got really frustrating," she recalls. "A guy who wrote one review of one comic would somehow get credited with editing my whole zine." During a trip to London, she met another girl zinester who told her about some girl zines in the United States that she had never heard of, and the need for a networking device became obvious. In 1992 Dyer started the *Action Girl* newsletter. It was one of the first resources for girl zines—a single photocopied page with the names and addresses of the few other zines made by young women at the time, folded in thirds, addressed, and mailed off with a single stamp to girls voraciously looking for their own zine community. Coincidentally, Riot Grrrl was born a few months later in Olympia, Washington, and what resulted, given the climate of free expression already engendered by the larger zine community, was a media revolution of unprecedented proportion.

Riot Grrrl, of course, was that anarchic web of punk girls who were outcasts a couple of seasons before "outcast" was "in," who decided that slumber parties and hand-holding were revolutionary activities, and who were rightfully delirious from their collective peeling away of the pretenses of American teenage girlhood. It was a grassroots movement of young women who decided that mosh pits, bands, fanzines, and revolution were not just for boys. They used the same organizational tools that feminists had wielded for decades—a cool name, a manifesto, a tattered phone list, meetings in crowded living rooms—to confront not only myriad problems in their punk scenes, high schools, and dysfunctional families but also the dogma of mainstream feminism and society.

Zines were the perfect outlet for expressing discontent and new beliefs, and thousands of them materialized alongside the Riot Grrrl juggernaut. There was *I'm So Fucking Beautiful,* with its diatribes against fat oppression, and *Oompa Oompa,* with how-tos on herbal abortion and becoming "cunt positive." There was *Bikini Kill* by the famed Olympia band of the same name, with a lengthy ten-point defense of feminism in the punk scene, and *Tales of Blaarg,* which lightened things up with a menstrual board game. There were *Mudflap*'s bike repair tips for mechanically shy girls, *Elf Lube*'s unabashed ode to The Smiths, and *Aim Your Dick*'s fawning homage to the anarchist Emma Goldman. Some zines were more political, some more personal, and many were just hodgepodges of everything. Dyer's *Action Girl* newsletter, which was one of the most accurate gauges of the rate at which the phenomenon grew, eventually received up to twenty-five submissions of girl zines each day. Overwhelmed by mail, Dyer quit publishing the newsletter in 1996 and recently donated her entire girl zine archive to the Sallie Bingham Center for Women's History at Duke University. The collection amounted to a hundred and forty pounds of paper.

So what happened between Dyer's first listing of a few disparate girl zines and a hundred and forty pounds of them being trucked off and archived as a side note to women's history? It's a question that has to be unpacked in parts. First, consider the girls who were reading zines, and for whom they were often lifesavers. Being fourteen or fifteen years old anywhere—rural, suburban, or urban—can be a pretty dismal and isolating affair, and getting these Xeroxed-and-stapled concoctions in the mail was, for many who got them, roughly akin to receiving alien transmission from outer space confirming that they were not alone in the universe. Alice Marwick found out about zines through *Sassy* magazine in 1992, when the edgy teen magazine started running a regular feature on zines. Marwick, now twenty-four, went to high school in upstate New York, where she and her friends would order the zines in *Sassy* for the cost of copying and stamps, and devour them as soon as they arrived. "Zines connected me to a lot of things I couldn't find in my hometown, to a larger like-minded community," she says. "It definitely fostered my own feminist consciousness by proving that feminism wasn't something for people my mother's age only, or a dead movement altogether. That was the feeling you got growing up where I did—as if feminism didn't have anything to offer anyone young, that it was something that had happened and was done. But finding out about girl bands and underground feminist filmmaking through zines made it something that was still going on. It was a huge inspiration to me."

Integral to reading zines was the implicit challenge to turn around and write them. Zines made clear that they were not just another product to be consumed but were unique contributions to a vast conversation which everyone was expected to join. Girls who wrote zines did so because it was activism, it was therapy, and it was fun. They did so, as Sasha Cagen and Tara Emelye Needham of *Cupsize* did, to make emblems of their friendship and beliefs. They did it to respond to other girls' zines and to engage in the larger discussion about what exactly constituted "Revolution Girl Style." Erika Reinstein was a member of the original Riot Grrrl chapter in Washington, D.C., and remembers meetings during which everyone would get together and talk and write simultaneously. Then one young woman who had a computer would type the copy, lay it out with pictures, and make copies. It was instant zine-making, created literally within the context and safety of the community, and as much about the process as about the end result. For Reinstein, a survivor of childhood sexual abuse, making zines was the most important aspect of Riot Grrrl because it gave her a way to start writing about her trauma. "Riot Grrrl was about people learning how to express themselves, which a lot of girls did through bands, but I think it's easier to write something down than to get up onstage and play music. Just writing down your thoughts is so empowering," she says, noting that, after almost ten years, she has produced about thirty zines on her sexual abuse. "At this point, I have an artistic body of work that chronicles my whole healing process. People have different rituals for putting out the mistakes they've made and suffered from, and sending them into the water. As I've made progress in my healing process, I've been able to share insights with other people through my zines."

And in this way the girl zine revolution boiled over on the subcultural stove, occupying a unique intersection of art, protest, confession, and therapy. It seemed deeply, if unknowingly, informed by the old feminist dictum that "the personal is political." It's difficult for me to think or talk about girl zines without peering through the lens of my own experience. Flipping through the stack of old zines in the bottom drawer of my desk, I can't remember which was the first one, but I know that reading it as a fourteen-year-old in suburban Ohio was like having the anesthesia pulled while still splayed open on the operating table—in a good way. I leaf through them now like artifacts in my own personal museum, as viscerally familiar with each grainy photograph, emotional rant, and cutout graphic as one is with the scent of an old lover.

Like Alice Marwick, I found out about zines through *Sassy*, and hunted relentlessly for the Riot Grrrl community that was generating these magical creations. I recall with extraordinary fondness staying up all night in high school making zines with others from my local Riot Grrrl collective. Our backpacks and Glue Stics and stolen copy cards strewn all over the floor of Kinko's, we would scour books picked up from yard sales—housewife manuals, Girl Scout guides, Barbie coloring books, anatomical diagrams—for the most ironic graphics. We were dizzying crucibles of emotion, creating ourselves as well as creating our zines—the two seemed interchangeable. Between the ages of seventeen and nineteen, I published my own zine called

Gogglebox: a rather candid and often explicit record of my travels back and forth across the country. *Gogglebox* achieved a respectable stature in the zine community, having been named editor's choice by the now-defunct zine bible *Factsheet 5*. It generated tons of mail from girls all around the country, who poured their hearts out to me and who bought three thousand copies of the last issue. For a young writer and feminist, it was an exhilarating experience. Zines basically represented pure freedom; there were no ideological police to say that women's liberation couldn't be alternately sexy, angry, emotional, feminine, combative, childish—and unapologetically contradictory.

Revolution Girl Style was touted with an almost religious fervor. It seemed that if we only churned out enough zines and screamed loud enough, people would listen and society would quake. I do think this happened, in the way that small revolutions happen whenever people challenge the status quo and demonstrate alternative models of living in the world. But there are ways in which zines were not revolutionary, ways that are instructive for those of us committed to writing and publishing as a positive force for social change. One major detraction was how the mainstream media, with its interminable fetish for the salient and absurd, quickly pounced on zines. "Get ready for Riot Grrrl magazines," warned *USA Today*. "Hundreds of small, photocopied pamphlets now circulate, offering gut-wrenching confessional poetry and angry honest prose on topics such as rape, feeling ugly, boys, sex, and masturbation."[1] *The Dallas Morning News* leveled that "girlzines have their downside—bad spelling and layout, an excess of concert reviews, and a tendency toward self-indulgence."[2]

Indeed, it was only a matter of time before Riot Grrrl was effectively subsumed by the cultural zeitgeist, and the girl zines it helped inspire became little more than social curios and collectors' items. Of course, they continued to be produced, but the much portended Revolution Girl Style that had seemed so imminent when girl zines, bands, and collectives first exploded soon seemed like little more than a blip on the radar of feminist history, a mere footnote to social trends of the nineties.

Besides the impact of being sensationalized, there was the weakening effect of capitalization. The entire zine movement was effectively over, one could say, almost as soon as it began, having been swallowed up by the great maw of popular culture with dollar signs flashing in its eyes. Like hip-hop, grunge, and punk rock, the language and style of Riot Grrrl were absorbed, repackaged, and marketed back to us in the most superficial form of its origin. Whereas Riot Grrrl's "grrrl power" was about doing it yourself and questioning authority, pop culture appropriated the message to sell a sanitized version of "girl power" that was essentially capitalism dressed up in baby doll dresses, blue nail polish, and mall-bought nose rings. Indeed, the values—fearlessness, independence, daring, and a solid middle finger to the patriarchy—on which many girls zines were built, and for which their writers were denigrated as "angry" and "self-indulgent," were flipped on their heads and used to sell everything from cars and cigarettes to athletic shoes. The selling of girl power illustrated, as Naomi Klein wrote in *No Logo*, how "the cool hunters reduce vibrant cultural ideas to the status of archeological artifacts, and drain away whatever meaning they once held for the people who lived with them."[3]

Girl power, harnessed for its market potential and translated into consumer culture, had something for everyone. For the little girls, there were the Spice Girls and their endless records, collectibles, and concert tickets. For the bigger girls, there was *Sex and the City* and a bevy of books, movies, and magazines affirming, as Michelle Goldberg wrote, that "shopping-and-fucking feminism jibes precisely with the message of consumer society, [saying] that freedom means more—hotter sex, better food, ever-multiplying pairs of Manolo Blahnik shoes, drawers full of Betsey Johnson skirts, Kate Spade bags, and MAC lipsticks."[4] It was not the form of the zines as much as the tone and content of their writing that was appropriated for commercial ends. But not always: the clothing store Urban Outfitters actually published its own authentic-looking zine at one point to reap the trend's coolness factor. "They had some really good writers," Marwick recalls, "but their ultimate aim was to get people into Urban Outfitters to buy clothes and to brand them as a cool, hip, edgy store."

Both the denigration and the appropriation of zine style certainly did something to preempt the movement. Both were attacks from the outside in which zinesters essentially became caricatures of their own vision. A deeper blemish, however, was one that actually grew from within: the movement's virtual homogeneity. Despite pools of copier ink spilled in earnest discussions of race and class, girl zines were largely a hobby of white, middle-class young women. Riding on the heels of a feminist movement that had long stood rightly accused of excluding women of color and poor women, Riot Grrrl and its attendant zinesters was still a young version of a ladies' lunch society—except that the ladies have blue hair and weird clothes. Participating in girl zine culture requires that one have the leisure time to create zines, a life generally uncluttered with the rudiments of survival, access to copy machines and other equipment, money for stamps and supplies, and enough self-esteem and encouragement to believe that one's thoughts are worth putting down for public consumption—all marks of a certain level of privilege.

Although they were the exception to the rule, zines by young women of color or working-class backgrounds still found their way to fruition, and they were excellent. *Bamboo Girl,* which is still in print, features sassy, smart indictments of the exoticization of Asian-American women, interviews with Filipina authors on queerness, and analyses of "superwomen of color" in Japanese comix. The writer of *Discharge* zine recounts coming from a working-class, alcoholic, gambling family in Detroit to the D.C. Riot Grrrl community, where the most pressing concern often seemed the achievement of an equal opportunity mosh pit. Claudia von Vacano, a Latina Riot Grrrl in New York, wrote scathing indictments in her zines of Riot Grrrl's failure to confront its own internalized racism—which was for many the first time they had ever heard the phrase. *HUES* (Hear Us Emerging Sisters) was one of the most successful and respected girl zines (though more of a regular magazine than a zine) made by, for, and about young women of every color and shape. However, its content made it seem less a peripheral element of the white-dominated zine scene than a literary element of the growing multicultural scene.

Many of my fellow zinesters never saw or spoke of excellent zines like *Bamboo Girl* and *HUES,* suggesting that even within the self-proclaimed "underground," there is both a mainstream underground and an underground underground. To be fair, the girls in the former category were often writing zines about genuinely difficult things in their lives. But even so, it is difficult to feel completely vested in a slogan like "Revolution Girl Style Now" when the girls shouting it almost all look the same.

I might be giving the impression that zines are a phenomenon that came and went, that their effects were briefly felt, and that they no longer exist, or that Riot Grrrl and the motivations behind the "girl zine explosion" have also petered out. None of these statements is true. Riot Grrrl chapters still exist all over the country, in third- or fourth-generation incarnations, many churning out zines as they always have. Do-It-Yourself (DIY) zine distributions are still operated out of bedrooms and living rooms, selling zines that reflect the distributors' personal favorites. Anarchist infoshops, independent record stores, and many small bookstores still carry racks of new zine titles. Bigger magazines (some of which have their roots as zines) like *Giant Robot* and *Bust* review new zines and tell people where to send their concealed dollar or two for a copy. Ericka Bailie started Pander Zine Distribution in 1995 and now distributes up to 150 zine titles through a website and mail-order catalog. Having been closely involved with the girl zine community since 1992, Bailie thinks that the zines have actually gotten better since the trend-watching spotlight moved on to other things. "There are so many more people doing zines now that it doesn't seem like a novelty anymore," she says. "People aren't doing it just to be cool, they're making zines because it's just another outlet. It's normal."

Still, zines are not quite what they used to be, and the most compelling explanation of what happened to them can be told in one word: Internet. Since the Net blew up to unpredictable proportions in the mid-nineties, the essence of zines—namely, that anyone with anything to say can say it to the world—was codified and implemented en masse online. Everyone got a homepage, and e-zines became the electronic equivalents of their paper predecessors. Alice Marwick, who had already been involved with the zine community for several years, started *I Reclaim Wack* online in 1995 and loved the world-wide distribution, instant responses from readers, ability to change and update content, and absolutely free production. Like so many others, she taught herself HTML and learned the rudiments of Web design as an outlet for her creative energy and personal expression, and she has relished watching so many others do the same. "I think it's really good that there are so many e-zines," she says. "And actually, even though there are a lot of feminist girls online, I don't find that most of the e-zines by young women have a feminist slant at all. Yes, some are explicitly feminist, but many of them are just personal zines about girls' lives. If I was fourteen years old and growing up now, I would be so excited to find that community online."

Marwick's view is an important commentary not just on the status of girl e-zines but on the status of feminism as well. She's right that most e-zines for young women—even of the fierce, seemingly feminist variety—don't mention the F word outright. But a quick perusal of content shows that they are largely smart, challenging, socially aware, and independent—in short, feminist in every sense. Sites like *Ruby Slipper* (www.dork.com/rubyslipper) and *Smile and Act Nice* (www.smileandactnice.com) grapple with sexual assault and praise clothing catalogs with realistically sized models. Sites for women like *Bust* (www.bust.com) and *Maxi* (www.maximag.com) are unabashedly sex positive, celebrate solo travel, and demand, for example, that the 1999 Woodstock concert rapists bear full responsibility for their actions. Several huge sites that primarily serve teenage girls, like *gURL* (www.gurl.com), take on everything from bisexuality to body image, and provide free homepages to hundreds of thousands of girls. For those who criticize these types of sites as being too watered down (one New York–based riot grrrl describes them as putting "*Cosmopolitan* girls in tough-girl gear yet still conveniently kissing the Man's ass"), it's not hard to find the direct descendants of the girl zines of the early nineties online, with politics, spunk, and cool clip art to spare. In the sense that feminism is a gendered analysis of society toward liberation from social dictates, all of these can rightly be called "feminist"—whether they say it themselves or not.

It would seem, then, that the Internet and the advent of e-zines have been nothing short of a miracle for girls who previously had to scrounge around indie record stores and punk shows for a portal into the zine underground. Positive things have clearly come from the proliferation of online zines, not least, as Marwick mentions, the ease with which isolated young women pining for like-minded peers can now find them. And although some zine aficionados may lament having lost the exciting sense of tree-house-club secrecy that once shrouded the zine culture, there is something equally exciting about their enormous visibility online. How vindicating is it that e-zines like *My Boot Against the World* and *BratGirl* can be located as easily as the webpage for, say, Amazon? The blank URL bar of an Internet window has proven itself in many ways to be the great cultural equalizer. A Google search for "girl zine" turns up thousands of results; "pro-choice zine" hundreds. The question nowadays is not where to find a good girl zine but rather how to begin sloshing through the glut of them.

And the girls and women making e-zines? Their motivations vary as much online as they do in print. Deanna Zandt never made a print zine and didn't even know they existed until she was in college. As the publisher of *GenerationGrrl*, however, she values helping younger girls foster a sense of themselves by offering an alternative to what she calls the "bullshit of glossy magazines." She says, "I remember reading those and thinking anything from 'I will never have skin that smooth!' to 'I will never have the money to spend two hundred dollars on a pair of jeans!' and also thinking that those things were really inherent to my self-worth as a person. Not to mention the zero-lesbian-visibility factor. Please! We are real girls and women producing these things, telling our life stories—we give life to our words through our designs and pictures. In a very broad sense, it's like being the big sister who shows you how to navigate the world, not just what lipstick to buy." Others see their e-zines more as conduits through which to connect with peers. After producing *Bunnies on Strike* as a paper zine in Holland for several years, Tanja put it online with the help of a Web designer friend.[5] Since then she has been able to connect with Riot Grrrls and like-minded young feminists all over Europe and North America, and in some parts of Asia and Africa. "E-zines themselves are just a step further in the already existing revolution of paper zines," Tanja explains. "Being online just makes your zine available to more people. It can be revolutionary once you meet other girls through the Internet and decide to take action."

Revolutionary is a powerful term, however, and one that just doesn't apply to what many girls are doing online. Homepages, for example, are pretty closely related to zines—rants, raves, diary entries, some photographs, perhaps some poetry, yet often nothing politicized. In this light, not everyone agrees that the realization of a soapbox for every young woman is the pinnacle of feminist achievement. The website gURL.com hosts around half a million homepages, and its cofounder Esther Drill suggests that while they may be an important rite of self-expression for teenage girls, they may also have gone overboard. "It's great if these girls are smart and have something to say, but if they're talking about stupid things, then it's just one more extraneous voice added to everything," she says. "Girls put up their diaries all the time, and after a while, I wonder if that's a good development. There are other important things for people to talk about besides themselves, and in general, the homepages are really self-focused. For all the good things, I also want to say, 'Guess what, girls, you're not the most important people in the world.'"

More troubling even than the possible overabundance of homepages and e-zines is the complete absence of them for those without access. The technological landscape reflects the homogeneity of zine makers. The 2000 U.S. census reported that among families with incomes of $25,000 or less, only 19 percent had access to the Internet, compared with 75 percent among families with incomes of $75,000 or higher. Only 33 percent of black homes and 34 percent of Latinos had Internet access, while 53 percent of white non-Hispanics had access, as did 65 percent of Asians and Pacific Islanders.[6] More recent reports, however, show that both the racial and class gaps are closing. By 2001 there were reports that Internet use among blacks had grown at an annual rate of 31 percent, while use among whites grew by 19 percent. During the same period that home access to the Internet increased among blacks, it increased as well for poor people of all races.[7]

Young women of color who do have Internet access are using the information superhighway to build community, express themselves, discover its infinite possibilities, and connect with people both similar to and different from themselves. The resources are certainly not anywhere as abundant as they should be, but they seem to be increasingly present, ranging from *Colorlines* magazine's information on the rampant incarceration of urban youth to Black Grrrl Revolution's *Problackgrrrlfesto,* which states that "still being ingrained in society's consciousness by academia [is] that black only equates African-American and male, and that woman only equates white"[8]—both hopeful signs that when the numbers of young woman of color online increase, there will be something there for them beyond Backstreet Boys fanpages and Caucasian beauty tips.

As technology activists continue working to narrow the digital divide, the critical imperative to do so shows no signs of letting up. Beyond zines and e-zines, young women are making films, producing music, publishing books, and otherwise carving space for the DIY ethic in the feminist sphere. Kara Herold interviewed forty-five girl zinesters for her film *Grrlyshow,* a documentary about girl zines and their relationship to contemporary feminism, and found that many identified as strongly as media activists as they did as feminists. "Since just a few corporations essentially own all the magazines, the whole point is getting your writing out there into the culture, even if it's just to ten other people," Herold explains. "If you have something different to say than the mainstream, it's feminist just by virtue of believing that what you have to say is important. That's why I think girl zines and e-zines will continue, because, really, you have to create your own venues. Nobody else is going to do it for you."

Holly Bass

Holly Bass is a writer and performer. She has written arts features for The Wall Street Journal, *the* Washington City Paper, *and* American Theater Magazine, *and her poems have appeared in* Callaloo, Cave Canem V, *and* Role Call: A Generational Anthology of Social and Political Black Literature and Art. *She also co-curates the New York City Hip-Hop Theater Festival. She received her B.A. from Sarah Lawrence College and a master's degree in journalism from Columbia University.*

Looking for Juliet

The hushed electric darkness of a theater. An audience collectively inhales. Lights rise. A scene of carnage, limp bodies scattered across the stage. A young man prowls among the corpses like an animal, nudging them with balled fists, detached yet human enough to feel that something within him has also died. The sound of several discs mixed and scratched by an orchestra of deejays ushers in a new scene. The lights flash viciously, rapidly, slicing the stage into visual sound bites

like the jump cuts in a music video. The dancers come to life
and begin to tell an old, old story: "Two households, both alike
in dignity/In fair Verona, where we lay our scene/From
ancient grudge break to new mutiny . . ."

But this is not the Shakespeare taught year after year by
countless English 101 teachers to countless uninspired students. The choreographer Rennie Harris, whose company Pure-
movement marries hip-hop and modern dance, offers a dark,
postmodern, multidisciplinary remake with shades of *West
Side Story*. Harris flips *Romeo and Juliet* so that it becomes not
a story about a boy and girl but a story of a boy and his *boyz*.
"Star-crossed lovers" becomes "star-crossed homies" in the opening rhymed prologue, and guns and knives replace poison and
sleeping potions.

Visually stunning, his "hip hopera," *Rome and Jewels,* incor-
porates live video and sound effects, intricate lighting designs,
slides, three onstage deejays, a nine-member company, and a
troupe of associated dancers. *Rome and Jewels* uses rhymed
poetic monologues replete with current hip-hop references
and beautifully staged dance sequences, as well as improvisa-
tion, to update this classic tale of ill-fated romance. It focuses
on the friendship and camaraderie among young black men
while delivering a haunting assessment of the violence that
permeates much of urban life. Hugely successful by performing arts standards, the piece was performed across the country
and internationally between 2000 and 2002.[1]

But what differentiates *Rome and Jewels* from Shakespeare's
original and the incalculable number of remakes is also its
most disturbing feature—there is no Juliet. The audience knows
of her existence only through references to her by the male

characters. When Rome delivers the famous "What light through yonder window breaks" monologue, a pool of white light appears onstage, and he looks upward as if Jewels were standing at her balcony looking down. He proceeds to woo her with a mix of schoolboy charm and mack daddy come-ons in a monologue that ends with a mimed sex scene. He starts off slowly, grinding his hips on the floor as he praises Jewels's sexual prowess and beauty. As the solo continues, his gestures indicate that Jewels has taken on larger-than-life proportions, like the Incredible Shrinking Woman in reverse, growing so much that in the end there is only her all-consuming vulva. He mimes diving inside it, breast-stroking through this imaginary vaginal paradise.

Through the comments of Rome's homies, we learn that Jewels is "a fine ass ho," though Rome counters his friends' crass assessment, saying that Jewels is truly "beautiful." And what makes Jewels off-limits is not family disapproval of Rome—as in *West Side Story,* her family doesn't appear in the play—but that she is the girlfriend of a rival gang member, Tibault. By the end of the piece, though still unseen, Jewels becomes the saddest of stereotypes—an unwed pregnant teen whose baby's daddy has been murdered in a case of black-on-black crime.

In response to questions, Harris has stated that he intended to show Rome's evolution from a hard-core, bragging, swaggering roughneck to a "fully human" person through love.[2] In the real world, outside of art and theory, Harris has been a vocal supporter of women dancers in hip-hop and has had several b-girls in his company. In *Rome and Jewels* he experimented with incorporating a female lead[3] but dropped her. The women function primarily as one of the boys, as the saying goes. In some ways this is a positive step—the b-girls in battle sequences, where dancers showcase their best moves, clearly are there for the quality of their dancing. But when Ben V., Tibault's best friend, refers to women as having "fallopian tombs" and tells Tibault that Rome was "all up in that cavity," meaning Rome was having sex with Jewels, the absence of a strong female counterpart is conspicuous. Juliet/Jewels, invisible and voiceless, never has a chance to speak for herself.

In the hushed electric darkness, I was looking for Jewels, looking for new theater that in some way mirrored my experience. She never took the stage.

My Definition Is This

When many people hear the term *hip-hop* today, it brings to mind bikini-clad, booty-shaking women surrounding a bejeweled rapper as he (or she) extols the virtues of conspicuous consumption and innumerable sexual conquests. But hip-hop is more than rap music and videos. Hip-hop is a culture with roots that can be traced back to ancient traditions of singing, dancing, drumming, oral history recitation, carving, and hieroglyphics.[4] Like its ancient cousins, this culture prioritizes both stories that urgently need to be told and the art of storytelling.

Hip-hop culture is born out of traditional village society (with its emphasis on ritual, circle, and inclusion) and the urban crucible of discrete, concrete boxes stacked one upon the other, tightly compressed squares where youth grow up with an acute awareness of all the things they do not have. In the projects or other racial ghettos, hip-hop has provided an outlet, a way to—using a pieced together art form—express brutal and otherwise unexposed realities. Hip-hop culture is postmodernism in its most organic form. It takes supposedly unrelated cultural forms and cuts, pastes, and collages them into completely new forms: turntables that scratch records instead of play them; dancers whose feet hang in the air as their hands, backs, arms, and heads spin on the ground; Beethoven transformed in the hands of the mixmaster Afrika Bambaataa. Although hip-hop culture has tremendous potential for political protest, it is primarily a means of artistic cultural expression. In its twenty-five or so years of existence, hip-hop culture has spilled outside Bronx and Harlem projects, basketball courts, and block parties. It has moved beyond American radio and television to infiltrate and infect popular youth culture worldwide.

Hip-hop theater is theater for the new century, but the form itself is not as new as it might appear. The narrowest definitions of hip-hop theater insist that it includes one or more of the primary elements of hip-hop—emceeing or rapping, deejaying, b-boying or b-girling (commonly called break dancing), and graffiti art. But not all hip-hop theater has to rhyme or be backed with bass lines and beats. Any production that captures the energy and feeling and drive of this hip-hop generation, its issues and concerns, its larger cultural aesthetic, is hip-hop theater. And hip-hop theater is more than just what's on the stage; it's who's in the audience as well. A theater work can have all the beats and rhymes and slick moves it wants, but if the production excludes the hip-hop community from the audience, it loses a valuable synergy. The interaction between the performer and the audience is a crucial element in the work. Hip-hop the-ater practitioners will often say that when they perform in front of the traditional theater audience—which is predominantly white, middle- to upper-middle-class, and over fifty—the crowd doesn't "feel" them the way a more diverse audience grounded in hip-hop culture might. If we turn down the bass-heavy beats and slow the rapid-fire rhymes, we see that hip-hop theater is a return to theater for the people.

Like hip-hop, theater in its earliest forms evolved from com-munal ritual, elevating everyday rites—death, birth, marriage, war—into shared spectacle. From elaborate drum, dance, and story circles in West African antiquity to poetry sung by masked choruses in ancient Greece, popular theater reflected the larger community and was generally accessible.

In our age of advancing technology and increasing class divi-sions, the performing arts have become primarily the domain of the educated and monied classes. The contemporary coun-terparts to Shakespeare's groundlings, the poor and working-class patrons who watched plays from the cheap seats below the stage, now make do with television and movies. Critics often rail against the deadening effect of technology—that computers, the Internet, and television separate and isolate people. But hip-hop theater uses technology—drum machines, turntables, live video montages, Internet marketing and pro-motion—to bring people together, shoulder to shoulder, in the flesh, and at cheaper ticket prices than those charged by most of the performing arts.

Of course, hip-hop theater is not the first to centralize an element of popular culture on the stage. During the Black Arts Movement of the 1960s and '70s, poets like Ntozake Shange and Amiri Baraka (né LeRoi Jones) transformed their staccato rhythms, protest poems, and lyricism into searing, highly politicized theatrical works, such as Shange's *for colored girls who have considered suicide/when the rainbow is enuf* and Baraka's *Dutchman*. The 1970s through the nineties saw the emergence of "rock operas" and musicals from *Hair* and The Who's *Tommy* to more recent musicals such as *Hedwig and the Angry Inch* and *Rent*. But as Broadway becomes a virtual subsidiary of the Walt Disney Company and regional theaters sustain themselves with high-priced tickets for sure-to-sell revivals of classic plays, a new theater that reflects and celebrates contemporary society, challenges the imbalances of power in our culture, and remains economically accessible becomes even more necessary.

Return of the Boom Bap

Early hip-hop shows of the 1970s almost always had a theatrical element, since artists at the time earned their reputations more from live performance than from their recordings. The classic hip-hop film, *Beat Street,* immortalized the high-energy theatricality of live hip-hop shows, notably in the Santa Claus scene performed by the Treacherous Three, complete with a velvet curtain, costumes, and Chaplinesque antics. GhettOriginal Production dance company, made up of members of the pioneering hip-hop dance crews Rock Steady Crew, Magnificent Force, and Rhythm Techniques, enjoyed an extended sold-out run at P.S. 122 of the "hip-hop ghetto musical" *So What Happens Now?* in 1992.

Probably the best-known piece of hip-hop theater is *Bring in 'Da Noise, Bring in 'Da Funk,* which started at the Public Theater before moving to Broadway, where it garnered two Tony Awards in 1996 for choreography (by Savion Glover) and direction (George C. Wolfe). The book for the musical, which was nominated for a Tony, pulsed with staccato rhythms, terse rhymes, and cleverly woven narratives detailing the black experience in America. The poet Reg E. Gaines, a product of the Nuyorican Poets Cafe and the New York slam poetry scene, was also nominated for a Tony for his hip-hop-inspired text and lyrics.

In many ways hip-hop theater represents a return to more holistic, open-minded, progressive ideas present in earlier manifestations of hip-hop culture, especially music. Hip-hop theater, for example, attracts a younger, more urban audience, and then encourages the audience to participate in the show in a form that resembles call-and-response. In this way, hip-hop theater brings us back to egalitarian hip-hop music, when the audience was encouraged to interact with the artists. And while the popularity of hip-hop theater will undoubtedly increase, the economic potential of theater is much lower than that of popular music, which means that it may be possible for hip-hop theater to retain its mostly progressive political themes without too much fear of commercial control.

Early rap music and manifestations of hip-hop culture tended to focus more on dance music and a party atmosphere. Even the competitive braggadocio rhymes dealt more with artistic prowess than with how much money or how many murder charges one had accumulated. Popular groups like Grandmaster Flash and the Furious Five addressed the economic hardships of working-class blacks in songs like "The Message" while counseling against cocaine use in "White Lines" without any loss of street credibility. An artist who put out an antidrug recording now would be laughed out of the studio faster than Nancy Reagan could "just say no."

In the mid-eighties, rap took on a decidedly militant tone with groups like Public Enemy, whose focus was black political empowerment, and Queen Latifah, whose women-centered messages echoed feminist concerns. But in the nineties, with the popularity of gangsta rap and artists striving to outdo themselves with wilder and more fantastic tales of sex, violence, and crime, hip-hop gained its largest audience but lost touch with its core cultural values. Currently, mainstream rap is all about the "bling bling"—the sound of gold and diamond watches bumping up against each other, the sound of champagne glasses filled with Cristal or Dom P clinking, the sound of cash registers overflowing with Benjamin Franklins. Rap music became profitable, and commercial artists were given little incentive to challenge the status quo. In this stage of rap, especially in music videos, the representation of women mirrors the status quo: they are primarily significant as sexualized backdrops—a little booty here, a skimpy bikini top there—and signs of wealth alongside the Benzes and Cadillac Escalades.

Although the mainstream rap industry is male-dominated, women have a stronger presence in hip-hop theater, particularly behind the scenes as producers, directors, technical directors, administrators, and graphic designers. That said, the actual presence and representation of women on the stage leaves something to be desired. Even with plays written and/or directed by women, the main protagonists are often male, replicating the tendency of the commercial rap industry to promote male artists more heavily than female artists and the media's obsession with "the endangered young black male." In some of the more progressive pieces by male artists, which artfully address issues of police brutality, violence within communities of color, consumerism, and racial discrimination, characters' misogynist comments sometimes go unchallenged within the work. Many artists argue that the misogyny in their work is simply a representation of reality, merely "keeping it real." But this easy-out response falls apart quickly when one examines the treatment of other issues, such as racism or crime, in which an attitude is presented as reality and then challenged and deconstructed. Sexist comments in and of themselves are not a problem, but when they are not refuted elsewhere in the piece, they are.

The most successful hip-hop theater shows featured male themes and male performers. There are many reasons for this: the social conventions that gender artistic expression (i.e., women should sing and leave rapping to the men) and the fact that most theater producers and directors are men. The roots of hip-hop culture also lie in activities that have always been traditionally assigned to men. If we view precolonial West Africa as a precedent, we see the roots of rapping, deejaying, graffiti writing, and breaking in the griot, the drummer, the carver, and the warrior trained in martial arts, all of whom were men.[5]

When women engage in hip-hop culture, the work they produce is often not considered hip-hop enough, especially in an environment which favors hard-core violence and the degradation of women. Among hip-hop theater aficionados, much work by female artists is considered alternative, and male artists who deliberately avoid violence and misogyny are labeled "soft." As hip-hop music and culture have become more popular, they have become more narrow-minded. Hip-hop theater artists who want to broaden the spectrum still have to fight the prevailing attitudes to have their work heard and accepted.

Will Power, a male performer originally from the California Bay Area who expresses very progressive feminist politics in his work, is one such artist. His solo show *The Gathering,* which debuted on the West Coast in 1999, explored different gathering places of black men, such as the basketball court, the barbershop, and the jazz club. In one scene Power portrays a gay man confronting an elderly minister about his homophobia. In another he takes on the persona of an upright bass player admonishing a young rapper about his misogynist lyrics, suggesting that bass itself, the foundation of rap music, is feminine. In resonant low notes while he mimes plucking bass strings, Power intones, "You can't be a bass lover and a woman hater, mmmm. Nothing is more powerful than the . . . bass. Nothing is deeper than the . . . bass." But more than his subject matter, Power's very way of moving onstage, the grace and lyricism of his choreography, along with his complete lack of machismo, separates him from other male artists.

Power's work disappoints those looking for the hard-edged attitude of hip-hop. In a summer 2001 performance in San Francisco with three other hip-hop theater artists, Power received less enthusiastic critical reviews than did his counterparts, whose work could be characterized as more edgy, angry, and in-your-face.[6] Perhaps the idea of a tall, graceful, young black man defending women and gays with unmasked sincerity in a hip-hop performance disturbs audiences and disrupts their notions of hip-hop, blackness, and masculinity. Even so, I would argue that Power's work lures the audience into a new way of looking—allowing them the space to process the ideas and images they are seeing onstage and to suspend their pre-conceived notions of what black male behavior should be.

Leaders of the New School

As the curator for the second New York City Hip-Hop Theater Festival, which took place in June 2001 at P.S. 122 in the East Village, I had the opportunity to work with many incredible artists during the festival's three-week run and the months of development preceding it. Prior to the festival, my work as an arts journalist, teacher, and performer allowed me to witness this art form from its early germination to its current furious flowering. And despite my belief that hip-hop theater will undoubtedly, like other art forms that receive big commercial backing, be lured into reflections of the status quo instead of criticisms of it, there are still cutting-edge feminist performers who are using their art to make thoughtful commentaries on our society.

In the independent theater world, two of the best-known performers are Danny Hoch and Sarah Jones. Along with Power they include progressive politics in their work and are emblematic of feminist hip-hop theater. Both Jones and Hoch possess an uncanny ear for character, voice, gesture, and accent. With only the slightest costume change (a baseball cap, a scarf), they transform seamlessly into vastly different characters. The effect is consistently stunning, with awed audiences leaping to their feet at the end of a show. But that's not, of course, what's politically meaningful about their work. Jones's and Hoch's characters attempt to speak most profoundly to a larger group than those who normally occupy theater seats. As in early hip-hop music, they are trying to make the world a better place by telling the stories of people who are often without voice—a homeless woman, the guy who works at the bodega, people in prison. As Hoch said in an interview published in *The Revolutionary Worker,* "I've seen all generations, colors, and genders moved by what I do . . . Their minds were opened. I could touch the possibility for a change in these people, particularly [those folks I've worked with] in jail."[7]

Hoch grew up in a working-class neighborhood in Queens in the 1970s. Raised by a single mother, he describes being surrounded by neighbors from Puerto Rico, the Dominican Republic, Russia, India, the Philippines, Senegal, and the Caribbean as well as Jews, blacks, and Italian Americans and combinations of the lot. After graduating from LaGuardia High School of the Performing Arts (the *Fame* school), he attended North Carolina School of the Arts. He dropped out in his second year and returned to New York. For five years he worked with New York University's Creative Arts Team, leading improvisational theater workshops to teach conflict resolution to young people in high schools, jails, and detention centers.

He made a name for himself with his solo performance play *Pot Melting.* A mind-dazzling collage of characters, the play premiered in the winter of 1991 in a run-down theater space with no heat. Word of mouth about Hoch's chameleonic abilities spread. He followed with *Some People* at the Public Theater in 1993, which won an Obie award and was turned into an award-winning HBO special. His 1998 piece, *Jails, Hospitals & Hip-Hop*, which tells the stories of ten characters, including a white prison guard, a heroin-addicted inmate with HIV, and a Cuban engineering student with a limited understanding of English enamored of American rap, was published as a book and made into a film.

Hoch is also an activist and uses his talent and other resources to benefit social justice causes.[8] After several critical successes, he turned down about $4 million worth of movie roles because the characters he would have portrayed lacked depth. As his popularity grew and he was booked into bigger venues, ticket prices went up, and the audience for his work changed. Uncomfortable with presenting stories of urban life to predominantly white, upper-middle-class audiences that had little or no connection to the experiences of the characters onstage, Hoch began to request that theaters invite youth groups and would sometimes pass out free tickets to teens in nearby neighborhoods. His activist ideals affect not only his work as an actor and playwright but also his approach to producing theater. For the NYC Hip-Hop Theater Festival, advertising money went to street team promoters rather than ads in major daily newspapers, and a third of all tickets were donated to High Five, an organization that provides high school students with theater tickets for five dollars.

Sarah Jones emerged from the downtown slam poetry scene in the mid-nineties. In 1997 she won the Nuyorican Poets Cafe Grand Slam Championship and was a member of the Nuyorican Slam Team, which made it to the semifinals of the National Slam. Like Hoch and many hip-hop theater artists, Jones is a teacher as well as a performer. She has taught workshops in poetry and theater at Rikers Island's Rosewood School, various New York City public schools, and universities in the United States and Europe. Her work has also been featured on various hip-hop albums, including *Lyricist Lounge, Vol. 1,* and *The Rose That Grew from Concrete: The Poems of Tupac Shakur.* Because of the language she uses to speak about women's rights, Jones's lyrics have been unfairly censored. In 1999, with the London-based hip-hop artist DJ Vadim, she recorded "Your Revolution," which appeared on *USSR: Life from the Other Side.* The song was a minor success in Europe and received some airplay stateside, mostly by small independents and college radio stations.

After the volunteer deejay Deena Barnwell of KBOO played Jones's recorded poem "Your Revolution" on *Soundbox,* a weekly program of music that addresses various social justice issues, a U.S. listener complained to the Federal Communications Commission. It took the FCC two years to act, but it ultimately prosecuted the Portland, Oregon, station "for willfully broadcasting indecent language." The station was fined $7,000, a hefty fee for a noncommercial radio station.[9]

A takeoff on "The Revolution Will Not Be Televised" by Gil-Scott Heron, with whom Jones toured, "Your Revolution" addresses the misogyny in contemporary popular culture and parodies lyrics to popular rap songs of the day, referencing platinum-selling rappers who degrade women in their songs:

> *your revolution will not happen between these thighs*
> *your revolution will not happen between these thighs*
> *the real revolution*
> *ain't about booty size*

the Versaces you buys
or the Lexus you drives

and though we've lost Biggie Smalls
your Notorious revolution
will never allow you to lace no lyrical douche in my bush

your revolution
will not find me in the
backseat of a Jeep with LL
hard as hell
doin' it & doin' it & doin' it well

your revolution will not be you
smackin' it up, flippin' it, or rubbin' it down
nor will it take you downtown or humpin' around
because that revolution will not happen between these thighs

you will not be touching your lips to my triple dip of
french vanilla butter pecan chocolate deluxe
or having Akinyele's dream
a six-foot blow-job machine
you wanna subjugate your queen;
think I should put that in my mouth
just 'cause you made a few bucks . . .

The radio station filed a countersuit, and Jones provided a statement explaining the political context of her work, along with testimony from academics and a petition signed by KBOO listeners. Both Jones and station employees thought the case would be dismissed and her work considered protected speech under the First Amendment. The FCC saw it another way.

Jones believes the FCC ruling reflects the commissioners' ignorance of hip-hop culture as well as the strident conservatism of the Bush administration. "This is a particular sticking point for me as a person of color and a woman. Too often what we put out is judged by our bodies; we're always in a position where we have to fight to have our identity as women and our sexuality," she says.[10] "In attacking my song in the same way they would a Foxy Brown or a Lil' Kim, they don't even realize they're participating in the same thing they say they are trying to stop. It's their own kind of sexist lens that keeps them from listening and seeing that the song is actually about empowerment."

The ruling doesn't require the FCC to stipulate which words were the cause of the offense. Ironically, the only other recording artist to have been censored under the new FCC rulings is the rapper Eminem, known for his violent, misogynist, and homophobic lyrics. The suit against him was filed after a listener complained when a radio station played the album version of one of his songs. Had the station played the "clean" version, in which potentially "offensive" words are edited out, the case would not have been brought at all. Ostensibly, the rock-rap group Limp Bizkit can boast on the airwaves "I did it all for the nookie." Eminem can rap about having sex with his mother and killing his girlfriend without penalty, as long as the actual offensive words are deleted, but Sarah Jones's reworking of sexually explicit songs by male rappers—songs that have been played freely on the radio—warrants legal censorship. In the cases of groups like Limp Bizkit or rappers like the Notorious B.I.G. and Eminem, even if everyone, including children, can easily, from the context, fill in the "real" words that are bleeped out, the FCC gives license to sing as much as groups want about blow jobs, bitches, and hoes. Nas's particularly misogynistic 2001 hit "Oochie Wally" describes a sex act in which a woman is passed from guy to guy. Even though the so-called offensive words are edited out, the meaning of the brutality comes across vividly. Jones's lyrics, by contrast, have the potential to reach young women who can't help but hear songs like "Oochie Wally" on the radio and to lead them toward self-empowerment and protection. In her theater works, Jones has much more freedom to say what she wants.

It was at the Nuyorican Poets Cafe that Jones developed her first solo show, *Surface Transit,* which went on to have extended, highly acclaimed runs at P.S. 122 and on Broadway at the American Place Theatre. In the show she portrays eight residents of New York City connected to one another by chance. A Polish immigrant who struggles to understand the racism directed at her biracial daughter works as a cleaning woman for another of Jones's characters, a conservative Jewish grandmother who complains about gays and rap music. A young emcee leads a twelve-step meeting for recovering rappers, while a sassy, round-the-way teen and proud virgin speaks out against curbside sexual harassment.

Jones's critically acclaimed solo piece *Women Can't Wait,* commissioned by the international women's rights organization Equality Now, premiered at the United Nations International Conference on Women's Rights in June 2000. In it Jones again depicts eight characters, composites based on real women who come together to address the UN in protest against sexually discriminatory laws in their home countries.

Jones wraps a sheer length of fabric, her only prop, different ways, around her head, diagonally across her torso, in a bundle like an infant baby, to evoke women from around the world. Praveen breaks the silence about being regularly abused by her husband in India, where a man cannot legally be convicted of raping his wife. Tomoko from Japan protests laws governing a woman's right to remarry. Hala from Jordan makes a case against the legally sanctioned abuse and murder of a woman for adultery by male relatives. Alma from Uruguay faces pressure to marry her rapist, who would then be legally pardoned for his crime. Shira from Israel fights to divorce her husband. Young Anna from Kenya doesn't want to be circumcised in a female initiation ceremony. Emeraude breaks the French labor law that prohibits women from working at night, while Bonita from the United States, a pregnant drug addict, faces criminal charges if she seeks medical attention.

Although Jones's work is clearly striking and powerful as it shifts the boundaries of what hip-hop theater is, and can be, she has to contend with "purists" in the United States who don't consider her recordings and theater hip-hop. Men who incorporate feminist messages into their work are perceived as "soft," but the question of "realness," or authenticity, is one that dogs women artists much more than it does men. Women artists in hip-hop not only have to excel at their art form but often have to prove their legitimacy to a community which judges them against an aesthetic standard set by the commercial rap industry. The multiplicity of voices within hip-hop and hip-hop theater tend to fall outside this narrow standard. In this way, women's voices in hip-hop theater are marginalized or delegitimized.

Keeping It Moving

As more progressive women artists begin to create work that reflects their particular experiences and political perspectives, it becomes necessary to develop a new context for understanding their work. Curators, directors, and theater producers play a significant role in determining what makes it to the stage and how the work is framed. More critical writing and scholarly exploration of these emerging artists will also help legitimize this kind of work, but the audience is the ultimate arbiter of success.

One piece in particular from the 2001 New York City Hip-Hop Theater Festival illustrates how women artists can manifest the creative energy of hip-hop in ways very different from men's. The Revival, a collaboration of four female artists, presents itself as a religious service at the Church of the Living Womb with the audience as congregation. The smell of burning incense greets patrons as they arrive. In lieu of formal programs, audience members are given paper fans like the ones typically found in traditional black churches with advertisements for local funeral homes.

The Revival recalls the "seminal" (ovular?) work of the performance artists Jessica Hagedorn, Robbie McCauley, and Laurie Carlos, who as the group Thought Music performed in experimental theaters in the late 1980s. The performers enter from behind the audience singing and playing tambourines, carrying bundles of burning sage. Encouraging call-and-response with the "congregation," each of the "preachers" makes her way to the pulpit to deliver a sermon. Tish Benson opens up by reading a passage from "the good book"—not the Bible, which also appears onstage, but Zora Neale Hurston's *Their Eyes Were Watching God*. She crouches low to the ground to hear the voice of her womb, which delivers Christ-like parables and truisms. Sistah Sebek, wearing an army helmet adorned with a large gold ankh, directs her message to the women in the audience. Her distinctive, low-pitched voice rolls from empathetic Oprah-like encouragement to guttural tongue-lashing as she puts her audience in the hot seat about everything from health and diet to child-rearing and financial management. Liza Jessie Peterson, as Sistah Merlina, has the most obvious hip-hop elements in her rhyming sermon, which addresses the creative and psychic power of people of color and the economic and political forces which keep people from using their full potential. The vocalist Imani Uzuri punctuates the piece with gospel choruses, speeding them up until they become percussive chants.

Some viewers questioned whether the Revival was hip-hop enough. With the exception of Peterson's character, the Revival uses very little rhyming, and none of the other primary elements of hip-hop—deejaying, b-girling, graffiti. Yet one clearly sees the techniques of hip-hop production—sampling, taking elements from one song (or text) to create the musical base for another work; the way the text turns on itself, repeats and builds; and deejay turntable techniques such as repetition, cutting, and scratching—in the group's work. In a brilliant reference to James Brown, the most sampled artist in the history of hip-hop music, Sebek shouts and moans herself into a fever pitch, ending on bended knee, prompting the other performers to drape her in a large velvet cape. The sung vocals, led by

Uzuri, act like musical hooks, the kinds of brief repeated choruses found in rap songs, connecting the various monologues
in the same way a hook would connect the rhymes of different
emcees taking turns on the microphones.

In the opening track to the album *Black on Both Sides,* the rapper Mos Def says he's often asked where hip-hop is going. "If
we smoked out then hip-hop is going to be smoked out. If we're
doing all right, then hip-hop is going to be all right. . . . We are
hip-hop, so hip-hop is going where we're going." The same is
true of hip-hop theater.

Over the years, rumors of a large-scale hip-hop musical or
film in the works crop up, but such a project has not yet been
realized. (MTV attempted this with *Carmen,* starring Beyoncé
Knowles, in 2001, but the ultimately disappointing film made
little impact.) Certainly there's a desire within mainstream
Hollywood and Broadway to cash in on the popularity of hip-
hop. The proliferation and sustained presence of hip-hop elements in television commercials prove that a viable market
exists, but the big-budget producers haven't yet found a vehicle for work that both has mass appeal and retains a kind of
street-level, grassroots reality.

Just as painters might belong to the Impressionist school,
the Cubists, or the Neo-Realists, hip-hop theater artists have
created a new school of theatrical performance. Its aesthetic is
characterized by rhyming, beats, breaking, aerosol art, and
deejaying. But it also represents an era, as the Harlem Renais-
sance does, and encompasses artists of many styles and ap-

proaches albeit with similar experiences, political values, and cultural perspectives.

The stage is wide open. This is the challenge and the beauty of hip-hop theater. A sliver of light bounces off the silver line of a lone mic stand center stage. You can rock the mic, or kick it a capella. Say your piece and pass it along to the next voice waiting to be heard.

THE NEW GIRLS NETWORK:
WOMEN, TECHNOLOGY, AND FEMINISM

Shireen Lee

An advocate for the empowerment of girls and young women, Shireen Lee helped to start SportsBridge, a nonprofit organization for girls, in 1995. In 2001 she also served on an advisory board for the Asian Pacific American Women's Leadership Institute. Internationally, she was one of the founding members of the Youth Caucus of the UN Commission on the Status of Women. She served on the International NGO Coordinating Committee for the UN General Assembly Special Session on Beijing + 5, an appointed body of twenty-five international women activists. She holds a bachelor of applied science honors degree in engineering science from the University of Toronto and a master's degree in public administration from San Francisco State University.

In history, we have seen technology out of our control: when the United States during the Second World War dropped atom bombs on Hiroshima and Nagasaki, killing thousands of people and destroying worlds, even the scientists who had helped create the bomb were dumbfounded by the results of their work. Soon after terrorists killed thousands of people by flying airplanes into the World Trade Center and the Pentagon on September 11, 2001, Americans experienced further panic when the biological agent anthrax started showing up in the mail, making some severely ill and killing others. But our technological future does not have to continue in the same way.

"Imagine," writes Anita Borg, president of the nonprofit Institute for Women and Technology, "a world in which information technology (IT) was used to its highest potential, being an engine for an efficient, ecological economy and providing new opportunities for more people based on more available knowledge. Imagine a political system based on open access to information, better education, more communication, and equal participation. Imagine connecting people around the world in the spirit of positive internationalism, where social goals such as universal literacy, basic education, and health care are achieved."[1]

Technology could help us reimagine societies, communities, and futures that move beyond the binaries—white-black; male-female; straight-gay; First World–Third World; future-past; technological-organic; work-play—of our contemporary world. As they achieve certain credentials in technology, women are participating in these reimaginings. But there continue to be barriers to women getting the right credentials, and to the careers where they can use them.

I grew up in Malaysia, where single-sex education is the norm. I benefited from being able to develop intellectually and physically in an environment free from the consuming social pressures of girl-boy interaction. Throughout my schooling I focused on math and science, and excelled. It seemed natural that I would become an engineer.

In Canada, where I attended college, graduating engineers are each presented with an iron ring in a secret ceremony designed by Rudyard Kipling and dating back to 1922. Engineers wear their rings on the little fingers of their working hands after taking an oath of ethics. At the age of twenty-three, I took off my iron ring when I stopped working at oil refineries, but I did not turn my back on technology.

An Environmental Scan

In 2001, the Bureau of Labor Statistics projected that between 2000 and 2010, eight of the ten fastest-growing occupations would be computer related, with computer engineers topping the list.[2] Yet, according to the National Council for Research on Women, women's share of bachelor's degrees in computer science dropped to fewer than 20 percent in 1999, after having reached a high of 37 percent in 1984.[3] A look at these numbers from the supply side suggests that the gap between male and female participation in the technology workforce, instead of closing, will actually widen in the near future. We are simply not graduating enough women to fill tomorrow's technological jobs: information technologists, computer applications specialists, games programmers, code writers in software development, and systems programmers, among others. The Information Technology Association of America predicts that, by 2010, 60 percent of American jobs will require technological skills.[4] Contrast this demand with the following current statistics: women leave engineering jobs—ranging from electrical and mechanical engineering positions to computer-related engineering jobs, such as hardware engineering—at double the rate of men,[5] and women are more likely to leave technological occupations altogether.[6]

The mantra of second wave feminists was "Let us in!" Their success opened the doors to educational opportunities and brought women into schools and the workforce in unprecedented numbers. The women of that generation butted up against centuries-old traditions of patriarchal governance and belief systems to gain financial and reproductive independence. What does the world look like today for the daughters of those 1970s feminists?

Gender and racial discrimination at the end of the twentieth and beginning of the twenty-first century is subtle yet still pervasive. It stems largely from unconscious ways of thinking that have been socialized into all of us, men and women alike. In the realm of technology, its influence spans the pipeline from girls in school to women in the job market.

The Education-Career Discontinuity

Back in 1992, the American Association of University Women (AAUW) published *The AAUW Report: How Schools Short-change Girls,* which claimed that there was a dearth of women in technology careers because girls were not taking math and science classes in school.[7] The approach to the problem at the time can be summed up as follows: If we can get girls to take the classes and excel in them, they will naturally choose corresponding careers. Nearly a decade later, Patricia Campbell, coauthor of the report and an expert on educating girls and people of color in math and science, reiterated the original premise of the report and took it a step further, when she said "Achievement is necessary but not sufficient."[8]

Campbell and Beatriz Chu Clewell, leading researchers in the field, tell us that girls, particularly those in the middle-class socioeconomic sphere, are now taking math and science classes in the same numbers as boys, and in some cases excelling in them. But they are *still* not choosing technology careers to the extent anticipated ten years ago. Girls do not seem to be making the link between math and science education and technology careers.[9] Campbell believes that many girls place greater importance than do boys on making a positive difference in the larger world. Girls apparently do not see the connection between technology jobs, which tend to be highly specialized and solitary endeavors, and changing the world.[10] Katie Wheeler, executive director of the Girls' Coalition of Greater Boston, a consortium of nonprofits, funders, and researchers interested in girls' issues, agrees. "Girls perceive technology and the hard sciences like physics as not involving people. They don't see in technology the potential to help people in the world. That's why most girls and women end up in the life sciences like biology rather than in high tech."[11] Compounding an already unfavorable situation, research by the Congressional Commission on the Advancement of Women and Minorities in Science, Engineering and Technology Development (CAWMSET) confirms what most people already suspect. Many girls do not see themselves reflected in the role models, men *or* women, in technology careers. The general image of technology workers and engineers as unusually intelligent, socially inept, and absentminded "geeks" or "nerds" is often a deterrent.[12]

For low-income young people of color, especially African-Americans, Latinos and Latinas, and Native Americans, the question of gender is moot—among them the overriding barrier is economic. Lack of educational resources in inner-city schools, where the majority of students are blacks and Latinos and Latinas, affects participation and achievement in math and science for both girls *and* boys.[13] In Massachusetts, for example, tenth graders are required to take the Massachusetts Comprehensive Assessment System test, or MCAS, in a variety of subjects, including math and science. In low-income areas such as Springfield, Holyoke, and sections of Boston where a majority of the students are of color, the rate of failure is startling. In Springfield, in the year 2000, 94 percent of tenth-grade Latinos and Latinas and 91 percent of black students failed the math section; in Holyoke, 95 percent of Latinos and Latinas failed; and in Boston, 86 percent of Latinos and Latinas failed, as did 82 percent of black students. Deficient inner-city public school systems make it almost impossible for students to consider fields in technology because they aren't even getting the basic education needed to participate fully in society. Many women and girls of color must fight prejudices against their race, gender, and class that keep them from entering any number of career fields.

Yet there is hope. Many companies that seek to promote ethnic and racial diversity in the workplace have begun to fund training programs which benefit people of color. These programs may not have an impact on a large scale, but they are making a difference in particular neighborhoods. In Washington, D.C., Edgewood Terrace, an 884-unit apartment complex, was once so crime-ridden that the local media referred to it as Little Beirut. After the Community Preservation and Development Corporation, a nonprofit organization, began work to make Edgewood a better place to live, good things started to happen. It created EdgeNet, an intranet-style system that networks users together and hopes to help residents gain computer literacy. The Gateway @ Edgewood Terrace, a CPDC computer learning center that has more that sixty workstations and four networked labs, began to help residents get logged on. In addition, the Gateway center offers classes in computer skills and applications and will offer network management and beginning Microsoft Certified Systems Engineers courses.[14]

Feminism has opened doors for those women who do not have to contend with race and class barriers, especially in fields such as medicine and law. In spring 2001, *The New York Times* reported that for the first time, incoming female students would outnumber male students in law schools across the country.[15] In engineering, however, men dominate: of all engineering bachelor's degrees awarded in 2000, 47,320 went to men and only 12,216 to women.[16] According to Campbell's research, even in colleges with the strongest outreach and support for women engineering students, enrollment of incoming female students has plateaued at about 20 percent over the last few years.[17] A similar pattern is evident in the workforce. In an article in the *San Francisco Chronicle,* Karen Calo, vice president of human resources for the IBM Software Group in

New York, observed that although women now make up 30 percent of lawyers and doctors, fewer than 10 percent of engineers are women.[18] Even fewer are women of color. Technology is still very much a pale male profession.

Subtle Messages, Major Barriers

A historical lack of women in technology careers has resulted in work cultures that have developed without them. According to Sokunthear Sy, a young female engineer at Accenture (formerly Andersen Consulting), there are more informal support structures for men. Male-dominated work environments do a poor job of retaining women once they begin working in industry. "Subtle things like golfing that happen socially because that's the thing to do . . . [to] hang out after hours. Most women don't golf. And women with families can't hang out. Relationships that form outside of work influence decisions at work especially when reviews come around."[19] A recent survey by Women of Silicon Valley, a joint project of the Community Foundation of Silicon Valley and the strategic advising group Collaborative Economics, confirms that 41 percent of women who work in technology, compared with only 23 percent of women not in technology jobs, feel that they have to "fit into a masculine workplace" to advance.[20]

The subtle messages that women don't belong extends even to seemingly trivial elements, like clothing. As a chemical engineer I had to visit oil refineries several days a week. Attire mandated by safety regulations included steel-toe boots and Nomex fire-resistant overalls, which back then came only in men's sizes. On my first day of work I was forced to show up in boots that were two sizes too big and overalls with sleeves and pant legs rolled up multiple times. I looked like I was playing dress up in my father's clothes—not the image that one wants to project walking into a control room that is 100 percent male workers. But these are details that no one tells a newly graduated female engineer.

Today overt gender discrimination in schools and the workplace is rarely tolerated, so most people, both male and female, believe that women are on equal footing with men. After-school and mentoring programs to support girls and women in technology are thus often viewed by girls, women, and their male peers as remedial. Sy maintains that "there is a fear that if you get involved in specialized groups, people will think, Oh, you need extra help. You can't do it on your own. For example, if you are in a women's mentoring group and you get promoted, people will say that's why."[21] Support programs can reinforce the stereotype that women are not as capable as men and need a leg up.

Programs targeted at groups that have historically been discriminated against, such as students of color in universities, or women in technology careers, serve to move us along a path of greater equity. It is not the *programs* themselves that need to be eliminated but rather people's *perceptions* of them. Contrast the opposition to affirmative action programs for women and people of color with the G.I. Bill, which provided higher education grants to veterans. The G.I. Bill, after all, can be viewed as a national, federally initiated affirmative action program—benefiting mainly young white men. According to Michael Haydock in an article for *American History*, "By the time the last

American World War II veteran was graduated in 1956, the United States was richer by 450,000 engineers, 238,000 teachers, 91,000 scientists, 67,000 doctors, 22,000 dentists."[22] Would the country also benefit from similar increases of women and/or people of color in these professions? This point seems particularly salient in the high-tech sector, where, according to CAWMSET, the demand for skilled American workers will continue to outstrip supply.[23] With the G.I. Bill as a model, one can imagine a grants program that could provide badly needed science and math resources for low-income girls and young women of color in urban public schools. Think of the possibilities—if political will is forthcoming.

Redefining Our Position: Women as Technology Innovators

The challenges facing women in technology fields are nothing new. Most commentary on women and technology—academic and otherwise—makes this clear. However, the focus is often on what women are *not* doing. That vantage point perpetuates a deficit model—women seem perpetually to fall short of expectations. Such an approach can become a self-fulfilling prophecy.

The spotlight rarely shines on what women are doing *right*. They are redefining their involvement with technology and using technology to empower and advance themselves and other women. Problems still exist, but there are many women who have adapted to their environment and found ways to succeed.

Nowhere is this more apparent than in the high-tech sector.

Here are the numbers we typically see: There are just three female CEOs among the Fortune 500 and only seven in the Fortune 1000; women hold only 4 percent of the top management positions in Fortune 500 companies.[24] No surprise. What the media usually don't tell us is that women account for 45 percent of the highest ranking corporate officers in Internet companies, and 6 percent of Internet companies financed by venture capital firms in 1999 have female CEOs.[25]

If you read only half the story, you see only a partial picture. Rather than butting heads with patriarchal corporate America, women are using a different leverage point—smaller, newer companies. That these startling statistics show up in the high-tech sector, an industry that burst into prominence after the feminist era of the 1970s, is probably no accident. High-tech has become the nexus for minirevolutions—linking women's leadership in small businesses and global women's activism to create a new form of feminist activism.

Women Business Owners: Today's Feminists

Women in general are no longer just banging on the doors of corporations saying, "Let us in!" We are taking matters into our own hands and creating new centers of power. Women are starting their own businesses in unprecedented numbers. Between 1992 and 1997, according to the National Federation of Women Business Owners (NFWBO), the number of women-owned firms increased two and a half times faster than all U.S. businesses.[26] As of 1996, one in eight women-owned firms in the United States was owned by a woman of color, and the number of these firms has increased three times faster than the overall rate of business growth in the past ten years.[27] What about younger women? Ta'chelle Herron, of San Francisco, is a twenty-one-year-old woman of color, a product of the urban public school system. She insists that women *can* use technology for their advancement. "Start your own business! Once you learn the fundamentals of how the systems work, you can switch that around and use it for yourself—to make money. I started my own graphic design business."[28] A 2001 survey on women in Silicon Valley confirms this trend. It found that many women in technology are leaving the corporate workplace. About 10 percent of women in Silicon Valley are independent contractors, and another 20 percent said they planned to start their own businesses in the next three years.[29] The U.S. Small Business Administration tells us that women now own a staggering 9 million companies—38 percent of all U.S. enterprises. They employ over 27.5 million people.[30]

Further, women are breaking down the binaries associated with pleasure and work, activism and work; they are living their activism in ways that they find fulfilling. Feminism, once synonymous with marching in the streets, is now part of the economic engine of the country. Thanks in part to what those marching women accomplished, contemporary women are making change from within institutions. Looking at her peers, Rebecca Tadikonda, a twenty-eight-year-old recent MBA graduate from Stanford University, observes, "Amongst high-tech start-ups where there is a woman CEO or where there are more women on the management team, there are more women in the company overall. If there aren't women or if there are fewer women on the management team, there are fewer women in the company overall."[31] This point seems consistent with recent research by the Stanford Graduate School of Business. According to the report, "Gender and the Organization-Building Process in Young, High-Tech Firms," women's early representation in core scientific and technical roles has decisive consequences for how emerging companies evolve.[32] This presence in turn could have positive implications for the development of women-friendly workplace cultures. As alluded to earlier, long-established male-centric cultures in large companies are often deterrents to women's advancement. Increasing numbers of women in leadership positions in high-tech companies will inevitably offer a more diverse array of role models for young girls and help them see that people in technology careers can be like them. Whether they are conscious of it or not, women leaders are also acting as activists and role models by paving the way for other women. Feminist activism may not look like it did thirty years ago, but it is definitely alive and thriving.

The High-Tech Sector

Women in the high-tech sector in particular are reimagining the possibilities for work, activism, empowerment, technology, and our future. Why? David Brooks gives a compelling argument for a new "bobo" ethos that has its ground zero in the high-tech industry. *Bobo* means "bourgeois bohemian"—a melding of capitalist bourgeois values and bohemian egalitarian ideals. Old society, with its insular isms—sexism, racism, ageism—has been displaced by educated, antiestablishment people with scuffed shoes who embrace change, welcome experimentation, challenge convention, and thirst for the new.[33] Bobos resist conventional ways of doing things. Women in high-tech are among the forces creating this new environment and are redefining capitalism in a more human way.

The Women's Technology Cluster is an incubator for women-owned high-tech start-ups in San Francisco. Founded by Catherine Muther, a feminist and former head of marketing for Cisco Systems, the cluster provides its companies with a cadre of advisers, partners, and peers who can make connections to funding and other resources. Built into this business model is a unique giveback component. Each business that enters the Women's Technology Cluster commits a small percentage of its equity to the charitable Venture Philanthropy Fund, which over time assists female entrepreneurs and helps sustain other women-owned companies in the cluster. This new collaborative business model embodies the feminist ideals of philanthropy and social equity. Hillary Clinton, in a tongue-in-cheek poke at the "old boys network," dubbed this movement the "new girls network."[34]

Despite their potential, women-owned high-tech start-ups still have a notoriously difficult time raising venture capital, a key source of funding for new companies. Venture capitalists provide financial backing and management assistance to new, fast-growing businesses. Unlike banks, which give loans that have to be repaid as debt, venture capitalists get a portion of the company that they invest in. In 1999 women-led companies received less than 5 percent of the $36 billion invested by venture capitalists.[35] This is not surprising since venture capitalists typically review proposals submitted by people whom they know, whom they know of, or who are like them—the old boys network in action.

In response, women have once again mobilized. In 2000, the National Women's Business Council launched Springboard, an annual series of forums to help women gain access to venture capital. In cities across the country, specially selected groups of women-led companies were coached to present their business plans to hundreds of corporate, individual, and venture investors during daylong events. In just one year Springboard companies raised a total of $450 million in venture capital.[36] According to Denise Brosseau, president of the Forum for Women Entrepreneurs, which cosponsored two Springboard forums in the San Francisco Bay Area, the long-term goal of showcasing women entrepreneurs is to put them on the venture capital map—essentially to give them a jump start into the venture capitalists' network.[37]

In 1994 there was another development just as groundbreaking as Springboard, perhaps even more so. Inroads Capital Partners started the first-ever venture capital fund targeting women entrepreneurs. Today four other funds—Women's Growth Capital Fund, Milepost Ventures (formerly Viridian Capital), Fund Isabella, and Axxon Capital—have followed suit.[38] These funds, all managed *and* founded by women, focus investments on early-stage companies that are led, founded, or owned by women, as well as companies that sell products or services catering primarily to women. Willa Seldon, cofounder and general partner of Milepost Ventures, recalls, "When we first started our fund, a number of people said, 'Why would you even think about doing that?'" Seldon and her peers must feel an enormous sense of satisfaction (and validation) since increasing visibility for women entrepreneurs has translated into real dollars. "There is direct investment [by VC firms] of course," she continues. "But it usually ends up being more after you take into account angel investors [wealthy individuals—women or men—who invest directly in start-up companies, business incubators for women, and additional resources like educational workshops]. Women VC firms have driven larger community backing."[39]

Full participation in a capitalist society is contingent upon private ownership—of money, property, and assets. The relationship is straightforward: ownership grants participation. This is a dynamic from which women have historically been, for the most part, excluded. In the past, legislation curtailed women's rights to ownership of property. Even since (white) American women received legal rights to personal property in the nineteenth century, their participation has been restricted by a culture that views men as the purveyors of monetary and economic matters. Many women continue to face limitations on their ability to participate fully in capitalist society.[40] Yet women with money who invest in women-owned businesses are supporting women's empowerment on many levels. Women can take charge of their own assets. They can invest with an eye toward empowering other women who are in turn starting their own businesses. All these women have the potential to be role models and philanthropists (not merely earners) for the next generation of women.

Virtual Organizing, Global Activism

After I left engineering, I joined a group of women who use technology for feminist empowerment. I bought a one-way train ticket from Toronto to San Francisco to help start a nonprofit organization for girls. Five years later, while I am fully immersed in local, national, and international advocacy for girls and young women, technology remains an integral part of my work, but like other women, I have redefined my involvement with it. Now, as one of the cofounders of the Youth Caucus of the United Nations Commission on the Status of Women, I use Internet technologies to fight for women's rights. In a sense, I have come full circle. I left a job in technology because there was no gender awareness or sensitivity there, and I now use the Internet to organize young women activists from around the world.

The Internet has revolutionized the way we organize. While e-mail, websites, Listservs, search engines, and newsgroups have improved communications for all groups, they have been particularly effective in serving a women's political agenda. All over the world, women's groups tend to be small, helping communities on a local, grassroots level. Historically they have worked in isolation, having little communication with one another. In the past three years, as access to the Internet worldwide has grown exponentially, this circumstance has changed drastically. Even in poor rural communities women may now have access to a computer with an online connection, albeit not with the frequency that we take for granted in the United States. Nonetheless, even sporadic access has globally facilitated information-sharing and coalition-building among women's groups in unprecedented numbers. Through Listservs that help build online communities, young women activists from Nigeria and Bosnia share learning about peer education models in HIV-AIDS prevention, and youth activists from Kenya and India exchange information about the state of girls' and young women's education in their countries.

The Internet offers possibilities for inclusion, diversity, and transparency that feminists have always aspired to but have sometimes had difficulty achieving. New technologies have sped up our communications, allowed us to share information on a grand scale, and given an immediacy to what we do. My favorite image of these new practices remains the computer room set up for the thousands of women's activists who converged on the UN in June 2000 for the Special Session of the General Assembly, also known as Beijing + 5. At each of the twenty or so computer terminals sat a women's rights activist from a different country e-mailing the latest information about the negotiations in New York back to her colleagues at home while hearing feedback on lobbying strategy from the dozens of activists from her country who could not be at the United Nations. If information is power, then that little room was power central.

The Internet has also changed how we interact with government, making it easier for us to influence legislation, demand accountability, and promote democratic participation. Women who have been reluctant to take a visible role in the women's movement now have the option of being "armchair activists" who can have an impact without leaving their homes or sacrificing anonymity. Rebecca Tadikonda epitomizes this new breed of women's activist. "I got an e-mail from a friend of mine about [the appointment of Attorney General John] Ashcroft and clicked on to the website," she says. "It only took five minutes—I wouldn't have done it if it was longer. I ended up forwarding the e-mail to a bunch of my women friends. Then I got another activist e-mail from another woman friend that I had forwarded the e-mail to. It creates networks and is an easy and personal way to get people involved in political activism—*especially* if the e-mail comes from someone you know."[41]

The Internet has definitely brought more women into the political process. According to Jennifer Pozner, founder and executive director of Women In Media News (WIMN), a media watchdog group, since President George W. Bush's inauguration, women have been embracing technology as a means of activism like never before. When President Bush reinstated the "global gag rule," which prevents government agencies from giving funds to private family planning programs outside the United States even if the money is not going to be used for abortion, Patt Morrison wrote a column in the *Los Angeles Times* denouncing it. Morrison sent the president a card that read, "President George W. Bush, in honor of President's Day, a donation has been made to Planned Parenthood in your name." People began forwarding the column via e-mail, asking that donations to Planned Parenthood be made in Bush's name. The e-mail spread like wildfire, and Planned Parenthood received $500,000.[42]

Toward an Empowered Future

When we think of technology, we often think more of the *use* of technology—using computers, e-mail, cell phones—and less of the *creation* of technology—designing computer software and hardware. The distinction is important because women now relate to technology much differently than men do. Women tend to be users more than creators of technology, whereas men are as much creators as they are users. Women have clearly used technology to their advantage in their activist work and business lives, but they are often shut out from creating the technology. Being good at using technology and adapting it for our political activism and financial independence is a huge step forward. But women must also play an integral part in creating the technology. To ensure that women are not left behind, we must develop ways to educate and graduate more women engineers and computer scientists and facilitate their participation in the workforce. Bridging this gap will ensure that future generations of feminists will not only express their activism from the outside, through existing technology, but also from within, through new technologies that are created with a gender lens and communities of color in mind.

How exactly will creating technology benefit women? Let's imagine. Thanks to new communications technologies, working from home at least part of the time is a growing phenomenon. This arrangement benefits women, particularly those with families, more than any other demographic group. Could this flexible approach to work have come about even earlier if women were responsible for designing the computers, networks, and faxes that make it all possible? Does it surprise anyone that when more women entered the medical profession, we started seeing more research on the impact of diseases on women and using women subjects rather than the male standard?

According to the Institute for Women and Technology, most product designers create products with themselves in mind.[43] As a result, most new products reflect the desires of the single, eighteen- to thirty-five-year-old men who design them. What if women were at the forefront of creating technology? We can imagine a spectrum of changes from the trivial—keyboards to fit women's smaller hands—to products with broad societal consequences. Will women engineers choose to perpetuate the multibillion-dollar military industry that keeps us locked in war games all over the globe? Or will they apply their intelligence and expertise to solving more pressing global problems?

As a movement, young feminists must continue to fight for meaningful representation and participation in the technology workforce and, equally important, continue to create their own workforces. But there is much work to be done. Gender equity in computer access, knowledge, and use cannot be measured solely by how many women send e-mail, surf the Net, or perform basic functions on the computer. The new benchmark should emphasize computer fluency—being able to interpret the information that technology makes available, mastering analytical skills and computer concepts, employing technology proactively, and imagining innovative uses for technology across a wide range of problems and subjects.[44]

PART II

※

NEW ACTIVISM

IN THE

GLOBAL CITY

EXPORTING VIOLENCE: THE SCHOOL OF THE AMERICAS, U.S. INTERVENTION IN LATIN AMERICA, AND RESISTANCE

Kathryn Temple

Kathryn Temple is a painter who lives in the mountains of western North Carolina. She has been active in the anti–corporate globalization movement since 1993, after having done community development work in Guadalajara, Mexico. In the late nineties she worked at a shelter for battered refugee and immigrant women. Her paintings have been exhibited in solo and group shows throughout the eastern United States and can be found in private collections across the country. She serves on the board of directors of OurVOICE, the Asheville area rape crisis center. She also works as a designer of crafts projects for children's books.

Part I

My mailbox is machine-gun black. And every day it reminds me of a seven-year-old El Salvadoran girl whose name I don't even know. I've named her a thousand times Esperanza, Luz, Memoria, Cantadora, Maestra . . .[1] The soil is moist and cool, and she can feel it through her dress against her back. The sun is low in the sky, and like the fabric between her legs, it seems to soak up the reds of the day's slaughter. The soldiers who have raped her, who have hung toddlers by their necks from trees, who have thrown infants into the air and caught them on the points of their bayonets are surveying their near-complete operation. They have killed nearly every child, woman, and man of the village called El Mozote. They raped women and children throughout the day. This seven-year-old girl kept her eyes fixed on the sky and sang strange spiritual songs even when the soldiers were taking turns with her tiny body. They made jokes of her singing even as her voice was muffled by an urgent soldier's chest. As the sun sinks lower and the evening air stills, the little girl's voice continues to rise, in atonal melodies and invented words. Frightened, a soldier fires a bullet into her chest. Faintly, she continues to sing. He fires another. She continues to sing, more faintly still. With his knife, he draws a decisive line through her throat.[2]

Six days out of the week I pull the mailbox door down, squeak metal against metal, and hear it click pop over the bend in the dented hinge. I hear the first shot. I shut the door over the metal dent. The second shot. Any day now I could receive a letter summoning me to appear in federal court. I could be facing six months in federal prison. I was arrested two months ago for nonviolent protest against the School of the Americas (SOA) at Fort Benning in Georgia, the combat school that trained ten of the twelve officers who spearheaded the massacre at El Mozote.[3] It was my third act of civil disobedience at the School of the Americas and my second arrest. Typically, they choose to prosecute repeat offenders. I flip through the envelopes: a student loan bill, two credit card offers, and a letter from my dad.

* * *

In 1995, at an Amnesty International conference in Atlanta, I saw a documentary about the School of the Americas. I remember this image from the film: the children's mass grave is being exhumed. The earth is divided into sections. A woman picks up a papery crumple of fabric. With a sleeve in each hand, she lifts it for the camera: a girl's dress, caked with earth, blood, and ten years of silence. The eyes, hair, and skin of tiny heads had long since been absorbed back into the earth, but the children's bones had persisted. Ten years of government denial, ten years of scant media coverage, ten years of the United States's refusal to launch a legitimate investigation of the incident hadn't touched the hard, gray bone of memory.[4]

I studied the massacre for months and learned the name of the only adult who survived: Rufina Amaya. She recounted how the men and women were killed in small groups, then dragged and piled into the church. She watched a soldier shoot and decapitate her young husband. It took two soldiers to pull her still-nursing baby from her arms. She hid inside the branches of a gnarled crab apple tree and endured the screams of her children as they were killed. She dug a hole in the earth, pressed her face into it, and wept to avoid being heard by the soldiers. She knew she must survive in order to tell the story of what had happened. The soldiers set the church on fire, and the air thickened with smoke and the smell of her loved ones' bodies smoldering inside. Her breasts filled the following morning, as if nothing had happened, aching to feed her baby girl.[5]

I was in college, a painting major. I painted the story of the massacre for almost a year. I built a tiny black coffin and painted an image inside of a baby boy, shot through the chest. A boy who survived the El Mozote Massacre remembers watching the soldiers kill his two-year-old little brother. *"Este es justicia!"* they shouted as they killed the children. I painted their words on the outside of the coffin: "This is Justice."

I read about the toys found during the exhumation . . . prized possessions stuffed deep into tiny pockets. I built a child's block and painted each side with a letter: "L-A-C-R-U-Z," the name of the highest hill in the village. La Cruz, "the cross," the name of the hill where the children were tortured, raped, and killed. The wooden block, hinged along each edge, unfolded into the shape of a cross. Inside, the image of the seven-year-old girl.

I slept little and cried often that year. The massacre at El Mozote was but one of a list of atrocities committed by the El Salvadoran military over the twelve-year "civil war." More than eighty thousand people, the majority civilians, were killed. Thousands of labor unionists, teachers, student activists, church workers, and peasants were disappeared, raped, tortured, and murdered.[6] A 1993 United Nations Truth Commission Report named more than sixty officers responsible for the most brutal atrocities committed during the war in El Salvador. More than two-thirds of these officers were trained by the United States at the School of the Americas.[7] In addition to this military training, the Reagan administration gave El Salvador's military $1 million a day (of U.S. taxpayers' money).[8] By the war's end, the United States had given the El Salvadoran government $6 billion in economic and military aid.[9]

The Reagan administration routinely cited the "communist

threat" as justification for heavy military involvement in El Salvador and other Latin American countries. Yet the brutal oppression enabled by U.S. funding and training was hardly more democratic than any supposed communist threat. The counterinsurgency techniques taught at the SOA were systematically used against unarmed civilians; the "insurgents" were often landless peasants, indigenous communities, labor unionists, and advocates for the poor.

The U.S. Army School of the Americas

The U.S. Army opened the School of the Americas in Panama in 1946. In 1984 the school was relocated to Fort Benning in Columbus, Georgia. In 2001 it underwent a name change that reflected no substantial change in its mission or curriculum. For more than fifty-five years, what is now called the Western Hemisphere Institute for Security Cooperation has trained the military elite of Latin American countries in commando tactics, counterinsurgency warfare, psychological warfare, torture techniques, interrogation tactics, and sniper training. The school's stated mission is to "provide military education and training to military personnel of Central and South American countries and Caribbean countries" in order to "promote democratic values and respect for human rights; and foster cooperation among multinational military forces."[10] A 1995 government report on the SOA emphasizes that "the School is strategically important to the United States and supports the short- and long-term U.S. economic, political, and military interests in Latin America."[11]

The school's sixty thousand graduates include the notorious

dictators Juan Velasco Alvarado of Peru, Romeo Lucas Garcia of Guatemala, Guillermo Rodriguez of Ecuador, Leopoldo Galtieri and Roberto Viola of Argentina, Hugo Banzer Suarez of Bolivia, and Manuel Noriega and Omar Torrijos of Panama. Each of their repressive regimes, bolstered by SOA-trained military officers, resulted in thousands of civilian deaths. The SOA graduate General Hector Gramajo was "the architect of strategies legalizing military atrocities in Guatemala that resulted in the deaths of more than two hundred thousand men, women, and children."[12] Graduates of the school have effectively overthrown democratically elected, reformist governments: in Guatemala in 1954, for example, and in Nicaragua in 1984. Graduates have been found responsible for countless human rights violations throughout Latin America, including the 1980 rape and murder of four U.S. churchwomen in El Salvador, the 1991 murders of nine university students and one professor in Peru, the 1988–91 Trujillo chain saw massacres in Colombia, and the 1994 massacre in Ocosingo, Mexico.[13]

When questioned about the brutal record of so many SOA graduates, school proponents, like the former SOA commandant Glenn Weidner, claim that a few "bad eggs" are inevitable. He insists that the School of the Americas "did not and does not teach torture or violations of the law." The school does "just the opposite," he elaborates; it "promotes U.S. values with respect to democracy . . . and adherence to international standards of human rights."[14] But the former SOA instructor Joseph Blair disagrees: "In three years at the school, I never heard of such lofty goals as promoting freedom, democracy, or human rights."[15] A Panamanian SOA graduate testified to the torture training that he received at the school:

They would bring people from the streets [of Panama City] into the base and the experts would train us on how to obtain information through torture. . . . They had a medical physician, a U.S. medical physician I remember very well . . . who would teach the students the nerve endings of the body. He would show them where to torture, where and where not, where you wouldn't kill the individual.[16]

In a campaign to expose the SOA's official policies of "murder, torture, and extortion," human rights activists, journalists, and members of Congress pressed for the release of the school's training manuals.[17]

Recently declassified documents confirm the U.S. government's awareness of, and involvement in, SOA-led human rights abuses. State Department documents released under the Freedom of Information Act, for example, expose U.S. collusion in the 1980 assassination of the El Salvadoran justice leader Oscar Romero. The SOA graduate Roberto d'Aubisson orchestrated the assassination, and a State Department official was present at the planning meeting. Soldiers drew lots to decide who would have the honor of assassinating the Roman Catholic archbishop.[18] An advocate of the poor, Romero had publicly addressed and implicated El Salvador's military: "I would like to make an appeal in a special manner to the men of the army. In the name of God, in the name of the suffering people whose laments rise to the heavens each day more tumultuous, I ask you, I beg you, I order you in the name of God, *stop the repression*." The following day he was assassinated.

Clearly the goal of the SOA is not to promote "democracy

and human rights." What, then, is the actual mission of the School of the Americas?

As the United States emerged from World War II, its elite enjoyed an unprecedented level of wealth and power. George Kennan, who did policy planning for the State Department from 1947 to 1949, explained, "We have about 50 percent of the world's wealth, but only 6.3 percent of its population. . . . In this situation, we cannot fail to be the object of envy and resentment. Our real task in the coming period is to *devise a pattern of relationships* which will permit us to maintain this position of disparity without positive detriment to our national security [emphasis mine]."[19] The world's elite were enjoying increasing luxury while the world's poor were being pushed further into poverty. Policy makers knew that such a vast inequality could be maintained only through aggressive economic and military strategy.

In 1944 the International Monetary Fund and the World Bank were established as part of a policy that would help to ensure the United States's economic dominance. These institutions have been instrumental in opening Latin American economies to foreign investment. In conjunction with free trade agreements, they have promoted corporate interests by eroding legal, political, and economic barriers that protect Latin America's people, land, and mineral resources from exploitation. United States foreign policy has historically been designed to protect the fortunes of the economic elite; the term "vital U.S. interests" is often synonymous with "corporate interests." As a self-described "implement of foreign policy," the SOA, and its gradutes, serves to protect those overlapping interests. Large corporations benefit most substantially from policies that bolster international economic disparity, but it is important to note that ordinary American citizens also benefit from the abundant supply of cheap consumer goods that this disparity guarantees.

The School of the Americas was opened in 1946 as the military component of a U.S. foreign policy that would prioritize the security of foreign investments. In George Kennan's words, "The time had come to cease to talk about vague and unreal objectives such as human rights, the raising of the living standard, and democratization."[20] Over the years, the official mission of the SOA has changed. It went from "professionalizing" Latin American militaries to defending the United States against the communist threat. These days military training and intervention are justified by the "War on Drugs," a campaign that SOA leaders claim helps "to ensure peace of the Western Hemisphere and promote human welfare through inter-American cooperation that is fully grounded in International law."[21] The packaging has evolved, but the philosophy that informs foreign policy has remained the same. U.S. foreign policy is still primarily focused on keeping our foreign investments safe.[22]

In August 1996, the U.S. General Accounting Office issued a report on the School of the Americas. It confirmed that the countries sending the most students to the school at any given time were also receiving the largest amounts of military aid; this was the case in El Salvador in the 1980s. The report explained: "When the United States was providing large amounts of foreign assistance, including training, to El Salvador's military . . . , about one-third of the students at the School came from El Salvador." It elaborated: "The predominant countries represented at the School typically reflect U.S. interests in the region at a particular time."[23] Evidence has consistently demonstrated that human rights abuses in Latin American countries increase with increased SOA training and military funding. In the mid- to late 1990s, the number of Mexican soldiers at the SOA reached an all-time high. At the dawn of the twenty-first century, Colombia, arguably the country with the worst record of human rights violations in the hemisphere, sends the most soldiers to the SOA. In both cases SOA training and military funding coincide with increased resistance (by peasants, union organizers, indigenous rights groups, student activists, and others) to corporate globalization.

Part II

Power and Control: Examining Corporate Globalization Through a Violence Lens

In 1997 I began working in a shelter in Atlanta for refugee and immigrant women who were escaping domestic violence. I met Maria when she was eighteen. Two years earlier she had waded through a polluted river that marked the border between Mexico and Texas; she was five months pregnant. With a third-grade education, Maria could seek work only in her small border town. There were a few foreign-owned factories, or *maquiladoras,* and the vast majority of *maquila* workers were women about Maria's age. But the *maquiladoras* were infamous for poverty wages, hazardous working conditions, sexist hiring and firing practices, and forced overtime. Many companies required pregnancy tests and made nonpregnancy a precondition of hiring. Maria left her family and her home hoping to make a better life for herself and the child she was carrying. She believed she could earn more money and give her child an education in the United States.

Knowing no one, and speaking no English, Maria made her way to Georgia, where her little girl was born. Several months later she entered a relationship with a young man. Charming and generous, he suggested they move in together. They rented a small room in an apartment. He discouraged her from learning English and became jealous when she made new friends. Maria found jobs in the undocumented workforce. At first work was sporadic. Eventually she got a steady job cleaning office buildings after hours for subminimum wage. Her supervisor transported her and a crew of workers in a windowless van from building to building; they were forced to work until all of the contracted tasks were complete, sometimes late into the night. When she came home, her boyfriend was enraged; he called her a slut and accused her of having an affair.

Although the physical violence began early in the relationship, it steadily increased in severity. Maria left when her abuser picked her child up by the hair and threatened to rape the infant. Maria lifted the back of her shirt to show me her own scars: some were fresh and pink, others had healed into white lines stretching the length of her back. She had endured the beatings *en silencio,* she said, so that the couple from whom they rented the room wouldn't turn them out onto the streets.

In survivor support groups and volunteer trainings, we often

referred to the "Domestic Violence Power and Control Wheel."
Developed by survivors of domestic violence, the wheel iden-
tifies a range of tactics that abusers use, in conjunction with
the constant threat of physical and sexual violence, against
women. The goal of the abuser, survivors concluded, was not
the physical violence itself but rather to maintain a position of
absolute authority over the victim. The power and control diagram is simple and effective; an outer circle is connected to an
inner circle by eight spokes. "Power and Control" are at the
center of the wheel. "Physical and Sexual Violence" mark the
outer circle. Various tactics mark the spokes connecting the circles. These tactics include

1. Using economic abuse
2. Using intimidation
3. Using isolation
4. Using children
5. Minimizing, denying, blaming
6. Using coercion and threats
7. Using emotional abuse
8. Using male privilege.[24]

Many of the refugee and immigrant women we worked with
explained how their abusers had prevented them from learning
English in order to isolate and maintain control over them.
Others lived in constant fear of their abusers' threat to report
them to the Immigration and Naturalization Service. Many
women reported that their batterers had refused to teach them
to drive or to take the bus and that the physical violence inten-
sified when they made any effort to empower themselves,

whether by going to English as a Second Language classes, getting a job, making a friend, or learning to use public transportation. Across the board, abusers use tactics that compromise and limit the internal resources of their victims, while increasing the victims' dependency on them. Violence increases when exploited people threaten to empower themselves or leave the abusive relationship.

Like batterers, those who design U.S. foreign policy understand that someone who is strong and self-sufficient cannot be easily controlled. I have modeled the Corporate Globalization Power and Control Wheel on the domestic violence wheel. The Corporate Globalization Power and Control Wheel diagrams a complex series of social, political, and economic relationships in which there are multiple beneficiaries and multiple casualties. The goal of the individual abuser is to retain power and control over his individual victim; the goal of the political and economic elite is to maintain unrestricted power and control over the world's profit-making resources, especially labor, land, natural resources, and capital. In both cases, abusers exemplify a patriarchal power model that equates power with one's capacity to control others. Like individual abusers, U.S. foreign policy makers, multinational corporations, and international financial institutions such as the International Monetary Fund and the World Bank use tactics that compromise and limit the internal resources of Latin American countries. At the same time, these countries increase their dependency upon international lending bodies and U.S. aid and currency. Domestic and global abusers use the tactics of relabeling violence, inverting blame, and renaming the victims. Soldiers who rape and stab children call their victims "little guerrillas." A man who batters and rapes his girlfriend calls her "slut."

Domestic violence, like SOA violence, occurs within a larger culture that supports it. We must see the abuse as part of a pattern, not as a deviation from a pattern. As long as we identify the soldiers who raped the seven-year-old girl or the boyfriend who beat his partner as a "few bad eggs," we deny that this kind of violence is systematic and maintains an institutionalized power inequity. Carol Adams explains that when one "identif[ies] with the abuser . . . the tendency is to see the violence as an aberration rather than as a chronic problem. This protects the offender."[25] In order to expose the offender, we must study his behavior and reveal the patterns.

Part III

Tactics of Global Abusers: Debt as a Tool for Establishing Dependency

In my experience with domestic violence support groups, a survivor often communicated that her relationship with the abuser began as a storybook romance. He had been charming, a gentleman, had wooed her with flowers. His protectiveness was comforting, and his jealousy was initially flattering. Once he had secured some level of her emotional, economic, or social dependency upon him, the abuse began. He became increasingly controlling and possessive and whittled away at her physical, psychological, and financial boundaries until he controlled nearly every aspect of her life.

Debt is a powerful tool of global economic abusers. The lender, holding the carrot of the next bailout loan, has the power to impose conditions in exchange for the money. In short, the lender gains an enormous amount of control over the debtor's domestic affairs, dictating how the debtor country will spend that money and how it will restructure its economy to make loan repayment its highest priority. Like domestic abusers, global abusers devise strategies to gain access to the internal resources of their victims. Free trade agreements and international financial institutions like the International Monetary Fund (IMF) whittle away at the healthy boundaries (labor protections, environmental protections) of the debtor countries in order to expose the countries' land, mineral, and human resources to foreign investment.

The debt crisis of the 1980s gave the economic elite an invaluable opportunity to secure greater control over the economies of Latin American countries. In the 1970s interest rates were low, and private (mostly United States) banks were looking for new borrowers. Many banks actually sent young bankers to Latin American countries to woo new borrowers with the low interest rates. Many Latin American countries accumulated significant debt; while some loans financed development projects, most went to finance corrupt governments and to fund excessive military spending. After the 1972 earthquake in Nicaragua, for example, the Somoza dictatorship appropriated most of the loan money meant for reconstruction. Argentina, under the leadership of SOA graduate generals, borrowed $10 billion for military expenditures.[26]

A dramatic rise in interest rates in the 1980s (the result of numerous factors, including excessive U.S. borrowing for war toys) was accompanied by a worldwide recession. Latin American countries were unable to make interest payments on their loans, and the private "First World" banks lacked the leverage to force debtor countries to prioritize debt repayment above all else. The IMF, a financial institution composed of member countries, was able to offer bailout loans to Latin American countries on the brink of default. The harsh conditions attached to bailout loans are called structural adjustment programs. They require borrowing countries to make debt repayment their top priority, even above the basic survival needs of their people.[27]

Structural Adjustment, Also Referred To as "Belt Tightening"

I cannot examine structural adjustment programs without thinking about domestic violence survivors, sitting in a circle, sharing the stories of their abuse. Many women said that their abusers constantly compared them to a Barbie doll standard of beauty. Women of all body types reported being called fat and ugly. Many abusers deemed strength and self-possession "unattractive." The ideal of attractiveness was emaciated, plastic, and white; and it didn't talk back.

Structural adjustment programs are designed to make a country's economy "more attractive" to foreign investors. Like individual batterers, global abusers value weakness, dependency, and vulnerability in the subordinate member of the relationship. The policies vary, but they all work toward the same goals. The programs weaken the purchasing power of Latin American people, injure healthy trade boundaries, and increase dependency on the international economic system as they make Latin America's people and natural resources more vulnerable to corporate exploitation. Communities that are economically and nutritionally self-sufficient are less vulnerable to exploitation.

Structural adjustment programs, free trade agreements, and Poverty Reduction Strategy Papers (PRSPs) represent the structural imposition of a value system that measures worth in terms of cash-generating capacity. Thriving ecosystems, self-sustaining communities, public lands used for subsistence farming, clean water sources, health care systems, and schools are all considered "unproductive" before being commodified and harnessed for profit. Some of the first structural adjustment programs imposed by the IMF require debtor countries to devalue their domestic currency, constrain or cut wages, and lift "nontarriff trade barriers," which include environmental protections and labor standards, such as a minimum wage. Like domestic abusers chipping away at their victims' self-esteem, structural adjustment programs weaken a country's healthy trade boundaries, environmental and labor protections, and purchasing power; the initial belittling paves the way for the abuser to secure greater access to and ownership of the victim's internal resources.

After currency devaluation, a Colombian peasant who earns 200 pesos a month might find her actual monthly buying power has been reduced to 150 pesos. When the local currency is devalued, the U.S. dollar is worth more. It is sleight of hand: the 25 percent loss that the Colombian peasant took on her monthly earnings magically winds up in the pocket of the American investor. He also benefits from the constraints on local wages. Not only is his investment dollar worth more, but he can pay an already underpaid workforce even less. Women, who exhibit superior fine motor skills while being paid less than men, become extremely attractive employees in factories and sweatshops.[28] Women between fifteen and twenty-two years of age compose 90 percent of sweatshop laborers and are paid 20 to 50 percent less than men.[29] Relaxed environmental regulations, which enable corporations to drill and strip-mine protected wilderness and pollute and dump without accountability, guarantee that laborers will be working in a more dangerous, more toxic environment.

Reductions in government spending imposed by the IMF result in cuts in health care, education, and food subsidies. Schools close, and poor families are unable to afford private education. Because of institutionalized sexism, girls are the first to be kept home from school when families make budget cuts. Children are forced to enter the workplace to supplement a household income that has already been devalued and reduced by structural adjustment programs.

Structural adjustment also requires the privatization of public companies and lands, which are sold to the highest bidder, often a multinational (and frequently U.S.-owned) corporation. The privatization of public utility companies results in the firing of public workers, rate hikes, and reduced access for poor people. As is the case with victims of domestic abuse, the poor are alienated from their own countries' resources and both literal and figurative power. Power companies in El Salvador, for example, chose not to extend service in less profitable and hard-to-reach rural areas but instead to export power to neighboring countries for increased profit.[30]

Public lands are often inhabited by indigenous people and worked by small-scale subsistence farmers. When such lands are privatized, the companies that buy them often convert them to cash-crop plantations or exploit them for potential oil and mineral deposits. People who had sustainably farmed and inhabited lands for generations are forced from their homes to make way for monoculture or drilling and mining. Indigenous wisdom defies profit-driven logic: the intact ecosystem is inherently valuable because of its life-sustaining power. Respecting the biodiversity of the earth, sustenance farmers can grow food without poisons and without destroying forests. By contrast, multinational corporations clear-cut forests and establish large-scale plantations of single crops like carnations or coffee that are defenseless against pests without the help of chemical pesticides and herbicides. Though the poisons compromise the long-term health of the soil, the water, and the people who labor in the fields, short-term profits are to be made by exporting the crops to the United States.

Women and the environment suffer. Women bear the brunt of increased food, utility, health care, and education prices that accompany structural adjustment programs. Privatization of utilities forces rural families to resort "to more traditional energy sources—especially collecting and burning wood—which contributes to deforestation and generates a significant additional workload (mostly for women)."[31] Women are the main producers of food within the subsistence economy; land privatization threatens the principal source of nutrition for themselves and their families. As "IMF-imposed structural adjustment policies make imported food more expensive and cut government support for food subsidies," the poor are pushed further into poverty.[32] As malnutrition weakens overall health and immune function, the need for health care increases. Unfortunately, as a survey conducted by the Women's Environment and Development Organization indicates, "privatization trends have reduced access to health services by the poor, with special impact on women, the elderly, and immigrant and minority populations."[33]

Despite the intricacies of structural adjustment, its effect is always the same: the poor, women and children in particular, pay the price for a debt that belongs to someone else. The elite do not feel the impact of "belt-tightening." Abusers, who violate boundaries and lose their sense of a difference between self and other, often say, "It hurts me more than it hurts you." The IMF explains that structural adjustment means "short-term pain for long-term gain." Yet economists such as Joseph Stiglitz, winner of a Nobel Prize in economics, judge structural adjustment programs a failure. They have not, he has written, brought "sustained growth" even to those countries like Bolivia that have "adhered to [their] strictures."[34]

Why Doesn't She Just Leave?

In domestic violence volunteer trainings, the most commonly asked question was Why doesn't she leave? He's abusive, he's not going to stop. Why doesn't she just leave? If a woman attempts to leave an abuser, the statistical likelihood of her abuser murdering her increases 75 percent.[35] Women often don't leave because they know there is a good chance they will be killed. They also know that the likelihood of the abuser being held accountable for his violence is very slim. Also, after they've suffered years of power and control tactics like limited access to education, money, and community, the cards are effectively stacked against them; their options and resources are often very limited. The question itself reflects how deeply colonized our thinking is. We don't immediately call abusive behavior into question or ask who colludes in creating an environment that supports the abuse and who benefits from it.

Training manuals released under the Freedom of Information Act reveal that soldiers are, as well, able to take advantage of the fact that they are not likely to be held accountable for their actions, which makes it difficult for their targets—groups and individuals who are working to organize labor, speak truth, and empower poor communities—to free themselves from the entanglements of war. Put simply, SOA graduates are taught to target people who are threatening to empower themselves to "leave" the abusive relationship. SOA manuals identify many indicators of what they call guerrilla insurgency: labor discontent; union organizing; characterization of government and political leaders as U.S. puppets; "accusations of brutality or torture by the police or armed forces"; strikes; "clergy embracing liberation theology"; economic discontent; protests against high unemployment, low salaries, or the national economic plan; "clergy involved in activities concerning political, rural, or labor organizing"; and "unusual meetings among the population." All of these indicators are legal and nonviolent means of challenging global economic and military abuse. Understandably, they occur with greater frequency in areas where poor people are feeling the effects of corporate globalization and unjust economic policies. These efforts are more often than not met with violence.

In 1989 the Ursulan nun Dianna Ortiz, a U.S. citizen, was

in the Guatemalan countryside teaching Mayan children to read in their own language. Ortiz's work was much needed; literacy is an important empowerment weapon.[36] On November 2, 1989, Ortiz was kidnapped by Guatemalan soldiers and taken to a remote prison for "interrogation." Horrifying and brutal, her story is unique only in that she survived to tell it:

> I was tortured and raped repeatedly. My back and chest were burned more than 111 times with cigarettes. I was lowered into an open pit packed with human bodies of children, women, and men, some decapitated, some lying face up and caked with blood, some dead, some alive and all swarming with rats. . . . The memories of what I experienced that November day haunt me even now. I can smell the decomposing bodies, disposed of in an open pit. I can see the blood gushing out of the woman's body as I thrust a small machete into her. For you see, I was handed a machete. Thinking it would be used against me, and at that point in my torture wanting to die, I did not resist. But my torturers put their hands onto the handle, on top of mine. And I had no choice. I was forced to use it against another human being. What I remember is blood gushing—spurting like a water fountain—and my screams lost in the cries of the woman.[37]

Largely because she was a citizen of the United States and news of her abduction became public, Dianna Ortiz is alive to recount the details of her torture and that of countless El Salvadoran people whose deaths remain nameless. She was arrested that day for the crime of teaching Mayan children to read.

Like domestic abusers, global abusers deny, minimize, and invert blame when their violence is exposed. In this case, as soon as Ortiz's abduction was reported, the U.S. Embassy in Guatemala initiated a smear campaign against her.[38] A U.S. court found the SOA graduate General Hector Gramajo responsible for Ortiz's abduction and torture. He denied the allegations and blamed her hundred-plus burn marks on a failed lesbian love affair. Two years after his involvement in Ortiz's kidnapping and torture, General Gramajo delivered the commencement address to an audience of graduate officers for the Command and General Staff College of the School of the Americas.[39] Like domestic abusers, Gramajo inverted blame for the rape and torture of Ortiz; he fabricated a story that exploited misogyny and homophobia to deflect responsibility and imply that Ortiz had been guilty of "aberrant" behavior and had "brought the abuse on herself." He understood that in many areas, a woman loving another woman is considered more criminal and aberrant than rape and torture. Also like most domestic abusers, Gramajo suffered no consequences for his violence despite the fact that he was found guilty by the same government that funded his violence. The SOA implicitly condoned his behavior by honoring him as a commencement speaker two years later.

In Colombia, the situation is complicated. There is a long history of violence, civil war, and nonviolent and armed resistance to government abuse. There is a long history of labor movements being met with violence. The land is rich in oil, and multinational corporations are eager to exploit it. There is a rich indigenous cultural heritage, which has been threatened and compromised by corporate globalization and armed conflict. The Colombian military, right-wing paramilitaries (who are connected to Colombia's military and corporate interests), and armed resistance groups like the FARC (Revolutionary Armed Forces of Colombia) have abysmal human rights records. United States demand for cocaine and heroin have exacerbated the growth of poppy and coca crops. The drug traders provide right-wing paramilitaries and leftist guerrillas with portions of their income.

Numerous policy analysts have observed that current U.S. policy toward Colombia seems to be repeating the El Salvador model of the 1980s. The communist threat has been replaced by the War on Drugs as justification for U.S. intervention. To date, Colombia has sent more students to the SOA than any other country: more than ten thousand Colombian soldiers have graduated from the school.[40] According to the 1996 General Accounting Office report, Colombia's high enrollment is accompanied by massive military aid. Whereas El Salvador was receiving about $1 million of military aid per day during the 1980s, Colombia is currently receiving about $2.5 million dollars of aid each day, more than any other Latin American country.[41] In fact, Colombia is the third largest recipient of U.S. military aid in the world, after Israel and Egypt.[42] Predictably, Colombia's incidence of human rights abuses has escalated with increased SOA training and military aid. Two-hundred forty-seven Colombian officers were named by the 1993 report *State Terrorism in Colombia* for human rights abuses; half of them were graduates of the SOA.[43]

In 2000 a massive foreign aid package called Plan Colombia began providing Colombia's government with over $5 billion in IMF and World Bank loans (and attendant structural adjustment programs) in addition to $860 million in aid from the United States. While U.S. government officials maintain the package is intended to promote "Peace, Prosperity, and the Strengthening of the State," 75 percent is designated for military and police aid, and less than 1 percent is allotted for peace efforts.[44] Robert White of *The Washington Post* observed that declaring war on the FARC actually "puts us in a league with a Colombian military that has longstanding ties to the drug-dealing, barbaric paramilitaries that commit more than 75 percent of the human rights violations" in that war-torn country.[45]

This enormous gift (of U.S. taxpayers' money) to Colombia's military and police purports to fund antidrug operations. Crop fumigation is the principal strategy; aircraft will spray coca and poppy crops with herbicides, thereby, the theory goes, reducing the supply of illicit crops. By attacking the southern crops, the theory contends that Colombia's military will reduce the FARC's source of revenue, weaken their stronghold on the region, and strengthen government control. However, the plan's logic is faulty in a number of ways. First, supply-attack strategy violates the doctrine of economic theory that policy makers hold so dear: the law of supply and demand. The *only* way to decrease overall supply of illegal drugs is to address demand for them; temporary reduction in supply may inflate prices, but it *will not decrease demand for illegal drugs*. A domestic demand-reduction strategy not only is desperately needed but also might actually prove effective. Half of the people seeking drug treatment in the United States are unable to get into programs.[46] Second, policy makers are ignoring the lessons of history. According to the drug policy expert Dr. Ricardo Vargas Meza, "In the entire history of the use of force against illicit crops, not one effort has succeeded in reducing the supply of natural drugs needed to fully supply the world market."[47] Third, the strategy ignores the well-proven "balloon effect"; if drug crops are effectively restricted in one area, crop production simply increases in another to meet demand.

Although Plan Colombia is completely ineffective in addressing the drug problem in the United States, it does effectively secure profits for U.S. arms, petroleum, chemical, and manufacturing companies. In conjunction with SOA training, the military aid serves to quell the social unrest that accompanies structural adjustment. The environment, the poor, and indigenous communities suffer the consequences.

Four hundred million dollars ($400,000,000) of the aid package was designated to purchase Huey and Blackhawk helicopters as part of the crop-fumigation strategy. These helicopters were also used in El Salvador in the 1980s and continue to be used in Mexico as a part of "counterinsurgency" operations. Sikorsky and Bell Technology, the two U.S. companies who produce these aircraft, contributed a combined total of $2.4 million to political campaigns in the two years preceding the passage of Plan Colombia.[48] Plan Colombia enabled two private companies to make a 16,000 percent return on their initial (campaign contribution) investment within two short years.

Through the plan, U.S. taxpayers are effectively supporting Occidental Petroleum, the company responsible for the 1970s Love Canal toxic waste disaster. The military aid of Plan Colombia will help clear the way for Occidental drilling by neutralizing resistance. Occidental's pipeline and drilling projects, closely associated with environmental destruction and the violation of indigenous lands, have met more than a decade of nonviolent and armed resistance in Colombia. Despite the struggle against it, Occidental remains determined to exploit Colombia's land for oil and profit. During House hearings on Plan Colombia, Lawrence Meriage, a vice president at Occidental, was one of the very few nongovernmental witnesses to testify.[49] Meriage is also the leader of the U.S.-Colombia Business Partnership, founded in 1996 to represent companies in the United States with business interests in Colombia.

Chemical companies like Monsanto, widely known for its environmentally and socially dangerous genetic engineering projects, will also benefit from the plan. It produces Roundup Ultra, a souped-up version of the hardware-store herbicide Roundup, one of the premier chemicals being sprayed over delicate Colombian ecosystems, including rain forest and cloud forest, as part of a crop-fumigation strategy. Other businesses with interests in Colombia include the American apparel manufacturers Liz Claiborne and The Limited. All of these companies enjoy the abundant cheap manual labor and relaxed labor standards guaranteed by trade liberalization measures and the structural adjustment policies that accompany IMF loans. They also benefit from the increased militarization that will enforce these policies in the face of social inequity and unrest.

Fumigation efforts have been particularly devastating to rural, indigenous communities. The spraying has contaminated water supplies, destroyed food crops, defoliated forests, eliminated alternative development projects, and caused illness including rashes, ulcers, fevers, diarrhea, and eye infections. In November 2000, planes began spraying the Indian reservation of Aponte. The local physician observed, "This is an epidemic. Since the spraying 80 percent of the children of the community have fallen ill." Most of them "have ulcers all over their bodies." Video recordings made by a local agricultural engineer show the planes dropping herbicide into the springs that are the community's water supply. Guided by the chief of the Aponte, the Dutch journalist Marjon van Royen observed, "The spring had dried up. Yet in a wide area around, no poppy field can be found." The Aponte chief introduced her to numerous peasants whose legal crops had been sprayed. Upon receiving a small loan, a peasant named Carlos replanted his small plot of poppy with barley. He told van Royen that even before the barley came out, the plants had been sprayed to death. Explaining that he is still expected to pay back the loan, he asked, "How should I do that? . . . Now we don't even have anything to eat." Carlos has resorted, once again, to growing a small plot of poppy alongside his food crops. He said, "I don't like it. But it is the only thing we can sell. . . . We grow our food ourselves, but for some things one needs money."[50]

Despite the climate of intimidation and fear, Colombian people continue their organized resistance. In October 1999, 10 million Colombians marched in hundreds of cities and villages, calling for an end to violence from all sides. The U'wa, an indigenous community that has inhabited Colombia's cloud forests for thousands of years, represent a profound challenge to the power of U.S. businesses. Since 1992 the U'wa have engaged in dozens of peaceful protests to halt Occidental's drilling for oil on sacred land. The U'wa people have stated: "We will in no way sell our Mother Earth. To do so would be to give up our work of collaborating with the spirits to protect the heart of the world, which sustains and gives life to the rest of the universe; it would be to go against our own origins and those of all existence."[51] Every aspect of the U'wa's culture is rooted in their sense of responsibility for protecting and continuing life. They believe that earth is a sacred mother, whose heartbeat provides the rhythm for their song and dance. The U'wa explain, "Oil is the blood of Mother Earth . . . to take the oil is, for us, worse than killing your own mother. If you kill the Earth, then no one will live."[52] The U'wa have vowed to commit mass suicide if the drilling plans continue. They are ready to sacrifice their own lives before sacrificing Mother Earth. Their nonviolent resistance to Occidental represents an effort to challenge and "leave" the abusive relationship; if they cannot stop Occidental's violation, they are willing to "leave" through mass suicide.

The peaceful resistance of the U'wa has consistently been met with violence. In 1997 Roberto Cobaría, the U'wa's elected leader at the time, was pulled from his bed in the middle of the night by a group of hooded men with rifles. He was beaten up and threatened with death. In 2000 the U'wa occupied Occidental's drilling site in the hope of preventing the project's advancement. The protesters were met with two brutal police attacks in which three U'wa children were killed.[53]

The U'wa and their allies have also suffered in the crossfire between the military/paramilitaries and armed resistance groups. In February 1999, the Colombian military launched an unprecedented attack on the FARC in which helicopters, gunships, and warplanes were used for the first time.[54] Several days later, in spite of Colombia's abysmal human rights record, President Clinton recertified the country as "a full ally in the

War on Drugs," thus authorizing further military funding. Two days after that, the FARC retaliated by kidnapping three activists from the United States who had been working with the U'wa to preserve their sacred land: Ingrid Washinawatok, an indigenous rights activist and member of the Menominee Nation; Lahe'ena'e Gay, a Native Hawaiian activist; and Terence Freitas, an environmentalist and founding member of the U'wa Defense Working Group. Several days later, Attorney General Janet Reno traveled to Colombia to guarantee the government $240 million in counterdrug and military assistance. On March 5, 1999, two days after her visit to Colombia, the FARC assassinated the activists. Some, including Menominee Tribal Chairman Apesanahkwat and the Indigenous Women's Network have theorized that the United States timed the attorney general's visit to destabilize hostage negotiations and increase the likelihood of the activists' assassination.[55] Apesanahkwat and the Indigenous Women's Network suggest that assassinations have provided justification for further U.S. funding and intervention in Colombia.

Occidental has refused to suspend its plans despite the U'wa people's vow to commit mass suicide.[56] During House hearings on Plan Colombia, an Occidental vice president claimed that only two groups are intent on blocking the project: leftist guerrillas who seek to undermine the country's democratically elected government and several fringe nongovernmental organizations in the United States.[57] Occidental knows that the U'wa are neither guerrillas nor fringe organizations in the United States. Much of the violence against Latin American civilians has indeed been justified by linking them falsely to leftist guerrilla groups.

The Nonviolent Resistance to the SOA

I held the nozzle with one hand and felt the pulse of the gas. The truck, packed full of my paintings and sculptures, was taking one big gulp after another. I watched the numbers on the pump change. It was 1996, and I was on the way to my first SOA protest. Leaders of SOA Watch, an organization devoted to monitoring and exposing the atrocities committed by School of the Americas graduates, had invited me to exhibit my El Mozote paintings just outside the gates of Fort Benning, as part of a nonviolent protest.

About twenty people were gathered at the gates when I pulled up. I set up the easels and tables and turned the sidewalk into a gallery full of my paintings and sculptures: *Rufina,* with the deep umber creases around her eyes, holding the empty swaddling blanket, her body sheltered by the gnarled branches of the crab apple tree; the *Child's Toy,* an oversized Jacob's ladder (click-clack) toy whose twelve surfaces are painted with images of the children's massacre and the exhumation of their mass grave; the *Vulva Box,* a small wooden cube painted in fleshy cadmiums. The *Vulva Box* is an homage to the seven-year-old girl at La Cruz. Each surface is painted with a stylized but identifiable yoni [sacred vaginal symbol]; the yonic shape on the top is hinged at the edges—the doors of the two lips open to reveal the face of a soldier. I spent the afternoon talking with protesters after they had looked at the paintings, opened the hinged doors, and held the works in their hands. Many of them were Catholic. I remember watching one clerical-collared priest open the doors of the *Vulva Box,* pause as he observed the soldier's face inside, and then shut them slowly. "What a beautiful heart," he said.

Later that afternoon, a handful of individuals prepared to risk arrest by entering the base and walking to the front door of the School of the Americas. One protester sang the names of victims of SOA violence. In Latin American tradition, we responded by singing, *"Presente. I am present, I am here."* To a slow and steady drumbeat, we honored the spirits of the children, women, and men who had been killed by SOA graduates:

> *Angelica Marquez, seamstress.*
> *Pre-sen-te.*
> *Maria Dolores Amaya, age five.*
> *Pre-sen-te.*
> *Girl child, ten months old.*
> *Pre-sen-te.*

A ribbon of hope against the wide gray road, the thirteen protesters walked deeper into the base and rounded the corner out of our sight. I wondered how far they could walk and still hear our singing. They were arrested, and some served time in prison. Like the protesters before them, they used the court hearing and the prison sentence to call attention to the SOA and the unjust economic agenda its graduates support.

The following November, hundreds of protesters gathered outside Fort Benning's gates. The next year, thousands came.

Around this time I began working in the domestic violence shelter in Atlanta. I continued to show my El Mozote paintings in various venues, including a feminist fine arts show organized to raise funds for domestic violence work. I began to see that batterers evade the consequences of their violence with such regularity that our entire domestic violence movement has been about helping survivors hide in secret locations rather than assisting their liberation into a safer world. In 1993 and 1998 I also watched Congressional bills designed to shut down the SOA fail by narrow margins. My letter writing, speaking, and painting felt ineffective. Though the exponential growth of the movement was encouraging, the fact that no structural changes had occurred in response to the public outcry underscored the power that corporate interests hold in our government. When the protests did get media attention, it was brief and relatively superficial, and it always underestimated the numbers of protesters. Against the overwhelming power of the corporate and government forces that supported the SOA, I felt I needed to up the ante. I prepared to increase my personal risk.

We sat in a circle in a fluorescent-lit Sunday school room of a Columbus church. I was preparing to participate in a civil disobedience action where there was a strong possibility of being arrested. In this meeting former prisoners of conscience would share their experiences with people considering arrest. I raised my hand to ask how safe the women had felt in prison, whether they had been harassed or threatened by male prison guards. An older nun leaned down to tell me that since I was such "a pretty young lady," I would have to worry about (here she lowered her voice to a winced whisper) the "lesbians in there." A forty-something nun with a Janet Reno haircut seemed embarrassed and said something like "Oh, now, Sister, they're not *that* bad, she'd be okay." Another former prisoner said she never experienced male or female guards as physically violent, but was constantly aware of their power and control.

"You don't have privacy when you get dressed or shower, and you are strip-searched after visitations. In order to demonstrate that you have not received any illegal substances or objects during the visit, you have to 'squat and cough' at the end of the strip search." She mentioned that some of the women with longer sentences "had sexual relations" with male guards, "you know, in exchange for favors."

There were fewer than fifty people at my first SOA protest in 1996. But only three years later, fifty of us were prepared to commit high-risk civil disobedience. Five thousand more went on to cross the line in lower-risk civil disobedience, and thousands more held vigil outside the gates of Fort Benning.

As one demonstrator called each victim's name, ten thousand voices responded *presente,* and the high-risk fifty began walking onto the base. We wore black shrouds and white death masks. We carried coffins of remembrance. Sister Kathleen and I balanced a long black coffin between us on our shoulders. Ahead of us, Clare, a war-tax resister and self-described parishioner of the church of the garden, carried a tiny white coffin, like a baby, in her arms. Behind us, a Veteran for Peace and a college student carried a coffin together. As the fifty of us walked deeper into the base, a river of thousands, five people abreast, walked behind us. The line stretched back over a mile. Though the lone voice that was singing names faded behind us, the response of *presente* echoed through the line of people, connecting us to those on the other side of the gate. As the drumbeat faded, I felt the fist of my heart beating steadily, though more quickly, in my chest.

I was afraid. I knew that, as is true for the people of Latin America, standing up and deviating from my place opened me to punishment. I could be arrested, I could be sentenced to prison. I could lose both my physical freedom and my illusions about the extent of my freedom. Thanks to the protections afforded by large numbers, media coverage, high visibility, and social privilege, I knew that the repercussions of our action would certainly be far less severe than those suffered by Latina peasants who organize and question authority. The dynamics of the power relationship between an authority and an outlaw, however, are quite similar.

We must have walked over a mile when we encountered the military police. Both sides of the road were walled off by dozens of buses. The police created a blockade with their bodies, shoulder to shoulder across the road. We had expected this. We slowly lowered our coffins to the ground. On cue, each of the fifty of us reached beneath the folds of our shrouds and pulled out bottles of red paint. We poured the "blood" over our bodies and collapsed onto the ground. My heartbeat quickened further, and I could feel my breath against the inside of my plastic mask. Sweat beaded on my forehead and upper lip. Through eyeholes in my mask, I watched the paint drip down my wrist into my open palm. As planned, we remained motionless when approached by the soldiers. I don't remember blinking. I kept my gaze fixed over the length of my outstretched bloody arm and saw only what passed through the limits of my masked frame of vision. Military boots passed inches from my eyes. I felt something (a hand? a boot?) prod my shoulder. "Ma'am. Ma'am. Get up. *Don't make us do this the hard way.*" I heard the MPs joke that it sure was an awfully hot day to be wrapped up in so much black against the asphalt. I wondered what the hard way was.

We laid motionless for more than an hour (or two? or three?), eye-level with the soldiers' boots. Their gun-wielding power was at once terrifying and irrelevant. They tried to wait us out. They tempted us with the easy way out, suggesting that we wouldn't be arrested if we would get up and cooperate. Realizing that arresting nonviolent protesters would attract media attention and further expose the SOA, they seemed to want to avoid making more arrests this year. Every moment I lay motionless was an act of discipline. The part of me that wanted to protect my physical freedom, that didn't want to risk spending six months in federal prison, felt tempted to stand up at the soldiers' command and to comply. Eventually the soldiers began cleaning up the massacre site. They escorted, dragged, and carried our fifty bodies onto a yellow school bus. We were frisked, photographed, and fingerprinted. A few hours later we were released with letters barring us from reentering the military base for five years.

The following November, I attended the protest with a group of fellow activists from Asheville. We formed an affinity group that would make consensus-based decisions about how to approach the protest. We needed to decide what level of risk we were willing to take. After determining it was not the right time to risk a six-month prison sentence but wanting to support members of the high-risk group, we crossed the line in a solemn funeral procession.

To the surprise of many, the MPs changed their strategy that year. They randomly arrested more than seventeen hundred protesters. We were a part of that group. It was cold and rainy, and they bused us deep into the base for processing. My shoes and socks were completely saturated, and I couldn't feel my toes. The buses pulled up to a complex of green canvas tents, holding cells for arrestees awaiting processing. In small groups they unloaded us and had us sit on aluminum bleachers in the rain while they waited for a tent to empty. They lined us up and counted us off as they waved us toward a tent. Our group was divided. Two members of my group and I made it into a tent together. We and the other thirty or so people crammed into the space shivered together as a soldier stood guard. Other soldiers passed through to relay messages to him, until they began ordering us into the hangar to be processed.

I looked around. Their system was beautifully choreographed. There was a frisking station, a fingerprinting station, desks set up with computers for processing, and bleachers jam-packed with wet protesters awaiting the next step of processing. Dozens of soldiers darted about, ordering arrestees from one station to another, delivering paperwork to colleagues, conferring with superiors, and calling the names of processed detainees. Several white men stationed throughout appeared to be higher-up officers: they wore different, more highly decorated uniforms and appeared to be in no hurry at all. The majority of the workers, on this Sunday, their normal day off, were young African-American men and women dressed neatly in fatigues.

After being called over to the computer-processing area, I noticed the digital cameras attached to the monitors, aimed at the chairs where we were politely asked to take a seat. As I sat, my face appeared on the screen. The computer recognized it as a match from the previous year. "She's a repeat," the white supervisor said to the younger African-American woman seated at the computer. She grabbed a red pen and marked an enormous X across the top of my file. Because of my past offenses, I was at a higher risk of prosecution. In earlier years protesters selected for prosecution had received a notice and order letter in the mail within a couple of months of the protest.

The letter was typed on heavy paper and crisply folded. It named a court date, prosecuting attorney, case number, and magistrate, but the sentence in capital letters in the center of the page was all I really saw: "UNITED STATES OF AMERICA VS. KATHRYN TEMPLE." Twenty-five other people from around the country had received such letters with their names typed in capitals.

For the next two months I grappled with how to approach the trial. The circumstances of my life and my thinking about nonviolent strategy were very different than they had been two years earlier, when I had prepared for arrest and possible prosecution. I began thinking about the martyrdom model that prison witness represents. For a woman steeped in a culture that teaches women to sublimate their needs and desires to those of a man, or a job, or a movement, how revolutionary would it be to spend six months surviving the emotional abuse and daily humiliation of the prison system? I reflected on the difference between what Starhawk calls the "Catholic Martyr Model" and the "Catholic School Girl Model." In one, you accept and suffer the maximum penalty for your "crime." In the other, you "get away with as much as possible." Starhawk said she was more of a Catholic School Girl and wanted to stay out in the streets as long as she could.

I thought about the women at the shelter who were forced to hide in a confidential location while their abusers walked free. These women, like Dianna Ortiz, Colombian poor people, and the victims of El Mozote, pay the consequences for the crimes of others; the men who commit the abuse get off scot-free. And yet doing prison time, effectively suffering the consequences for the crime of another, had been an effective strategy for raising consciousness about SOA abuse and building the movement. I found myself doing a cost-benefit analysis of spending half a year in a federal women's prison. Would the benefit to the movement be worth the personal cost to me, my family, and loved ones at this point in the movement? I realized that I don't believe suffering, especially for women who have suffered so much already at the hands of patriarchy, is inherently transformative. I don't think martyrdom is inherently righteous. I do believe in the practical benefits of prison time as a strategy: it is an excellent way of attracting media attention to an issue that has been marginalized by the corporate-owned media. It is an effective means of raising consciousness. And while I might be good at doing radio interviews, writing, and exhibiting paintings on the outside, how much of an audience would these efforts capture if it weren't for the sacrifice of prison witnesses?

I contacted the national SOA Watch office to flesh out my strategic options. The prosecuting attorney was not interested in plea bargains or willing to offer a reduced sentence in exchange for an agreement not to commit the same offense. Most of the

SOA Watch staff I spoke to agreed that my only real choice was how to plead. They told me the prosecutor was not accepting no-contest pleas, so my choices boiled down to "guilty" and "not guilty." They reminded me that not once in the history of the SOA Watch had a defendant pled guilty. By pleading "not guilty," defendants had used the trial to expose SOA atrocities and put the school itself on trial.

Pleading guilty might reduce my risk of a prison sentence, but would it be effective strategy for the movement? If I pled guilty, I learned, I would still have a hearing and an opportunity to speak in court. Guilty didn't equal silence. I wondered how the group would respond to someone who broke the "not guilty" tradition. Was it possible that breaking the tradition might open up more doors, a wider spectrum of risk options, so a larger community of people might be involved? Still, a guilty plea was no guarantee of a reduced sentence. There were others in the group of twenty-six who had not expected to be arrested that November and were shocked to receive news of their indictment so many months later. They, too, were deciding how to plead. Secretly, I hoped some other heretic would pave the way for me and plead a pragmatic "guilty."

One by one the fence-sitters decided to plead not guilty. A former prisoner of conscience remarked to me, "I just think it's so amazing the way people were not prepared for this but are willing to follow through on what they believe." I flashed back to a scene from middle school: at a Christian summer camp the counselors were inviting campers down to the stage to "accept Christ as their personal Lord and Savior." Most of the kids had gotten saved over the course of the week, and this was the last night of camp. Several of the resistant kids made their way down to the stage in a sea of hugs, tears, and amens. I remember one other kid and I who guiltily remained seated.

On May 21, 2001, I stood alone before Judge G. Mallon Faircloth in federal court in Columbus, Georgia. The courtroom felt like a church, looming and cold. In all his robes, Judge Faircloth had to climb several steps to reach his chair, perched like a throne at the front of the room. The prosecuting attorney's table was at the front of the courtroom, facing the judge. The defense table, my table, was directly behind the prosecution. The seats behind me were packed: my supporters were there along with the twenty-five other defendants and their friends.

I carried the child's toy that I had made as part of the El Mozote body of paintings. At first I felt like a five-year-old on the first day of school, clinging to my lunch box. But as I began to speak, I felt calmed, powerful, as though the voices of the dead were with me. I told the judge about the year I painted the El Mozote massacre. I told him Rufina's story. I told him how the children were killed at La Cruz, and about the toys found in pockets during the exhumation more than ten years later. I held the block up for him to see and unfolded it to reveal the seven-year-old girl. The image of her tiny body hung in the shape of a cross in federal court. The judge asked me to hold it up again, to bring it closer. He was visibly moved.

Two days later, after the trials of the twenty-five others, sentencing began. First the judge sentenced Dorothy Hennessey, an eighty-eight-year-old nun, to six months in federal prison. While sentencing another of my codefendants to six months, he implied that he intended to give me a three-month prison sentence. He sentenced my friend Clare to six months in prison and a five-hundred-dollar fine. Seven and a half hours and twenty-five sentences—most of which were the maximum six months—later, Judge Faircloth asked me to stand. He questioned me for fifteen minutes. I'd already answered the questions about my marital and maternal status. I didn't belong to a man or a family. Just before delivering my sentence, he asked me if my parents were present. I said, "Yes, they've been here every day." At last I belonged to someone, I was somebody's daughter if not somebody's wife or mother. This seemed to make the difference. "I hadn't planned on doing this," he said. "I sentence you to two years probation and a five-hundred-dollar fine."

I check in with my probation officer once a month. I have to report how much money I have made, how much I've spent, whether I've moved or changed jobs, who I'm living with, anyone I've associated with who may have a criminal record. I can't leave the Western North Carolina Judicial District without permission from my probation officer. I have to tell him where I'm going, the purpose of my trip, how long I'll be staying, the license tag of the car I'm driving, and the telephone number where I'll be staying. I have to carry a written permit with my picture on it everywhere I go while I'm gone, just in case I'm questioned by a law enforcement officer who can pull up my criminal record in his computer. I can't help but think of the SOA training manuals, which suggest restrictive measures like travel passes and restricted areas. The manuals target people who make accusations of brutality or torture by the police or armed forces, participate in protests about the national economic plan, or say things against the government, the armed forces, or the United States. One manual emphasizes various control techniques: "By controlling the subject's physical environment, we will be able to control his [*sic*] psychological state of mind."[58]

My probation officer and his supervisor decided it wasn't a good idea for me to travel to Columbus at all during my sentence so I wasn't at the protests in November 2002, or at the trial in December, where eight of thirty-seven pled guilty. Ten others pled not guilty but admitted to their participation in the protests. The options are expanding. Some might see this as the juncture at which the movement loses cohesion, but I see it as a hopeful, creative moment. This diversity of tactics, like the diversity of the rain forest, makes the system stronger, more stable, more resistant to blight.

This movement is not going to look like a monocrop. It must reflect the rot and bugginess of the deep forest, the canopy and the ground cover, the wet sounds that delight and frighten us. Unlike the U'wa, who literally sleep within that earthy wholeness upon the very soil they are trying to protect, we are trying to uncover it, trying to find our way back to it. In a culture that teaches us to pave over what is wild, how do we learn (or remember) strategies, ways of relating, modes of transportation that don't also destroy what we are trying to heal? The answers are not clear-cut. We must feel our way through this unfamiliar terrain. We must uncover what has been paved over, even as we drive down I-85 toward Columbus.

DOMESTIC WORKERS ORGANIZE
IN THE GLOBAL CITY

Ai-jen Poo and
Eric Tang

Ai-jen Poo and Eric Tang are organizers with CAAAV: Organizing Asian Communities. Formerly known as Committee Against Anti-Asian Violence, CAAAV was founded by Asian women in 1986 as one of the first organizations in the United States to mobilize Asian communities to work against anti-Asian violence. The group focuses on conditions and institutional violence that affect immigrant working-class communities, such as worker exploitation, concentrated urban poverty, police brutality, Immigration and Naturalization Service detention and deportation, and criminalization of workers and youth. By organizing across low-wage and poor Asian communities in New York City, CAAAV exposes and struggles against violence to help increase communities' capacity for self-determination. In building coalitions, CAAAV contributes to a unified strategy for a broader, multiracial, and multi-issue movement for social change.

On May 2, 2003, Justina Dumpangol, an immigrant house-keeper, told her story of abuse to a panel of New York City

Council members. She spoke of going to an employment agency in Manhattan and being told she would never get a job because she was too old. Out of desperation, Dumpangol decided to take any job she could get. She told the council members how she once boarded a train for Long Island to begin a job with a family that she knew nothing about—there was no interview, no references. Despite the danger involved in taking jobs that are not screened by employment agencies, Dumpangol believed that this was her only opportunity to support herself and her family members overseas. Finally, she described the treatment she received from that Long Island family. She spoke of wages that amounted to less than a dollar per hour, of the way the family confined her to her quarters, and of emotional and physical abuse.

Little did Dumpangol know that less than a week later her story—and those of thousands of her domestic worker sisters—would push the New York City Council to pass the first bill in the nation addressing the exploitation faced by domestic workers. On May 14, 2003, the council unanimously voted in favor of a bill mandating a standard contract for domestic workers that includes, among other provisions, a minimum wage requirement, overtime pay, and vacation and sick leave, as well as full protection under the federal occupational health and safety laws. The bill is a product of over two years of struggle waged by Domestic Workers United, a grassroots, worker-led movement. It sends a clear message: domestic workers are laborers in the fullest sense of the word; they are not—as some employers like to believe—a luxury service to be purchased and exploited in the "privacy" of one's home.

This chapter is a tribute to all those domestic workers in the global city who struggle for dignity and respect. It explores the local and global ideologies that have for so long confined domestic work to the sphere of privatized "nonlabor," even in the eyes of supposedly progressive unions. It then describes how the globalization of capitalism has expanded the private exploitation of contingent workers, epitomized by domestic work among Third World immigrant women surviving in the First World metropolis. Finally, it examines the dynamic vision and action of domestic workers in New York City who are forever changing the terrain of domestic labor.

It is a known fact. Those labors considered "women's work"— cooking, cleaning, raising and rearing children—are drastically undervalued. Domestic workers often assume the roles of caregiver and housekeeper. Because so little value is placed on housework, those who perform the tasks associated with it are generally devalued as well. Third World women—migrants from the Philippines, the West Indies, Jamaica, Trinidad, Guyana, St. Vincent, St. Lucia, and Barbados—who work as domestics play a central role in New York City's economy. They provide a range of services (housekeepers, caregivers, private tutors, nannies, and personal assistants) for the city's global elite. And, like housewives, they are treated with little respect for the work that they do. They are denied minimum wage and sometimes paid the equivalent of only a few cents per hour. Although the mean income for domestic workers in New York City is $2.12 per hour, the legal minimum wage is $5.15. They are often virtually imprisoned in the homes of their employers, threatened with deportation, physically and sexually abused, prevented from learning much English, and prohibited from establishing friendships with others from the countries of their birth. They have few political and legal resources at hand for their protection.

Despite their importance to the functioning of the global city and their particular vulnerability as immigrants, Third World women domestics' location on the radar of the traditional labor movement (the UAW, AFL-CIO, Teamsters, et cetera) has until recently been nonexistent.[1]

Forced Migration

In New York City, poor Asian immigrant women have essentially one option in the labor market—the sweatshop. New York City sweatshops take many forms: garment factories, restaurants, nail salons, Laundromats, and the most intimate of spaces, the home. These workplaces often have no regulations, harsh surveillance, low wages, long hours, and threats of physical and sexual violence. Women in them endure substandard working conditions and abusive environments that mirror the very working conditions many of them tried to leave behind in the countries of their birth.

Many of these women have worked in the free trade zones of the Third World—highly unregulated areas set aside by governments for the manufacture and export of goods by companies that are usually foreign-owned. Tax incentives, cheap rent, relaxed legal standards, and free utilities are just some of the mechanisms used to encourage foreign investment and the installation of companies. Because free trade zones tend to be located in poorer countries with very high unemployment rates, the companies have access to large pools of cheap labor. Within these zones, companies wield enormous power, ranging from the right to bust unions to the right to violate local laws. For corporations, free trade zones are akin to the Wild West, where anything goes, but for the workers who labor in them, they are often fraught with perils. The majority of laborers in many free trade zones are women who are forced to work long hours for little pay, accept sexual harassment and abuse, and endure environmental hazards, with little hope of changing their situations. As a result, many of them are compelled to emigrate in search of alternatives to labor in these zones. As the scholar-activist Grace Chang noted in her book *Disposable Domestics,* U.S.-controlled free trade agreements induce Third World nations to open themselves to lawless free trade zones and their accompanying oppressions in order to relieve dire economic plights. But such agreements also allow U.S. multinationals to capture low-wage labor, particularly the labor of women workers, from the Third World.[2]

Once in the United States, Asian and other Third World domestic workers extend the wealth of the global city by laboring in the homes of the city's elite, thus allowing their employers extra disposable time and income. In addition to cleaning and providing security and child care, domestic workers shop, wait for deliveries, drop off and pick up dry cleaning, and escort children to gym classes. They feed and bathe children as parents go to exclusive fitness centers, enjoy the opera, visit day spas, and travel abroad. Domestic workers are, in fact, the key link in a highly integrated service economy for the city's wealthy class.

In this way they are the foundation upon which the luxuries of wealth can be enjoyed. This is more than a mere metaphor— lines of cell-like rooms (servant quarters) can be found along the ground floors and in the basements of many of the immaculate buildings lining the Upper East and West Sides of Manhattan, housing women from Latin America, the Caribbean, and the Philippines. Yet despite their role as caregivers to the most important elements of their employers' lives—families and property—domestic workers are often paid less per week than many of their employers spend on a new pair of shoes.

Locking Them In

Physical isolation is perhaps the most effective and damaging form of control that many migrant domestics experience. Unlike African-American domestics of the early to mid-twentieth century, today's Third World migrant is a truly transnational worker with few ties to her ethnic community in the United States. She is often sent from her homeland directly to the employer's residence and thus immediately and completely isolated from any ethnic enclave. The employer often holds her passport, visa, and access to cash, and in many cases controls the degree of contact the worker has with the outside world.

Shamela Begum's story exemplifies the lack of mobility that many transnational domestic workers suffer. A domestic worker from Bangladesh, she was employed for nearly nine months in 1999 by a high-ranking diplomatic family from Bahrain. She was forced to work seven days a week for $100 a month and was forbidden to leave the house alone. With the help of Andolan, a South Asian organization in New York, she eventually retrieved her passport, which had been taken from her, and escaped.

Carolyn H. de Leon, director of the Women Workers Project of CAAAV and a former domestic worker, shares a similar story. She recalls how her first employers used isolation as a tactic:

> I was isolated for a long period of time. I finally contacted a friend who came before me from Hong Kong. She came to visit me in the suburbs and showed me where the train station was, and how to get to Queens. So the following weekend, I bought my ticket to New York City, and I met my friend at Grand Central Station. We got on the Number 7 train to Queens, and I searched for my [Filipina] community. When I returned, my boss was shocked to find that I went to Queens. She told me never to go there again because "it's a very dangerous place. If anything happens to you, I'll be responsible." This was the same woman who had me freezing to death because she wouldn't provide me with a winter coat.

Carolyn had left the Philippines at the age of twenty-three to work as a domestic in Hong Kong before moving to the United States with an American family who were returning to New York. At first glance, Carolyn's travels suggest a certain freedom of mobility that few workers seem to have. Yet she was able to travel only because she was bound to her employers by U.S. immigration laws that allow corporate executives to bring along their domestic employees as they move through the circuits of global capital.

The Politics of Visas

Among the many challenges that Third World domestic workers must negotiate is a complicated immigration bureaucracy. The vast majority of domestics in New York City are undocumented. Employers use the promise of sponsorship to keep workers in abusive conditions for years; an even more common threat is incarceration or deportation. Most workers endure numerous hardships to be able to work and send some money home. The fear of being delivered to an Immigration and Naturalization Service (INS) detention center or sent back home empty-handed or in debt is enough of a threat to silence them.

Migrant domestics from Asia come to the United States on a number of employment-based visas, including B1, A3, and G5 visas. Every year more than 200,000 B1s are issued in the United States. These visas are held by people desiring to enter the United States temporarily for business, as well as domestic workers who come with those businesspeople. Most B1 visa holders are either corporate executives here to work temporarily or their bound domestic workers. In this case, the term *bound* has multiple unintended meanings. They are bound by immigration laws in the United States that essentially give employers full control of their labor: if the worker ceases to be employed by the foreign company or person, her B1 visa is voided and she becomes undocumented. (In other words, the domestic worker cannot quit her employment without losing her visa—and she likely cannot afford to leave the country on her own.) Finally, Third World women workers are bound to their low-wage jobs because their race, gender, and undocumented status leave them few other options. A B1 visa-holding domestic thus has no way of resisting her own exploitation.

By contrast with B1 visa holders, A3 and G5 visa holders are domestics who work for employees of the World Bank, International Monetary Fund, or a foreign government. These visas also bind workers to their employers, as they are specifically for "staff of" the foreign employers. In addition, these employers often hold diplomatic immunity, making it nearly impossible for workers to seek justice against them in the case of abuse.

One of the first cases that CAAAV's Women Worker's Project (WWP) took on involved Maria Vidania, a domestic worker on a B1 visa from Hong Kong who was made to work as a live-in nanny and housekeeper, seven days per week, seventeen hours per day, by Edmund Bradley, an executive of Credit Lyonnais Securities Asia, an international financial institution. With the WWP's help, Vidania secured the pro bono legal assistance of the National Employment Law Project (NELP), a nonprofit advocacy group, and charged the Bradleys with minimum-wage and overtime-requirement violations. The lawsuit, filed in November 2000 in U.S. district court, was an unusual step for an immigrant worker because it put her at risk for deportation. The WWP's efforts succeeded in attracting media attention to the case and facilitated legal recourse.

The WWP focuses on broad change as well as discrete cases of injustice, and it encourages multinational companies to educate executives about local labor laws. The project is also working in coalition with the Asian American Legal Defense and Education Fund, NELP, and the New York University School of Law's Immigrant Rights Project to change laws that enable the abuse of domestic workers.

CAAAV has documented a general pattern of slavery-like conditions for diplomats' employees. Of course, abuse of domestic workers is not limited to those who fall within these visa categories. Rather, these cases are emblematic of a larger set of U.S. immigration policies and practices that have created a climate of pervasive fear among immigrant workers.

No Legal Protections

Because of their tenuous legal position, it is often difficult for domestic workers to seek redress in U.S. courts. Local and national employment and labor laws do not provide sufficient recourse. Not only do labor enforcement agencies turn a blind eye to abuses in the domestic work industry but many laws protecting workers' rights specifically exclude domestic workers. The Occupational Safety and Health Act protections do not extend to live-in employees. Domestic workers are explicitly excluded from both the federal labor law known as Title VII of the Civil Rights Act of 1964 and the New York State Human Rights Law, which protect individuals from employment discrimination based on race, color, religion, sex, or national origin. Title VII applies only to employers with staffs of at least fifteen, while the New York law applies to employers with staffs of four or more. Further, the Fair Labor Standards Act—perhaps the single most important piece of legislation for workers in the United States, which establishes minimum wage, overtime pay, child-labor protections, and the forty-hour workweek—excludes live-in workers from overtime pay despite the fact that they are probably most in need of such protection.

Although all domestic workers have the right to be paid the minimum wage, enforcement depends upon either the worker's power to demand lawful pay or the employer's goodwill. In addition, because a great majority of domestic workers either are undocumented immigrants or have uncertain national status, they are subject to the punitive actions embodied in the Immigration Reform Acts of 1996, including INS detention and deportation.[3]

The National Labor Relations Act, a hard-won victory of the labor movement, was passed in 1935 as part of the New Deal. It gave workers the right to organize and bargain collectively for better working conditions and protected them from retaliation by their employers. The only two groups of workers excluded from this act's protections were domestic workers and farmworkers. This exclusion holds true today.[4]

One of the most recent pieces of legislation to curtail domestic workers' rights even further was California's Proposition 187. An anti-immigration provision that denies immigrants access to public education and all nonemergency medical care (rights that were once considered fundamental in this country) has had a disproportionate impact on domestic workers. Proposition 187 is aimed specifically at undocumented immigrants and their children, and it represents a pointed effort to identify female immigrant reproduction as a source of state (and national) disruption. Because so many domestic workers are undocumented female immigrants, this legislation has had an enormous impact on domestic workers, removing many of the resources that were available to them and their families.

Taken together, the persistent exclusions of domestic workers from legal protection not only reflect a lack of recognition of domestic work as a legitimate form of labor that warrants protection but also serve to alienate domestic workers from the mainstream labor movement.

Alternative Citizenship

Among the many tasks for today's social justice movement in the United States is the need to develop new organizing strategies, a new political language and culture, and coalition politics that can effectively expose the fault lines of contemporary global capitalism and build resistance where these fault lines are most deeply experienced. These include the Third World migrant women domestic workers and other workers who subsist in the temporary, domestic, and flexible global economy. Workfare workers, prison laborers, garment sweatshop workers, and the piece workers whose living rooms have become floor shops for major garment and technology corporations (to name a few) face the same issues of exploitation as do domestic workers and, for the most part, are not represented in today's labor laws and immigration policies.

Yet as various sectors of social justice activism, particularly the core labor movement, experience a self-proclaimed rebirth, it is apparent that, save for a few notable examples, undocumented migrant laborers are at best marginal voices in the supposedly immigrant-friendly union movement. While labor has recently given some lip service to legalizing undocumented workers, they have yet to take a firm stand against their neoliberal allies who have facilitated passage of some of the worst anti-immigrant policies in modern American history. These include English-only measures like Question 2, which eliminated bilingual education in Massachusetts in 2002, and the "Alien Absconder Initiative," which gives local law enforcement power to track down more than 300,000 immigrants who allegedly have orders to leave the United States. At best, the renewed labor movement seeks a judicial granting of citizenship to immigrants who have proved themselves good producers and earners for the U.S. economy.

This view ignores the fact that the very presence of undocumented and superexploited migrant workers in the United States is a direct consequence of Third World economies that have been deeply ruptured by the United States and its First World counterparts. Such violence has occurred through a narrow form of American citizenship, which carries as its primary tenets the right to consume inexhaustibly, to compete without limits, to own (both property and labor) without interference, and to privatize without restraint. The U.S. labor movement, with its continual talk of living wages (in the public sphere) for working (read nuclear) families, upright citizens, and decent folk who believe in the promise of the American dream, has yet to challenge what is fundamentally oppressive to the undocumented migrant worker: American citizenship itself.

Despite these obstacles, Third World women domestic workers *are* getting organized. In the process, this labor force is becoming visible through the creation of alternative communities. Much more than autonomous political sites, these alternative modes of organizing constitute networks where women can begin to explore and script different forms of citizenship and political participation. These women are questioning the very concept of citizenship "illegality" and fighting for their rights as human beings. It is through these modes that a new set of resistance politics is emerging—one that takes into account the voices, the history, and the experiences of Third World women and serves as the basis for a new labor-movement vision.

The group CAAAV: Organizing Asian Communities (formerly Coalition Against Anti-Asian Violence) was founded in 1986 at the first New York City–area Violence Against Asians in America forum. The forum, attended by 250 people, was a culminating point for CAAAV's founding members, primarily younger activists from several other organizations, including the Asian American Legal Defense and Education Fund, the Coalition of Labor Union Women—New York, the Japanese American Citizens League—New York, the Khmer Association in the United States, Korean Americans for Social Concern, Korean American Women for Action, the Organization of Asian Women, Organizations of Chinese Americans—New York, and the Young Korean American Service and Education Center. These activists created a multi-issue coalition that would seek to assist poor and low-income Asian immigrant communities in contributing to the broader movement for social change and justice.

Since 1998 the Women Workers Project of CAAAV and Domestic Workers United (DWU), a New York City–wide multiracial movement, have gathered to challenge punitive anti-immigration legislation and exclusive labor practices. In 1999 the WWP drafted a model contract and a series of guidelines for employers; DWU pressured employers to use the contract. Members conducted regular outreach to workers throughout Manhattan and Brooklyn, distributing leaflets at subway exits, in parks, and in ethnic enclaves in Queens and

Brooklyn. In this way DWU organized monthly strategy meetings. Workers identified three main goals: (1) respect and recognition for domestic workers; (2) an industrywide standard; and (3) multiracial unity among workers. Domestic Workers United formed a multiracial steering committee to provide leadership for the campaign, and, within three months of the group's formation, its membership base grew to more than 150. As a result of this important groundwork, the 2003 bill passed by the New York City Council mandates a standard contract for domestic workers. It is the first of its kind in the country. After working on the campaign for a model contract, members are now developing training curricula, conducting surveys of their peers on working conditions, and researching both contract enforcement strategies and possible legislative initiatives at the city and state levels.[5]

For the domestic workers who organize in CAAAV and DWU, the task is not only to fight for dignity, workplace rights, and appropriate monetary compensation but also to bring forth an alternative citizenship. At stake for these women is an opportunity to challenge the citizenship of consumerism, ownership, privatization, and exploitation that characterizes globalization and has led to the further destruction of their homelands. Political organizing is how this alternative citizenship comes to fruition. Organizations such as Domestic Workers United recognize these women as transnational laborers who are not confined to the boundaries of the nation-state. Given the fact that domestic laborers must transgress national borders in order to do their jobs, their rights must be reconsidered within a different citizenship paradigm. The whole notion that one belongs to one country as a citizen and to another as an invader is brought into question when the global city facilitates trafficking of workers from nation to nation. These workers cannot, in other words, simply be regarded as "illegals" or "noncitizens" when they seek recourse for unjust treatment by their employers. They must instead be able to obtain legal redress, and both international and national laws must take into account domestic workers' transnational realities.

The dawn of the twenty-first century poses many questions for a renewed feminist movement, indeed for a renewed popular left. We struggle with staying faithful to an activism that takes into consideration race, gender, class, and sexuality. The past twenty years may have taught us to recite this mantra adequately, but our practical commitment to it, in the form of organizing, activism, and the culture of the movement, leaves something to be desired. The revitalized labor movement, civil rights/antiracist agendas, and contemporary feminist interventions have each found their own way of marginalizing those who reside at their common intersection: women of color, particularly those who migrate from the Third World. But if the popular left has grown tired of being reminded how race, gender, and sexuality intersect, if it is weary of devising ways to break down the distance between the center and the periphery, then it has missed an essential shift in the global economy. Working women of color around the globe are already at center stage. Now is the time to recognize them and organize.

Elisha María Miranda

Elisha María Miranda is a filmmaker, educator, writer, and activist. A self-described two-spirited "Puerto Rican in exile," she grew up in the working-class Mission barrio of San Francisco. She is cofounder of Chica Luna Productions, a socially conscious multimedia collective for women of color. She is in the master's of fine arts program in film at Columbia University and has just finished a short film, For the Love of Patria, *a political love story between two women—one a Nuyorican activist, the other a U.S. marshal in Vieques, Puerto Rico. Her feature script* Outside the Wall, *a coming-of-age story about a Mission homegirl, was a finalist in the Sundance 2003 Feature Film Lab. She is also finishing her documentary film about Vieques,* Baptism by Fire.

> I did not come here to kill. I came here to die.
>
> —Lolita Lébron

I stumbled across Lolita Lébron's reiteration of the old Puerto Rican battle cry during my first year of college. On March 1, 1954, she and three men entered the U.S. House of Representatives with weapons. While she strode with her fist held high and wrapped in the flag of Puerto Rico, the group opened fire, wounding four congressmen. Lébron was sentenced to fifty-seven years in prison for assault and conspiracy to overthrow the government of the United States.[1] I became obsessed with this woman who had sacrificed her personal freedom for the love of her *patria*.

For me, an eighteen-year-old Puertorriqueña, Lébron and her comrades were heroes, freedom fighters, armed only by necessity in a desperate, last-ditch effort to change the oppressive relationship between the U.S. government and the Puerto Rican people. They were not the criminals portrayed by the mainstream American media. Nearly a decade later, I still feel deeply connected to Lolita Lébron's startling and symbolic actions. I carry her with me while doing my work and living my life—teaching high school students, organizing, running antiracist trainings, sitting with my mother and grandmother around the kitchen table drinking café con leche, loving my partner, challenging mass consumerism in the ivory towers of higher education, and most recently, directing and coproducing a documentary film on Vieques, Puerto Rico, titled *Baptism by Fire*.

I begin with this description of what would certainly be now, and probably was at the time, called a terrorist act against the United States not to idealize the killing of government officials, civilians, or anyone, but to provide some context for both my experience and the experience of my fellow Puertorriqueños, particularly those who inhabit the island of Vieques. In 1952 the U.S. Congress decided not to grant Puerto Rico statehood.[2] It was designated a commonwealth instead, a status that would alleviate the United States' obligation to report to the United Nations about its relationship with Puerto Rico as a colony. The distinction between commonwealth and colony, however, was of little consequence. The groundwork for an oppressive relationship had already been laid. The military occupation of Vieques had begun in 1941, and the Puerto Rican people had protested ever since. Lolita Lébron, an unrepentant *independista,* is emblematic of the tooth-and-nail fight to free Puerto Rico from imperialist domination by the United States. A Puerto Rican in exile, born in America, I am one result of what happens when people are uprooted, their resources abused, and their political and national autonomy subverted. Like the migrants of the world, I am a person in limbo, a person raised in one place while yearning for another, even if the place that I desire and can feel in my bones no longer exists.

Puerto Ricans in Exile

In 1996 I traveled for the first time ever to Puerto Rico, to make a movie. This visit took me to the barrio of my family, Orocovis, and on a trip that spanned the circumference of the island. The power of this homecoming was overwhelming. I felt as if the Orishas had sliced open my wrists and allowed my *sangre* to pour as an offering to my ancestors.[3]

My grandma's grandparents, poor sugarcane workers, were

forced to leave Puerto Rico a few years after the beginning of the twentieth century. The United States had just acquired Hawaii—another colony that needed cheap labor. My great-grandmother told me that her mother and father were promised that in Hawaii people would speak Spanish, that they would be able to afford a home, and that they would find a better life for their children. They owned no land in Puerto Rico and had recently been forcibly evicted from their home. So they embarked on a boat with hundreds of other Puerto Ricans. For two months they traveled, from Puerto Rico to New Orleans by boat, from New Orleans to Los Angeles by cargo train, and from Los Angeles to Hawaii again by boat. My great-great-grandmother lost two children to sickness on this voyage and gave birth to my great-grandmother upon arriving in Hawaii. She never returned to Puerto Rico.

The stories my great-grandma, or G.G. as we referred to her, told were always about the pride of being Puerto Rican. She never saw Puerto Rico, but her eyes danced when she spoke about her *patria*. She moved her feet in salsa steps as she listened to Don Ho sing "Tiny Bubbles." She ate *arroz con gandules* with soy sauce, a meal emblematic of her hybrid cultural existence. She told me how her father organized the workers to strike against the Portuguese landowners and how her mother made moonshine to sell to the other cane workers for extra income. Money was so scarce that my G.G. was forced to quit grade school and help her mother around the house.

During World War I, G.G. moved alone to San Francisco and found work in the factories. She married my great-grandfather, who was also a Puerto Rican Hawaiian. Their daughter, my grandmother, Eva Simona Vega, married Francisco "Panchito" Luis Miranda, a seaman who had joined the Merchant Marine because employment opportunities were limited for a man with a fourth-grade education. Eventually, my grandfather divorced my grandmother and moved to New York, leaving her a single parent on welfare with five children. He died of cirrhosis of the liver, never quite able to cope with leaving his family and Puerto Rico.

My homecoming in 1996 was not just for me—I could feel my entire family upon my shoulders as I stepped off the plane at the Luis Muñoz Marin International Airport. I could hear my G.G. saying, "Mamita, you open the doors for all of us."

I wanted to feel a release upon arriving in Puerto Rico, but instead I grew angry. Being both a filmmaker and an activist, I knew all too well that—despite the United States' contention to the contrary—colonialism was alive and well in Puerto Rico. Still, I hoped for a moment of peace, a gentle coming home, a little paradise. Instead, I was bombarded with the same emblems of American consumerism from which I had retreated—the McDonald's, the Kmarts and Blockbusters, the pharmaceutical companies, the fancy chain hotels and restaurants that only the privileged could frequent, the racism against my people, and miles and miles of poverty. It could have been any barrio or ghetto in the United States, only it was surrounded by beautiful Caribbean beaches.

I ended my trip to Puerto Rico visiting the small island of Vieques, off the eastern coast of San Juan, with my partner at the time; we were seeking a "queer friendly" space to retreat to for a few days. Arriving in Vieques, I was reminded of what Puerto Rico must have looked like fifty years ago, without department stores, fast-food restaurants, traffic lights, or even a movie theater. The beaches were crystal clear, and the bay glowed in the moonlight from a species of bioluminescent plankton that was slowly being contaminated by military bombings. That evening I awoke to a loud thump that made the land gently rumble. I inquired in the morning to find it was the bombing maneuvers. All I wanted was a little bit of peace, but I ended up right in the middle of an *invasion*.

Even the Dead Must Go

Puerto Rico was under Spanish colonial rule until 1897, when Spain granted the island self-government. In 1898, at the end of the Spanish-American War, the United States acquired the island, and installed a military administration. In 1900 the United States instituted civil government but continued to exercise controlling power.

During the Second World War, the U.S. Navy arrived on Vieques to protect the country from Communist infiltration. But when the Communist threat was no longer a reality, the occupation remained. The Navy continued to use the island for military exercises on a regular basis, firing rounds of shells loaded with depleted uranium (only 25 percent of which are recovered). They also fired cannons, hellfire missiles, and napalm bombs that destroy the island's delicate ecosystems. Toxins from the bombs still rain down, contaminating the air, the land, and the people. Women, men, girls, and boys continue to suffer from much higher than normal rates of cancer, lupus, thyroid deficiencies, and asthma. And the people still fight to get their stolen territory back.

Although Navy documents state that they paid $1.5 million per acre for an area amounting to two-thirds of the island, the question is: To whom did they pay it? Most sources that document the resistance to military bombings on the island concur that the government paid residents between twenty-five and fifty dollars for their land (an amount which some displaced residents claimed they never received), gave them forty-eight hours to vacate the premises, then bulldozed their houses. One Viequense I interviewed for my film spoke of the military knocking on his family's door, demanding that they leave immediately. The evacuation, he said, "looked like a herd of cattle being gathered through my young eyes." In taking possession of the land, the Navy displaced thousands of families. Many islanders were forced to move to the mainland of Puerto Rico, and to St. Croix, St. John, and St. Thomas. Like families sold in the slave trade one hundred years before, Viequense families were forever separated during this transition. Today the civilian population that remains—more than nine thousand Viequenses—is clustered in the middle third of the island.

No displaced resident of Vieques was given the deed to his or her home, suggesting that the Navy's real intention was to relocate the entire population. The government also proposed digging up those buried in island cemeteries, and it attempted to eliminate Vieques as a birthplace by blocking the development of a hospital or health clinic.[4] In 1947 the Department of Interior first proposed to relocate the entire population of Vieques to St. Croix. Mass opposition in Puerto Rico defeated this proposal. But in 1961, the Department of Defense again proposed, this time to President John F. Kennedy, the relocation of the population of Vieques. The governor of Puerto

Rico, Luis Muñoz Marín, wrote a letter to President Kennedy asking that the United States adhere to the constitution of the Commonwealth of Puerto Rico, which "requires an Act of the Legislature and a referendum of the voters in the affected area as a condition of abolishing a municipality."[5] Marin went on to argue that "unless this constitutional procedure is followed prior to the appropriation of the property and lands in Vieques by means of eminent domain, the evacuation of Vieques might be subject to a charge of illegality."

In 1948 Pedro Albizu Campos, revolutionary leader of the Puerto Rican Nationalist Party, wrote a visionary article titled "To Defend Vieques," which accused the United States of "carrying out the dismemberment of our nation. Vieques is dying. It is becoming extinct in the face of cold, deliberate, and intentional attack from the U.S. government." Campos asked, "Why has the United States chosen Vieques as the site for the manifest re-creation, before contemporary civilization, of the crime of genocide, that is, the deliberate physical or cultural destruction of a nationality?" He cited the public hearing on the Tydings Project, which was carried out by the U.S. Senate Committee on Territories and Insular Affairs in 1945 and claimed Puerto Rico as a strategic base for naval operations. The United States declared that Puerto Rico was needed as "a strategic zone" and that the U.S. would be the "sole judge" of whether or not to destroy any municipality in Puerto Rico, thereby, according to Campos, "throwing its population to the vicissitudes of a forceful exile."

This forceful exile resulted in a loss of national identity. Nationalism as an identity, as a question, has emerged as a central point of investigation among scholars in a wide range of fields: international relations, cultural studies, literature, and anthropology, among others. Benedict Anderson wrote that the nation is an "imagined political community" that is "both inherently limited and sovereign." What happens when the sovereignty of a nation is usurped by another power, made into a nation without a nation, a place and a people that imagine themselves as a nation but possess no political power over their own state? Governor Muñoz Marin in his letter to President Kennedy made a direct answer to this question: "The project involves the destruction of a community which is a political and juridical entity to which people have strong emotional attachment. The people of Vieques regard themselves as Puerto Ricans, but they also regard themselves as specially identifiable on the basis of residence in Vieques." If, as the theorist Ernest Renan wrote, "the nation is a soul, a spiritual principle,"[6] then the implicit consequence of the destruction of Vieques has been, and will continue to be, the destruction of the soul of a people.

On January 31, 2000, President Bill Clinton gave a directive to the Secretary of Defense that the future of Navy training on Vieques be determined by a referendum of the registered voters of the island. On July 29, 2001, the people of Vieques cast their votes: 68 percent demanded the "immediate and permanent termination of the military exercises and bombings of the Navy in Vieques, withdrawal of the Navy from Vieques, and the cleaning and return of Viequense land to its citizens." In 2002, sixty years after the expropriations began, the United States made plans to halt all military and bombing exercises and did so on May 1, 2003.[7]

The Colonized Body

Wherever a Puerto Rican is, it is the duty of a Puerto Rican to make revolution.

—Gloria Gonzales of the Young Lords

Now that the pressure to end military exercises on Vieques has been met with victory, what will be legacy of the occupation? Many Puerto Ricans hope that Puerto Rico will one day be an independent nation. If, and when, independence is won, Puerto Rico will struggle with what it means to be Puerto Rican like many postcolonial countries struggle with their identities. The women of Puerto Rico in particular suffer long-term consequences of colonial history.

The link between colonialism and patriarchy has long been theorized. One theory suggests that the same impulses toward domination that fuel patriarchy fuel colonialism. In patriarchal societies, women, like land, are perceived as property—a possession or an accumulation to add to one's wealth. The occupation of land—often described as virgin land when it has not been occupied before—has been compared to the occupation of a woman's body, the attempt to tame it, control it, regulate it, and retain it within its physical and psychic limits.

And, the regulation of women's bodies is critical to any colonial or imperialist effort that seeks to eradicate the cultural and national identity of a people. By controlling women's reproductive freedom, the growth of the population can be thwarted, and enforcing birth control is by degrees more acceptable than lining people up and gunning them down. In Puerto Rico, this crass analogy of conquest applies; the land of Vieques was taken and women's reproductive health has been strictly controlled through, at the height of the practice, the sterilization of 46 percent of low-income Puerto Rican women of childbearing age.[8] This number is considerable, since over 60 percent of Puerto Ricans live below the poverty line.

During the years following World War I, the U.S. government, the medical community, and the local government of Puerto Rico colluded to sterilize a large percentage of the female population. The goal was one-third of women by 1965 and the "continued use of sterilization on a broad scale by Puerto Rican women as a form of birth control."[9] As a result, Puerto Rican women have the world's highest sterilization rate.

In *La Operación,* her documentary film about the sterilization of Puerto Rican women, Ana María García illustrates that contrary to what U.S. officials have stated, the sterilization process was not always voluntary. Dr. Helen Rodriguez-Trías says that the United States implemented a social policy in Puerto Rico that targeted a group of people who "shouldn't have children."[10] In one family, every woman had been sterilized. García's film highlights the grief of the elder woman in the family, who cried for those who could never be born. A twenty-two-year-old woman was told by her doctor that sterilization was her only choice of birth control. She was given no other advice, information, or options. Another woman thought that the procedure was reversible. Had she known the truth, she would not have agreed to be sterilized.

It is not only, of course, through sterilization that the women of Puerto Rico have been subjugated, but through a range of techniques in which women bear the double burden of being women and being colonial subjects. With the increased military presence of the 1950s, the number of rapes rose greatly. For my documentary, *Baptism by Fire,* I heard testimonies of local women who didn't leave their homes at night for fear of being raped by drunken American soldiers. Because of a proliferation of such attacks, the Municipal Assembly of Vieques passed a resolution in 1953 condemning the military presence on the island and requesting the return of occupied lands for civilian use.[11] Today many American soldiers are now confined to the military base.

A Contemporary Struggle for Justice

I think Vieques has brought together a new level of consciousness in Puerto Rico.

　　　　　—Dylcia Pagán (Former Puerto Rican political prisoner)

The time comes when justice arms the weak and puts the giants to flight.

　　　　　—Pedro Albizu Campos

On April 19, 1999, the U.S. Navy dropped two five-hundred-pound bombs on the eastern tip of Vieques. A civilian guard, David Sanes Rodriguez, was killed, and four others were injured. Since Rodriguez's death, hundreds of civilians have risked their lives to protest the bombings by living in encampments on the military's bombing ranges. Until April 2000 many of these protests, organized by the Committee for the Rescue and Development of Vieques (CRDV), a local grassroots group, had successfully deterred bombings. However, on April 28, 2000, U.S. authorities sent one thousand Marines to help remove Puerto Rican protesters.

On May 4, 2000, forty-five years after Lolita Lébron fired shots in the U.S. House of Representatives, she was arrested with 212 other activists in Vieques for resistance against the federal government. Protesters were arrested for camping on land that had been forcibly taken from Viequenses. "Puerto Rico has been invaded again," said New York City Councilman Jose Rivera as he was led away by law enforcement.

Throughout the history of the United States in Vieques, there have been public hearings, broken government promises, and numerous Puerto Ricans killed or imprisoned for their support of the independence of Puerto Rico. For a decade the United Nations has agreed that Puerto Rico is a U.S. colony. The UN has also repeatedly reaffirmed "the inalienable right of the people of Puerto Rico to self-determination."[12] Over sixty years ago Pedro Albizu Campos was already talking about the cultural destruction of Vieques and Puerto Rico. Lolita Lébron, along with many courageous others, sacrificed years of imprisonment. Yet it has taken the death of David Sanes Rodriguez for many to shift their eyes momentarily toward Vieques and Puerto Rico. Intense media coverage has made Vieques a household word. Rodriguez is now a part of a pantheon of heroes, many of whom remain unsung.

*   *   *

On September 11, 2001, thousands of innocent people were killed by a terrorist attack on the United States. Many Americans were both horrified and surprised that we were not safe on our own soil. Yet for those of us who deal with police brutality, racial hatred, violence against women and queer people, religious violence, immigrant bashing, and the criminalization of youth of color, terrorism is embedded into the fabric of daily life. I do not say this to minimize the pain inflicted upon the many people of different nationalities on September 11. However, as I write this, the people of Vieques have to contend with the aftershocks of the bombing, and many are subject to slow deaths from cancer and other diseases. As Dr. Jorge Fernández Porto notes, "Each detonation in Vieques forces up into the atmosphere the 'poison soup' that everyone knows gets into the air that the people of Vieques breathe."[13] It is difficult to prove that cancer on Vieques is directly connected to the Navy's bombing exercises because doctors know so little about the disease. Like the so-called known terrorist groups, the criminals here are both visible and invisible.

How far have we come from the image of Lolita Lebrón sacrificing all for *la patria*? The image I captured on film of a Puerto Rican police officer crying while she arrested a female Puerto Rican civilian protester in Vieques is the first that comes to my mind. These two images side by side bring tears to my eyes as I look at what's left of my fragmented people. Then I am reminded of a quotation by the activist-writer Betita Martinez who says, "Think what may seem unthinkable and envision revolution. Think *sin fronteras*—without borders."[14]

Most Puerto Ricans have grown up in a colonial culture that has increasingly become a culture of consumption. But if the United States is disseminating a culture of consumption throughout the world, as revolutionaries we must learn to spread a culture of consciousness. We do not have to water down our radical ideology or action, just rethink and reinvent our strategies for resistance. We can define anticolonial, antiracist, anti-ism in a way that will make people believe my survival is critical to your survival. We can create a political movement that uses entertainment to "edutain," thus providing a vision for Latinos that goes beyond the taco-peddling Chihuahua dog, the uneducated savage, the oversexed exotic, or the numbed out addict. We can bust down the borders, expose the truth, and create a new vision for liberation all at the same time. ¡*Yanqui Basta Ya, Vieques Vale Más!*

WHEN TRANSGENDERED PEOPLE SUE AND WIN: FEMINIST REFLECTIONS ON STRATEGY, ACTIVISM, AND THE LEGAL PROCESS

Anna Kirkland

Anna Kirkland is a twenty-nine-year-old Ph.D. candidate in jurisprudence and social policy at the University of California at Berkeley, writing her dissertation on personhood and group identity in U.S. law. She earned her J.D. from Berkeley in 2001 and formulated the research and arguments for this article as a law student. She teaches gender and law in the Women's Studies Program at the University of Michigan.

Transsexual and transgendered men and women, despite their exclusion from most civil rights laws in the United States, occasionally prevail as plaintiffs in litigation. (I use the term *transsexual* to refer to people who identify as such and who seek to alter their bodies through surgery or hormones to bring them into line with their social and emotional gender. The term *transgendered* captures a broader category of gender variant people who have not necessarily sought to alter their bodies but feel a disjunction between their biologically and

socially gendered selves.)[1] What should contemporary feminists make of these victories? How do transsexual and transgendered plaintiffs have to describe their gender and sexual
identity in court in order to win child custody, attend public
school in the clothing of their choice, or keep a job? This essay
presents several legal strategies that gender variant plaintiffs
have used successfully and places them within a critical feminist framework. Many feminists have long been suspicious of
using the law as a strategy for social change because of its
patriarchal history and relatively conservative structure. For
extremely marginalized groups like transsexuals and transgendered people, however, grasping for basic legal rights is still
very important, and these rare victories mean a great deal.
Nonetheless, there is widespread disagreement over what real
gender liberation would look like, and whether law helps or hinders its achievement. Closely examining the options the legal
process offers can help us to navigate these debates and produce solutions that extend gender freedom for all people.

One feminist attitude toward transsexuals has been prominent since the 1970s, when cultural feminists argued that
male-to-female transsexuals were just men who had mutilated
themselves, and because of their still-remaining male psyche
and upbringing, they should not count as women for the
purposes of women-only music festivals or meeting places.[2]
Transsexuals should be treated with suspicion and excluded
from the ranks of woman-centered feminism, this account
goes, since they continue to exhibit traits of their male dominance (in the case of males to females, who would be, of
course, still men) or (in the case of females to males) have dis-
carded their womanhood to join the patriarchy. A more soft-

ened view would simply maintain that there is no reason for feminists to be interested in transsexuals because they are not interested in changing gender norms; transsexuals simply aspire to move from one patriarchal and oppressive category to another.

So while "womyn-oriented womyn" have historically despised male-to-female transsexuals as patriarchal interlopers, they are now forced to share the tent with other gender theorists who focus on the power of eroticism to break down sexual and gender norms and celebrate the transgression of boundaries, and for whom transsexual and transgendered people represent the best of freedom.[3] These scholars have substituted an explicitly sexual style of writing for the more traditional strategy of arguing for rights through political and legal processes. D. Travers Scott, for example, makes his point about the need to get rid of identity boundaries by referring to the ways sexual desire refuses to contain itself: "How can a rigid Gay Male identity cope with that really cute guy, who used to be a baby butch dyke, and is still involved in a primary relationship with a woman, but considers herself basically a gay man?" he asks.[4] Sexual desire is the conduit that leads across all restraining boundaries; it is the way to understand "otherness" and to rethink our own sex-gender rigidities. Pat Califia notes another popular strategy of gender transgression besides erotic talk, advocated by Kate Bornstein: camp, humor, trickery, and spiritualism. "I think," Bornstein writes, "that anyone who regularly walks along a forbidden boundary or border (gay/straight, sober/drunk, male/female, black/white, etc.) has the potential to attain some degree of spiritual awareness."[5] Whether or not these views employ erotic talk or other narrative forms, what unites them is the conviction that "border crossings" are primary sites of freedom, knowledge, and power, and that one ought to dwell in them.

These directions in gender theory exemplify the new twist on feminism's old suspicion that rights-claiming under the law is not ultimately very effective or liberating. It is not just that, say, civil rights laws are more conservative than they should be but rather that to grasp at a protective category (woman, African-American, disabled, gay) is necessarily to place one's identity under regulation by an inherently conservative legal system. If freedom is about breaking down categories, then seeking protection through legal definitions is unlikely to secure genuine liberation. The fear is that engaging with the law will only domesticate gender variant people and downgrade their unique legal claims. The problem for feminists is that this view seems to dismiss law entirely, but many of us still accept that it is necessary for everyone to enjoy basic legal protections. It is unhelpful to say simply that law's categories are per se good or bad, liberating or oppressive. The real question is: When, under what conditions, for which plaintiffs, and for what kinds of claims might they be either liberating or oppressive? We have to understand the legal framework for these claims, and we must assess the different (and often conflicting) accounts of what law ought to do for gender variant people.

The law surrounding sex changes often relies on highly simplified ideas about sex and gender. In terms of contemporary civil rights and antidiscrimination law, cloaking herself with a rights claim often requires the transsexual plaintiff to, as one judge put it, "definitively identify the protected class in which she claims membership."[6] Because transsexuals are not protected per se, every lawsuit begins with an inadequate description (usually that the discrimination occurred because of "sex," meaning biological status as male or female). This "check-a-box" type of requirement immediately demands traditional gender classification of a plaintiff whose entire legal problem arises precisely because she does not have one. Right from the start, her unique challenge is downgraded because of the need to comply with pleading requirements. To reject this categorization is to have one's lawsuit fail immediately on a 12(b)(6) motion from the other side (for failure to state a proper legal claim).[7] The choice to go forward with a claim that may not be the most philosophically pleasing but will advance the lawsuit may win peace, protection, and public identity confirmation for a transsexual plaintiff, but what are its long-term effects?

Claiming to fit into a statutory definition (as Title VII discrimination "on the basis of sex" requires) or arguing for the application of a higher level of judicial scrutiny for burdensome laws or policies (as the Fourteenth Amendment's equal protection clause extends to certain classifications) is the beginning of a civil rights strategy. But many critical scholars have complained that doing so solidifies a certain "story" of a social group and its subordination that ultimately becomes co-opted and used against that group. This story may build up its tolerance for the group through references to the unchanging and stigmatic nature of the trait, and ultimately some judicial understanding becomes part of the truth of what it means to be African-American, or disabled, or a woman. The Supreme Court's equal protection jurisprudence is sometimes linked to the very brand of essentialism that much of contemporary feminism rejects—defining an individual's equal protection status by reference to one unchangeable trait that links him or her to a suspect class, such as a racial group. Traits that are immutable (some would say "beyond help") are more likely to trigger judicial sympathy than those that agents could change if they wanted to. For example, popular attention to the issue of a "gay gene" comes from the notion that if gays and lesbians are born gay, it would be unfair to discriminate against them.[8] Feminists, however, prefer to emphasize the ways that gender and sexuality are contingent and socially produced in relations of unequal power; thus, the gay gene debate simply distracts from the real issues surrounding gay and lesbian equality. If feminists are reluctant to embrace rock-solid definitions of gender identity and sexuality while they must assert rigid characteristics to their rights in court, then we are certainly in a bind. It seems as though we abandon the transgressive power of feminist politics if we rely upon traditional legal categories, however much we need them to win cases.

Perhaps, though, it is not so necessary to rely on arguments which risk conceding that there is something unfortunate and deviant about being a transsexual or transgendered person. One could frame a legal argument for protecting gender variant people around the history of their exclusion and oppression, drawing attention to the cruelty of society rather than to the features of gender variant people themselves. There would be no need to describe the causes of transsexualism (in the language of medical abnormality, for example), and such a strategy would help to facilitate group pride. Adopting a legal category for identity group promotion is therefore unproblematic, and not necessarily allied with the troubling theoretical implications just described. Under this view, it would be desirable to add the category of "transgender" or the words "sexual or gender identity" to antidiscrimination statutes next to "race," "gender," "religion," and so on. Gender liberation would be advanced by the recognition of a new social label, in other words, and the extension of public sympathy toward it. We would speak of "the transgender community" in the same way we hear of "the gay community" now, and we would not be confused about whom we are talking about. In this view, feminists (the ones who are straight and happy in their gender, specifically) should care about this effort because it helps expose the social power of gender and sexual norms, though perhaps only in a way parallel to rather than convergent with their own interests. We would hear many new stories of suffering and the history of "a people," and gradually we could hope to make alliances with and establish legal protections for this community.[9] But how would the legal system really treat this community, and is the alliance with feminism really so clear?

It may, however, be dangerous for feminists to adopt even this softened understanding of law's categories, especially in those brief moments when they seem to reward. We ought to bear in mind feminist scholar Wendy Brown's questions: "When does identity articulated through rights become production and regulation of identity through law and bureaucracy? When does legal recognition become an instrument of regulation, and political recognition become an instrument of subordination?"[10] Even when law cedes the point to transsexual and transgendered claimants that biological sex and gender role are not necessarily the same in the same person, it manages to preserve the two main categories of the masculine and the feminine as the only options for supposedly transgressive switching back and forth. Likewise, there is a danger that stories of the "transgender community" will become less than flattering in judges' hands. One powerful example is legal scholar Janet Halley's analysis of the rhetoric of *Bowers v. Hardwick,* in which the Supreme Court declined to protect private homosexual activity from arrest under Georgia's antisodomy statute.[11] By stigmatizing and isolating sodomy (defined as any oral-anal-genital contact) as a strictly homosexual perversity, the Court both protected heterosexual ideas about sex and reified its own version of gay identity. Halley explained how the trap worked:

> Recent, expansive readings of *Hardwick,* with their crudely essentialist notion of how the class of homosexuals is established, sound a weird echo of an argument repeatedly adopted by advocates of gay and lesbian rights. For until recently, gay rights advocates have fairly consistently argued that homosexual orientation is so unitary, fundamental, irresistible, and inalterable that homosexuals meet a supposed requirement of suspect classifications, that of immutability. After *Hardwick,* the argument for heightened scrutiny under the equal protection clause is now undermined, not bolstered, by claims that homosexuality is a fixed and immutable attribute of a rigidly demarcated class.[12]

Arguments that sexual oppression is like racial oppression, or that discrimination against transsexuals and transgendered people is like sex discrimination, have been appealing because these analogies draw upon understandings of subordination "that are widely understood to be widely understood," as Halley puts it, and because they have formed the basis for past development of legal protection.[13] But she cautions against simply absorbing new claims based on sexual identity into the rhetoric of legal rights, because doing so concedes that those whose claims do not fit the "like race" paradigm should not be protected and because "it promotes the idea that the traits of subordinated groups, rather than the dynamics of subordination, are the normatively important thing to notice."[14]

Halley also argues that it may be wrong to assume that all feminists and all queer or gender variant people share the same understandings about what kind of social change would be best. "Transsexuals, particularly male-to-female transsexuals . . . have entered onto the political scene insisting that gender is conflated with bodily sex," she notes.[15] To the extent this characterization is true, there may be thinner grounds for alliance between transsexuals and contemporary feminists than has been admitted, since it has been a feminist aim to separate these concepts. Further problems with identity groups and coalition-building are evident in the debate over the place of the *T* in *LGBT*—that is, gay and lesbian activists have also had their disagreements about how transsexuals and transgendered people fit in. As Shannon Minter, a staff attorney at the National Center for Lesbian Rights, points out, gay and lesbian concerns have not been automatically assumed to apply to transsexuals or transgendered people, and in fact there is a great deal of dissention about what the relationship between them should be. "Depending on one's perspective," he observed in a recent article, "transgender people have been depicted as misguided interlopers who have suddenly wandered into gay politics by mistake, or as the long awaited vanguard of a radical new politics of gender transgression."[16] But if theorists of gender and sexuality of different affiliations do not agree about what to make of transsexuals, they do raise the same question: Are transsexuals subject to the same gender regulations as the rest of us and thus just as susceptible to law's iterations of traditional gender norms, or are they somehow special, the key to dismantling a sex and gender regime? Are they all revolutionaries simply by being, or are they a diverse population including gender role conservatives ("I just want to become a real woman"), radicals ("Gender is over"), and all in between?

Feminist legal theorists who attempt to learn lessons from transsexual litigants must accept and understand how fragmentated transsexual and transgender activists themselves are on these questions. Otherwise we may fall into the trap of simply praising any iteration of transsexual existence and any win in litigation as progressive. Research gathered through therapists and support groups shows that many transsexuals simply want to come to peace with their "true" gender identity and get medical help to actualize it on their bodies.[17] Moreover, many judges look benevolently upon a transsexual whose "real" sexual identity is "trapped." The language of entrapment also occurs throughout the therapeutic and narrative literature on transsexualism. Legal rights-claiming is a perfectly unproblematic strategy for the transsexual who believes that her authentic sexual self is "out there," and that the state (as well as a surgeon) can enable the union of self and true sex.[18] Self-descriptions like this one from the transsexual Jan Morris are not uncommon:

All I wanted was liberation, or reconciliation—to live as myself, to clothe myself in a more proper body, and to achieve Identity as last. . . . To myself I had been a woman all along, and I was not going to change the truth of me, only discard the falsity. . . . I was about to adapt my body from a male conformation to a female, and I would shift my public role altogether, from the role of a man to the role of a woman. It is one of the most drastic of all human changes, unknown until our own times, and even now experienced by very few; but it seemed only natural to me, and I embarked upon it only with a sense of thankfulness, like a lost traveler finding the right road at last.[19]

In sharp contrast, the leadership cadre of transgender writers often draws back from endorsing a romantic view of transsexual identity, and thus it would seem that not all transsexual or transgendered people would want to promote themselves as a "like-race" social group under the law. Some transgender scholars are busy constructing a unitary narrative of transsexual identity throughout history, but many of these writers despise categories of all sorts because of the danger of reification of their contents. Riki Anne Wilchins, for example, does not want to claim a transsexual identity or start a transsexual movement that "will merely end up cementing the idea of a binary sex."[20] She does not support the strategy of emphasizing the special place within gender systems that transgendered people occupy, in which they are treated as uniquely transgressive and coherent as a category of people over time. Historical figures such as the Native American *berdache* ("two spirit" person) valorized in Francisco Valdes's and Leslie Feinberg's work make Wilchins "deeply uncomfortable."[21] "I don't want to bear the burden of being especially good any more than I want to bear that of being especially bad," she explains.[22]

It is critical to link any conclusion about the usefulness of rights strategies to the wide variety of perspectives that gender variant people have articulated. In the cases I describe, I ultimately defend a middling approach that adapts much of Janet Halley's criticism of social group construction in the law while maintaining the ethical force needed to prevent most of the garden-variety suffering that transgendered and transsexual people experience (that is, job loss and beatings). The legal analysis that follows reveals the pitfalls and the possibilities on the way to developing such an approach.

Protection Through Medicalization: Legal Victories, Feminist Misgivings

The judicial decision to order public funding for sex reassignment surgery rests upon a great deal of expert witness testimony that the surgery is "medically necessary" as a cure for illness. Transsexuals cannot make legal claims for state medical benefits as psychologically normal people who are simply gender variant (akin to, say, a person who has lost a limb and would like a prosthesis but who also wants to resist the pitying and stigmatic label "handicapped"). Their lawsuits are successful only insofar as petitioners characterize themselves as people in need of a clear surgical gender assignment, thereby making it impossible for advocates to question our society's strict system of gender classification and serve their clients' needs at the same time. In *B. v. Lackner,* a transsexual plaintiff won a case ordering the California medical welfare program, Medi-Cal, to pay for her sex-change operation.[23] The Medi-Cal director had refused the applicant's request on the grounds that the surgery was essentially cosmetic. The director's written decision noted that "the proposed operation as described by the claimant's doctor is a description of a cosmetic operation that would change the appearance of the claimant's external genitalia" and therefore "it must be considered a cosmetic operation that is not covered under the Medi-Cal Program."[24] In its judgment reversing the director's order, the court applied the definition of cosmetic surgery approved by the California Medical Association: "Surgery to alter the texture or configuration of the skin and its relationship with contiguous structures of any feature of the human body." The court, rejecting the director's argument, reasoned that "castration and penectomy cannot be considered surgical procedures to alter the texture and configuration of the skin and the skin's relationship with contiguous structures of the body. Male genitals have to be considered more than just skin, one would think."[25] The court's willingness to accept broader descriptions of the transsexual's need for surgery is initially promising. The petitioner's argument—that the surgery is a cure for an illness and properly matches her body with her true gender—was successful in this court of law but is problematic from a post-essentialist feminist view.

At the end of *B. v. Lackner*, the court ruled that it is "clearly impossible to conclude that transsexual surgery is cosmetic surgery."[26] Based on the expert medical testimony, the court concluded that the transsexual's request for Medi-Cal funding for her surgery was "necessary and reasonable" to relieve her condition of "gender identity dysphoria"(now termed "gender identity disorder").[27] In a 1980 Iowa case similar to *Lackner,* the court of appeals struck down the state's policy of denying Medicaid benefits for sex reassignment surgery because it constituted an arbitrary denial of benefits based solely on diagnosis, type of illness, or medical condition.[28] The ruling depended on the court's finding that sex reassignment surgery was the only medical treatment available to relieve the problems of a "true transsexual." In the Americans with Disabilities Act of 1990, however, Congress specifically excluded transsexuals from protection, along with pyromaniacs, voyeurs, pedophiles, and various other individuals whom legislators feared would claim legal rights based on deviant behavior despite the fact that law otherwise views "true" transsexuals as mentally ill and in need of a cure.[29] Our legal system simultaneously demands that transsexuals petition for benefits as ill people (open to being effectively cured) in one law and writes them out of another because their illness is not of the proper sort.

In these cases and others like them, the distinction between mere "cosmetic" changes to the body (which the state refuses to pay for) and those which are medically necessary to fix a disorder is determinative. As is evident in *Lackner,* the rhetoric of "cosmetics" versus "medicine" dominates the case law that pertains to funding for sex changes. The Medi-Cal director argued that transsexuals merely want the state to pay for a cosmetic change to the contours of the body, akin to smoothing away a bump on one's nose. The physicians responded with the "illness" model: unless this person gets sex reassignment surgery such that her genitalia and hormones match her sexual identity, she occupies the legal category of an untreated ill person who is entitled to Medi-Cal benefits. The legal category of transsexual may be highly problematic, but "untreated ill person entitled to Medi-Cal benefits" is one the courts recognize with sympathy.

What happens, however, when medical experts begin to disagree about whether sex reassignment surgery is "medically necessary"? In 2001, after finding that "the efficacy of the surgery has been questioned within the medical community," an Eighth Circuit federal court found that *Pinneke v. Preisser,* an earlier decision granting coverage for sex reassignment surgery to qualified Medicaid patients, had been superseded by Iowa Department of Human Services rules. The decision not to fund the rest of John Smith's (a pseudonym) surgery was held by the court to be the result of a reasonable regulation by the Department, even though his psychiatrist urged the state to provide the operation. There were other available treatments, the court noted, and a federal survey of treatment guidelines and practitioners revealed a lack of consensus about the surgery.[30] Has the contemporary debate over the ethics and efficacy of sex reassignment surgery become a means of retrenchment for a conservative court? It seems to behoove transgender activists to insist upon the efficacy of surgery and to marshal as much expert opinion behind this proposition as possible; otherwise judges seize upon disagreements as reasons to deny individual plaintiffs the surgery they want.

Another sympathetic grounding for transsexual and transgender rights that has enjoyed some recent success (without depending upon rigid medical conclusions) is the claim that suffering from gender dysphoria places one in the protected class of disabled people. In the 2001 case *Doe v. Yunits* (also discussed later for a different point), a Massachusetts state court interpreted its disability civil rights law more broadly than the federal Americans with Disabilities Act and ruled that a fifteen-year-old transgendered girl with male physiology could be covered under the state law in her suit against her school district, which had prohibited her from wearing feminine clothing to school.[31] The judge in *Doe* likened the process of broadening the legal concept of disability to include this youth to the expansion of Enlightenment rationality and tolerance: "[The state of Massachusetts] . . . recognizes that . . . persons who were previously thought to be eccentric or iconoclastic (or worse) and who were vilified by many people in our society may turn out to have physical or mental impairments that grant them protection from discrimination."[32] The fact that the plaintiff's tendency to wear girls' clothes is defined as a disorder by psychiatrists in the *Diagnostic and Statistical Manual of Mental Disorders* (*DSM-IV*) bolsters the judge's argument that she should be protected (as does the possibility, considered in a footnote, that she may have a genetic condition that caused her transgenderism).[33] Judges writing opinions in cases like *Lackner* and *Doe* seem to lack the legal vocabulary to uphold the transsexual's claim in any way but to affirm, first, the illness of transsexual and transgendered people and, second, the notion that one's genitals must properly match one's sexual and social identity. Both these solutions focus upon the traits and behavior of gender-transgressive people and measure the degree to which they deviate from social norms of maleness and femaleness, leaving the norms themselves untouched.

Feminists must not forget that legal victories, however obtained, help develop life plans that transsexual plaintiffs have doggedly pursued for years. By the time the plaintiff enters the court to ask for sex reassignment surgery, she has already spent several years demonstrating her desire to actualize her "true" sexual identity. To have come this far in the process, the plaintiff must have convinced psychiatric experts that she fit under the definition of transsexualism or "gender identity disorder" in the *DSM-IV,* Category 302.50.[34] In addition, the physicians' Standards of Care for the treatment of gender dysphoria mandate that the patient be in therapy with a clinical behavioral scientist for at least six months before she can get the expert recommendation to undergo the procedure.[35] The patient must also live as the opposite sex for at least a year before surgery. The surgeon is guilty of professional misconduct if she operates without at least two written recommendations in favor of the patient's sex reassignment, one from a doctoral-level clinical behavioral scientist and one from a professional who has known the patient for at least six months.

These standards are much more rigorous than usual in medical ethics of informed consent, even as they are applied to significant and irreversible procedures such as sterilization, organ or marrow donation, or radical plastic surgeries. Thus, it cannot be simply the permanence and wide-ranging implications of a sex change that justify such stringent gatekeeping mechanisms. The patronizing lack of regard for transsexuals as patients with clear desires seems apparent under a comparison of the rules. The medical profession controls access to sex-change surgery more stringently than other life-altering, irreversible procedures. It is reluctant to accept the transsexual's self-reported intentions, and law requires medical professionals to testify at length as expert witnesses on both sides, under continual threat of malpractice litigation or revocation of their licenses to practice if they fail to adhere strictly to the medical and legal requirements.

Judges may also exhibit a skeptical and insulting attitude toward transsexuals who are litigating one of the many issues that arise on the way to surgery, such as changing one's name. One judge refused to grant a name change petition in August 2001 because the "appellant's decision to change his name was made without regard to the possibility that he would change his mind once going through the real life experience."[37] It was reasonable, the Ohio appeals court found, for the trial judge to protect transsexuals from themselves because "sex reassignment surgery may be requested by persons who experience short-term desires or beliefs which may change with the passage of time."[38] The main reason both courts found the transsexual's intent flimsy was that he was not yet scheduled for surgery. A small bit of research would have revealed, however, that the process of obtaining sex reassignment surgery usually takes several years, so it would not have been reasonable to expect a date for the surgery at that point in time. Here, medical procedures conflicted with judicial understandings and blocked the sex-change process for reasons primarily based upon ignorance and distaste. Both the psychomedical and the legal establishments sometimes exhibit distrust of transsexual people's life plans.

But must feminists also exhibit a lack of regard for the reported desires of transsexuals? Most of us simply do not believe that what makes one a woman is a deep-seated inner woman-truth, that we are lucky to have the external sex traits to match up with it, and that this proper union has meant a more peaceful inner life. Is the only other option simply to ratify the desires of anyone who seems to be gender transgressive, out of sympathy or perhaps in the hope that anything is better than the gender status quo? Does feminist mistrust of the mystical "inner truth" understanding of transsexualism mean that making these legal arguments on behalf of people seeking surgery is always distasteful? Nor is there an obvious way for a feminist legal theorist who wants to support transgendered clients to know what is best simply by polling transsexuals or gender activists. There is, not surprisingly, a lot of debate among transsexual and transgendered people over the appropriateness of submitting to the medical and psychiatric establishments. Activists have spoken out against the normalization of the treatment process as it is currently practiced. James Green, a prominent FTM organizer, speaker, and writer, recently characterized that process as a "coercive dynamic [that has] perpetuated many inaccurate stereotypes about trans people, including the widespread misconception (which is unfortunately shared by many GLB people) that transsexual people are homophobic and reactionary and have no political goals other than being accepted as 'normal' heterosexuals."[39] Riki Anne Wilchins, cofounder of Transsexual Menace and executive director of GenderPAC, turns the entrapment metaphor on its head: "The problem with transsexual women is not that we are trapped in the wrong bodies. The truth is that that is a fairly trivial affair corrected by doctors and sharp scalpels. The problem is that we are trapped in a society which alternates between hating and ignoring, or tolerating and exploiting us and our experience."[40]

Yet feminists and gender activists must come to terms with the fact that transsexuals themselves often identify as ill people who need to unite their bodies with their real gendered self (which is often a fairly stereotypical version of a gendered self). Gender scholar Kim Stuart's two-year study of seventy-five transsexuals who consented to extensive personal interviews is a detailed and sensitive presentation of "the myths and real-life experiences of transsexuality" aimed at the general public. The individual cases certainly exhibit variation, but the men and women she interviewed do not seem at all like postmodern, performative, transgressive-gender activists, nor do they share these activists' suspicion of the medical establishment. Some of Stuart's observations, such as the fact that "large breasts are a fairly high priority for many male-to-female transsexuals," indicate that some transsexual women pursue the values of patriarchal culture just as anxiously as many non- or antifeminist women.[41]

Stuart summarizes the complaints that she found most prominent among her interviewees, and these also reveal a highly assimilationist attitude. The transsexuals wanted to obtain more and better information about their condition; to dispel ignorance about transsexualism among gender professionals and the public; to receive better services; to lessen the financial burdens of having surgery; and to be treated with the same respect as patients with other conditions.[42] These are certainly laudable goals; if achieved, they would relieve a tremendous amount of suffering in a vulnerable group of people. They are also compatible with an understanding of gender and sexual identity that is highly conventional, medicalized, and reductive.

If feminists want to transform the legal sphere in which we fight on behalf of gender variance, we should be reluctant to pledge allegiance to arguments for the legal right to change into the "right" body from the "wrong" body. By playing along with the idea that we can choose the sex which best matches our true self, we allow ourselves to forget that there is no self wholly unformed by the power of the state, the community, and the laws, and that we must investigate these forces.

Protecting Transsexual Parents

While preoperative transsexuals must present themselves as ill, after surgery they must convince the court that they are perfectly normal women or men. Postoperative transsexuals who successfully maintain child custody, for instance, do so by convincing judges that they fit properly into a distinct gender category (the same one their new genitals suggest) and that they are therefore normal parents. The law seizes upon the transsexual's desire to make her genitals fit her self-identification with palpable relief. Transsexuals have donned the correct gender, so to speak, and now must demonstrate their appropriateness as parents according to law's definition. Petitioners seeking protection for their family relationships are forced to seek it on the state's terms.

In *Christian v. Randall*, Duane Christian, a father of four
girls in Colorado, challenged his former wife's custody rights
on the grounds that she was undergoing sex reassignment, had
changed from a female to a male name (Gay to Mark), and had
married a woman.[43] Mark Randall was now a man in body as
well as in social role as father and husband. The trial court
granted Christian's petition for custody and removed the girls
from Randall's home, where they had been living since their
parents' divorce. The standard for the Colorado trial and appellate courts (and for most other jurisdictions) for deciding
which parent gets custody of a child is the "best interest of the
child."[44] The Colorado court is permitted to consider the mental health of all the individuals involved as part of that standard
of review. In this case the trial court had changed the custody
order purely on the grounds of Randall's sex change. The
appellate court, however, strongly rebuked the trial court's
decision: "Our review of the record persuades us that, there
being no evidence to support its conclusion [that the children
should no longer live with Randall], the trial court clearly
abused its discretion."[45]

The appellate court found for Randall on the grounds of
"uncontradicted evidence of the high quality of the environment
and home life of respondent and the children." Specifically,
social services investigators stated that all the girls had good
report cards, and each had special achievement awards in areas
such as art and music. The oldest, Lou Ann, had been elected
Cherry Queen, and all the girls had many friends and enjoyed
school immensely. Mark Randall submitted into evidence a letter from a school principal who said that he thought the chil-

dren were "wonderful" and that the older three girls ranked "very high on our Iowa Tests of Basic Skills." The children's high level of social adjustment (including success at a traditional feminine goal, the beauty pageant) convinced the appellate court this was a normal family that deserved to stay intact.[46]

The Randall custody dispute has a happy ending—a transsexual parent keeps custody of his children. When we contrast this legal tale to others, however, we see how a court might treat a transsexual who does not so readily abide by traditional norms. A Nevada court denied a transsexual father, Suzanne Daly, the right to see her thirteen-year-old daughter on the grounds that there would be an inevitable conflict between the "traditional" upbringing enjoyed by the child at the hands of her mother and the father's indication that the daughter should know lesbians, homosexuals, and transsexuals. Mark Randall posed no such threat, but Suzanne Daly wanted her daughter to understand her *as a transsexual*. The judge in *Daly v. Daly* described the audacity of Suzanne Daly (formerly Tim Daly, the natural father of Mary) in "introduc[ing] Mary to the community of alternate lifestyles by taking her to a session at the Pacific Center where other transsexuals gather for support and counseling and discuss their experiences with one another."[47]

Daly's action was taken as evidence of disruption of her daughter's life, rather than of a desire for an honest relationship with her daughter. According to her mother, when Mary learned of her father's plans for sex reassignment surgery she became withdrawn, began wetting her bed, and became inattentive at school. But Mary knew of her father's intentions months before he underwent the surgery, well before her symptoms of anxiety began. It is possible that her distress was a response to her mother's rage at Daly's plans and the tension between her parents: Mary's symptoms didn't appear until her mother began expressing her anger.

Whatever the source of Mary's anxiety, an expert witness who examined the child testified that if she had to be in her father's presence Mary risked serious injury. Though the nature of the harm is unclear in the opinion, the expert's testimony may have sealed the case against Suzanne Daly. In a telling phrase that may indicate a belief that transsexuality is inherently menacing to children, the judge equated being a postoperative male-to-female transsexual with bowing out of parenthood. The judge noted (using the appellant's former masculine name), "It was strictly Tim Daly's choice to *discard his fatherhood* and assume the role of a female *who could never be either mother or sister* to his daughter."[48] In the eyes of the court, Tim Daly simply could not simultaneously discard his penis and remain Mary's father.

Suzanne Daly wanted to maintain a transsexual identity after surgery. Perhaps even more unsettling to the courts are those transsexuals who not only change their sex but also switch from heterosexual to homosexual identification.[49] Riki Anne Wilchins recounts the enormous pressure she felt to fill a heterosexual woman's role: "Determined to be a 'successful' transsexual, I worked earnestly at being straight, at developing the proper attraction to men. . . . I faithfully reported each foray into heterosexuality to the hospital's noncommittal therapist, desperate to be the good patient upon whom she would confer surgery when my waiting time was up."[50] Heteronormative pressure can be just as strong in the litigation context, especially when child custody is at issue.

Another transsexual father—by all accounts a loving and responsible caretaker for her two sons—was barred from custodial relationship with her sons after her sex change and divorce from the children's mother. In this 1997 Missouri divorce litigation, the trial court had ordered that Sharon (in anticipation of some joint custody arrangement that never materialized) "shall not cohabit with other transsexuals or sleep with another female" during her temporary custody. She admitted that she was currently living with two other women, one of whom was also a transsexual, and had slept with another woman (though she denied sexual relations). Sharon (last name confidential) had not even wanted the divorce but rather hoped that the couple would remain legally married as two women after her transition (with the boys calling her Aunt Sharon). Noting that "there must be consideration of what conduct a parent may inspire by example, or what conduct of a child a parent may foster by condonation [*sic*]," and citing possible harmful effects on the children's "moral development," the appeals court judge denied Sharon joint custody.[51] This judge explicitly aimed to prevent her from having the chance to show the boys another way to live one's gender and sexuality.

The winning strategy for a transsexual parent, then, is to show how well she has adapted to the traditional role of her new sex, and to convince the court that the children will be socialized according to those norms. Admittedly, Suzanne Daly had not been a model parent before surgery. She was behind on child support and had only occasional contact with Mary. However, for her part, Nan Daly (the birth mother with primary custody) had violated the separation agreement by keeping Suzanne from seeing Mary. Suzanne had once even been frightened off from a visit to Mary when her former mother-in-law appeared with a gun.[52] Suzanne Daly was a supposedly cured transsexual, but her wish that her daughter interact with the transsexual community was a determining factor in the case against her parental rights. Her pride in her gender variance and her unwillingness to cut off all ties to the transsexual community provoked contempt and fear in the courtroom and in her family. The price she paid was losing the right to see her daughter.

Sharon's parenting abilities, however, were never criticized, even as she went from straight father to lesbian-transsexual divorcée. But she had reordered her intimate life as a woman-loving woman and would have helped raise her sons in that environment. She also lost the right to see her children. Any feminist who hopes for family structures and sexualities that overturn traditional patriarchal family organization should take note, and be wary. One critical race theorist has argued that we can tell how white Americans really feel about their fellow nonwhite citizens (whom it is now out of fashion to criticize openly in racist terms) by examining attitudes about nonwhite immigrants (where an "open season" approach is more permissible, venting true feelings by proxy).[53] Could feminists read behavior toward transsexuals, who are extremely vulnerable to undiluted gender-based hatred and disgust, as a concentrated form of what might be in store for lesbian moms or even single heterosexual mothers who eschew traditional marriage and parenting?

Protection for "Men in Dresses"

In the employment context as well as in family court, the plaintiff seems most likely to win when she can describe herself as a postoperative transsexual who is a successfully cured gender dysphoric—once ill, but now brought into line. In her analysis of *Ulane v. Eastern Airlines,* sociolegal scholar Lisa Bower observed that Karen Ulane (a transsexual airline pilot who evidently performed pleasantly as a "girl" after her surgery) won her employment discrimination trial at the district court level in large part because of expert testimony that she had adapted remarkably well to the gendered role of a woman.[54] (The victory was later overturned.) Dr. Jack Berger of the University of Chicago Gender Identity Board offered psychiatric testimony to Karen's femininity: "Her surgery, together with her actions, her movements, her automatic behavior and so forth—you don't think Karen's anything but a girl when you talk to her or see her."[55] The *Ulane* lower court victory, like Mark Randall's victory, demonstrates how transformed transsexuals can win their cases but at the same time how correct performance as a stereotypical woman or man can simply shore up traditional gender role expectations. Karen Ulane's lawyers meant well, of course. Their presentation of her as just a regular girl (straight, of course) was their attempt to rebut the defense lawyers' contention that this employee was too psychologically unstable to pilot an aircraft because of her transsexualism. This reasoning should give little comfort to those "psychologically unstable" females who refuse to act, move, and automatically behave as a real girl should.

Very recently, however, some of the more liberal state courts have begun to interpret their workplace antidiscrimination laws in a way that protects transsexuals and transgendered people based on the "sex stereotyping" theory first announced in the 1989 Supreme Court case *Price Waterhouse v. Hopkins*. In this case, a woman who was a candidate for an accounting firm partnership was advised to "walk more femininely, talk more femininely, dress more femininely, wear make-up, have her hair styled, . . . wear jewelry," and attend "charm school" in order to rise in the ranks. She successfully sued the firm on a Title VII sex discrimination theory, and the case has come to stand for the idea that employers' expectations of gender norms in the workplace should not work to the unlawful disadvantage of employees. As Justice Brennan explained for the majority, "In the specific context of sex stereotyping, an employer who acts on the basis of a belief that a woman cannot be aggressive, or that she must not be, has acted on the basis of gender."[56]

According to the law professor Mary Anne Case, feminists should observe the way law treats men who display feminine characteristics after *Price Waterhouse*, because we will find a consistent devaluation of the feminine as expressed in both males and females. At the time of Case's writing, in 1995, there was little indication that the sex stereotyping theory from *Price Waterhouse* could be used in the courts to protect gender-role-transgressive people, though she argued then that it should. "Shocking as it may be to some sensibilities," she wrote, "not only masculine women such as Hopkins, but also effeminate men, indeed even men in dresses, should already unequivocally be protected under existing law from discrimination on the basis of gender-role-transgressive behavior."[57] Instead, effeminate men were often assumed to be gay and thus excluded from civil rights protections.

In 2000, however, a federal court indeed embraced this broader understanding of gender discrimination, holding under the Equal Credit Opportunity Act that discrimination against a man in his application for a bank loan because he was wearing a dress would amount to sex discrimination.[58] It is interesting that the court noted that if he were gay (and presumably also if he were a transsexual, which the court did not consider), he would not be protected under the *Price Waterhouse* standard, which applies only to the enforcement of traditional gender norms. The Ninth Circuit has argued, however, that after *Price Waterhouse* it is clear Title VII does not differentiate between discrimination based on sex (the biological) and that based on gender (the social), and therefore previous case law hostile to transsexuals has been overruled.[59] Being a man but taking on the social role of a woman—*berdache* style— would then be legally protected.

Two interesting cases involving transsexual or transgendered people make use of new applications of *Price Waterhouse,* and the question becomes: Does this legal theory really fit the circumstances of transgender discrimination cases? What are the powers and limits of such a theory of transsexual-transgender protection? In the 2000 case *Broadus v. State Farm Insurance,* a male-to-female transsexual in transition filed a Title VII sex discrimination suit against State Farm, alleging that his supervisor's treatment of him constituted a hostile work environment. Karen Broadus's lawyer-drafted complaint alleged sex discrimination on a *Price Waterhouse* theory of sex stereotyping (a woman should not look like a man), but in his deposition testimony he attributed the negative treatment to his "transgender issues and sexual orientation." Sex stereotyping is actionable, whereas disgust at an employee's sex change is not, so the complaint was made to fit the pleading requirements. The supervisor allegedly gave Broadus odd looks, refused to make eye contact, did not care to discuss his transgender status, tried to minimize interaction with him, failed to compliment his performance after a presentation, and generally made his disapproval known. The federal trial court declined to hold that this conduct constituted a "hostile work environment" for Broadus, however, and dismissed his suit.[60]

The problem with Broadus's suit was that the supervisor's conduct seemed like a restrained form of contempt rather than an egregious example of torment, and thus on the facts Broadus could not meet the legal requirement for proof under Title VII. The court was clearly ready to entertain a *Price Waterhouse* theory of sex stereotyping, however, and perhaps with "better" facts the argument would have been successful. Such a case would establish a precedent that it is unlawful to treat a *woman* badly because she *looks like* a man, but not that it is unlawful to create a hostile work environment based on disgust at an employee's sex change or transgender status.

A victorious application of a *Price Waterhouse*–type theory came in October 2000, when a Massachusetts state court, relying on state constitutional provisions, issued an injunction barring a public junior high school official from disciplining a fifteen-year-old transgendered girl (with male anatomy) for coming to school in girl's clothes. Though the case was decided under Massachusetts state law, the court invoked

Price Waterhouse to show federal agreement with the proposition that federal nondiscrimination law covers those who transgress the norms of their biologically assigned gender. Pat Doe (a pseudonym) had previously been sent home and repeatedly suspended for coming to school in makeup, short skirts, high heels, padded bras, and wigs, and for using the girl's bathroom. School officials complained that her clothes and behavior, which included a full array of diva displays, such as flirting, blowing kisses at boys, grabbing a boy's buttocks in the lunch line, and primping in class, were disruptive. In granting the injunction, the court concluded that it was likely the plaintiff would prevail in a trial on the merits. The school was justified in punishing sexualized and disruptive conduct, the court found, but it was not permitted to punish Doe simply for being a boy in girl's clothes. The school's argument based on disruption was discriminatory because "if a female student came to school in a frilly dress or blouse, make-up, or padded bra, she would go, and presumably has gone, unnoticed by school officials." The distraction came only because of the gender role inversion: "Defendants do not find plaintiff's clothing distracting *per se,* but, essentially, distracting simply because plaintiff is a biological male," the court noted.[61] If it is suitable for biologically female girls to wear such clothing, then it should also be suitable for the biologically male plaintiff to wear them.

This theory of sex stereotyping as applied to transgendered plaintiffs differs significantly from the judicial approaches discussed earlier. Winning these cases would not depend on the plaintiff's characterizing herself or himself as ill. Announcing and maintaining a proud transsexual or transgendered identity would also be compatible with winning one's case under this theory. *Price Waterhouse* stands for the proposition that *abnormal* gender conduct cannot be the basis for poor treatment, and thus a winning plaintiff would not have to describe herself, like Karen Ulane, as "just a regular girl." Judicial sympathy, especially in *Doe,* rests on an understanding of how difficult it must be to find oneself gender variant in a world of traditional norms, rather than on sympathy for the sick or the pathological.

But what are the limitations of the *Price Waterhouse* theory as applied to transsexuals or transgendered plaintiffs? It requires employers, coworkers, and other people in public spaces to tolerate men who act like women and women who act like men. What is not captured in this jurisprudence, however, is the very thing that makes the most common form of transgendered or transsexual identity possible: the notion that one may have the genitals normally associated with one sex but actually *be* of the other sex. So Pat Doe is not a "boy dressed as a girl"—to take her seriously would be simply to conclude that she *is* a girl and happens also to be dressed as one. But of course all the fuss came about because school officials did not accept that she was a girl; if they had, her dressing as one would have been completely unremarkable and there would have been no dispute.

Thus, a *Price Waterhouse* theory directly addresses the social attitudes that make life difficult for transsexual and transgendered people—others' refusal to accept that they really are members of the gender group with which they identify—but also shuts out the possibility of getting at a more genuine description of how many plaintiffs actually understand themselves. Such a legal theory, which protects a boy dressed as a girl, suffers from the same flaw that Mary Anne Case pointed out about the *berdache* model of sex and gender: it is not necessarily more liberating to move back and forth between two gender spheres (even when the link to biology has been severed) because doing so still maintains a "package deal" concept of what it is to be a man or a woman.[62] That is, being a man or a woman still goes along with a certain "package" of behaviors—proper clothes, ways of talking and moving, the choice of an opposite sex partner—that are socially compelled, even for those who were born as members of one sex but have made the transition to the other. Does "border crossing" seem so liberating now?

On a broader theoretical level, the *Price Waterhouse* theory also forecloses a version of the appealing (but ultimately rather mystifying) argument that sex and gender should be disaggregated in the law. Professor Case also argued for the disaggregation of sex from gender, but the transsexual subject pushes her analysis further than simply "the effeminate man" who is still recognized as a man. Case, putting forth what I characterize as the "social norms" version of disaggregation, argues that a "man" should not be penalized for being "effeminate"; that is, sex and gender should be separated as a matter of social practice. Is that not different from arguing that she should not be mistreated because she actually claims to be a feminine woman? What I call "ontological disaggregation"—in which the reality of *being* one sex is not connected in any necessary way with one's presentation—would have the interesting effect of moving the Pat Does of the world back into straightforward Title VII cases in which women are treated badly *as women*. But what on earth would it mean to "really be" of a sex with no necessary social or physiological markers? Here is the mystifying aspect of ontological disaggregation. Could one just assert it in order to have it be true? Imagine that Pat Doe had not adopted feminine behaviors and clothes (preferring T-shirts and jeans, as girls often do), but still wanted to use the girls' bathroom and be accepted at school as a girl. She would probably appear to be a boy in every conventional sense, however. Is this a useful kind of unintelligibility to imagine, or is it just baffling and unappealing?[63]

Case's effeminate man analysis would still apply, of course, to nontranssexual effeminate men, who need rigorous defense on other terms. The *Price Waterhouse* theory pulls us back from the brink of having to figure out, as a matter of legal analysis, how we could treat sex and gender as ontologically disaggregated and leaves us with the more easily understandable protection for those people whose sex and gender are disaggregated in the social norms sense ("men" in "feminine clothing"). It is not so comfortable, after all, to defend the concept of being a woman as mysteriously, personally ontologically given (announced irrefutably, the way one would say, "I'm really a cat person") rather than socially formed.

The crux of the problems gender nonconformists face may lie, however, not in the vagaries of moving these pieces labeled "gender," "sex," and "sexual orientation" around but rather in the widespread and visceral disgust most people experience when they contemplate a man who cuts his penis off to try to become a woman. Actually pursuing an existence in a sex category other than the one genitally assigned at birth horrifies people in ways that effeminate men do not. And remember, for a transsexual who conflates sex and gender, getting the genitals right is much more important than performing as a woman in a dress, which is just a step along the way of attaining surgical change. The specter of the transsexual confronts people with physical alterations that repulse them and an aura of deception that scares them (whether a spouse knew about a long-ago sex change is always the pivotal emotional issue in inheritance cases, for example). It is not clear that the *Price Waterhouse* sex stereotyping theory addresses these feelings about transsexuals and transgendered people, which may account for much of such people's mistreatment. A man in pursuit of penectomy is quite different from a "man in a dress," but a sex stereotyping account of the harm being done requires us to pretend that he will be received in the same way at work, for example.

The *Price Waterhouse* theory is capable, however, of defending transsexuals and transgendered people in ways that do not depend upon insulting or normalizing them. Law frequently adapts over time by drawing upon inexact analogies and muddled comparisons, and feminist legal scholars ought not to demand a philosophical perfection that it is simply institutionally incapable of giving. We ought to take note of the complexities that a *Price Waterhouse*–type theory papers over and be watchful for a future chance to improve upon law's descriptions of transsexual suffering and inequality. For now, however, this development provides some helpful destabilization in the jurisprudence of sex and gender, and a reason to be pragmatically hopeful that at least some transsexual and transgendered plaintiffs are transforming the law rather than being transformed themselves.

Conclusion

What does it actually mean to be a "victorious" transsexual before the law? What grounds should feminist legal theorists use to decipher when rights-claiming advances sexual and gender liberation and when it simply props up old and hurtful notions? These cases show feminists some of law's possibilities, and prompt us to think more clearly about our goals before we try to effect legal change. We have discovered (or rediscovered), first, that positioning oneself before the law as a rights-claimer may not be an act of emancipation but may simply give conservative forces in the law an opportunity to retrench patriarchal expectations about gender roles.[64] I have described some of the myriad requirements, character traits, and postures that transsexuals must display in order to be successful in the courts and demonstrated that many of them are wholly retrograde from a feminist perspective. There is little room for the kinds of plaintiffs feminists would like to see win their cases: a nontraditional parent, an exuberantly healthy gender misfit, an unrepentant queer, an unruly girl. While seeming to enable transsexual rights, courts actually reward those who fit into constrained and patriarchal roles. Depending on the facts of the case, feminists can learn what kind of treatment other sorts of nonconformists might face if legal protections were not in place. Transsexuals' vulnerability allows their enemies to vent their feelings without the self-consciousness that civil rights laws protecting women and, to some extent, gay men and lesbians have imposed.

What is there to be said about those transsexuals who are gender conservatives, and whose posture in litigation undermines feminist progress toward protecting the characters I have described above? It should not be surprising that transsexual and transgendered people express the same wide variety of views about gender and the self that everyone else does. These plaintiffs remind feminists that there is no inherent connection between someone's gender identity and her political goals. Alliances should be distilled from conceptual agreements rather than from simple descriptions of identity. It also follows that accusations of "false consciousness" would be out of place, since there seems to be only thin ground upon which to base a "true consciousness." But while some transsexuals maintain gender fundamentalist positions in litigation and elsewhere, a pluralistic and compassionate form of feminist politics demands that we use the law to protect them from continued suffering despite the danger of reifying traditional stereotypes. Rather than backing away from the legal in favor of the personal, the aesthetic, or the erotic, feminist legal theorists should try to salvage as much as possible from these victories, amplifying the most positive snippets of judges' decisions in the hope that they may be useful in later cases.

Should feminists be reinvigorated by law's transformative potential, on display in the new application of *Price Waterhouse?* On the one hand, transsexual and transgendered people are more than men in dresses or women in suits. The true focus of most employers' disgust is not simply the fact that a male employee begins wearing dresses (because then at least he is still a *man,* in a dress, violating a cultural dress code) but the fact that "he" claims to *be* a woman and is intent on enlisting others' help in *transforming* himself into that role physically, sexually, and socially. This act of transformation, which must be a social process as gender is a social practice, is precisely what civil rights law does not protect.

As Mary Anne Case has illustrated, some of the most sympathetic receptions that transsexuals receive in their communities arise when they make a firm transition from one "package deal" to another: that is, for instance, when a male adopts an extremely queeny, effeminate existence in the *berdache* model. The fixity of the package deal remains even though gender is no longer anchored by biology—there are only two choices. Case wishes that the gender packages we currently have would go the way of medical theories about bad humors that dictated one's looks and personality, becoming structures that simply do not explain and direct our world anymore.[65] For now, however, even jurisdictions that seem favorably disposed toward transsexual plaintiffs continue to rely on them, and have not yet managed to articulate a legal theory of transsexual experience that is really representative.

However, law can protect against basic hurts and indignities that transsexual and transgendered citizens confront every day. Anxiety over imagining penectomy or horror at a teenage boy in a dress express themselves in predictable forms of sadism: harassment, exclusion, and violence. Even if only feminist legal academics care so much about how the jurisprudence is parsed—indeed, it is luxurious (but not thereby unimportant) to be able to do so—our intellectual misgivings cannot stand in the way of protecting transsexual and transgendered people from harm. A safer world for gender variation is something even currently gender-comfortable feminists want, and perhaps this freedom could create opportunities for living a self of which we are not now aware. As Pat Califia asks everyone, not just transgendered people, "What drag is hiding in your personal closet, kept there by the threat of violence or ridicule?"[66]

BEARING THE BLAME: GENDER, IMMIGRATION, REPRODUCTION, AND THE ENVIRONMENT

Syd Lindsley

Syd Lindsley is a feminist activist and a member of the Committee on Women, Population, and the Environment. She has been active in the reproductive rights, immigrant rights, and environmental justice movements. She is currently living in Seattle, where she works at Cornish College of the Arts.

On June 26, 2000, *Time* magazine ran a cover story called "Border Clash," which described the so-called antics of Arizona rancher Roger Barnett, who patrols his five-hundred-acre property armed with an M-16 automatic rifle in search of "illegals." *Time* asserted that "for many Americans who believe citizens have the right to defend their property and privacy with firearms, these ranchers [Barnett and his friends] are true patriots, doing a job the government is too weak-kneed to carry out." Barnett himself recounts an incident that he apparently finds amusing:

"You always get one or two that are defiant," says Barnett, who chuckles, remembering an incident a few weeks back. "One fellow tried to get up and walk away, saying we're not Immigration. So I slammed him back down and took his photo. 'Why'd you do that?' the illegal says, all surprised. 'Because we want you to go home with a before picture and an after picture—that is after we beat the s—— outta you.' You can bet he started behavin' then."[1]

Barnett has yet to be investigated by any U.S. enforcement agency for such brutal threats and assaults on the suspected "illegals" he hunts in southern Arizona. At the same time, at least three immigrants had been killed near the U.S. side of the United States–Mexico border that year, and many others seriously wounded. The murders and assaults at the border marked the end of a decade during which anti-immigrant sentiment had escalated, and immigrants' human rights were increasingly at risk.

Only a couple of weeks after the *Time* article hit the press, *E-Magazine,* a prominent environmental publication, published its own article on immigration, this one linking immigration to environmental degradation in the United States.[2] The article made no mention of the rising tide of violence against immigrants at the United States–Mexico border. In fact, it avoided the human aspect of immigration and cast it as a "numbers only" issue that is causing population growth and thus environmental problems in the United States.

The *E-Magazine* article represents a growing movement to blame immigrants for environmental problems in the United States. Anti-immigrant "environmentalists" came of age during the 1990s, gaining national attention and strongly influencing both anti-immigrant and environmental communities. The argument that immigrants cause environmental degradation by contributing to the country's population growth was popularized by a number of environmental organizations, such as

Negative Population Growth (NPG), Zero Waste America, Carrying Capacity Network (CCN), Population-Environment Balance, Californians for Population Stabilization, and Eco-Future, that focus solely on halting or restricting immigration. In addition, conservative immigration "reform" organizations, such as the Federation for American Immigration Reform (FAIR), began to use this environmental argument along with social and economic reasons for limiting immigration.

Scapegoating immigrants for environmental problems reflects fears that the reproduction of poor people of color worldwide threatens white dominance. Although the U.S. government has no direct "population policy," population control comes in many forms, including the "family cap" for welfare recipients; the marketing of long-acting, provider-controlled contraceptives (such as Norplant and Depo-Provera) to young women, poor women, and women of color; the development of dangerous contraceptives such as quinacrine sterilization in the name of stemming overpopulation; and private programs that pay drug-addicted women to be sterilized or receive long-acting contraceptives. Anti-immigrant environmentalism is part of the domestic population control movement and targets the reproduction of immigrant women, dismissing their health and rights in the name of environmental protection.

The Greening of Hate

In the spring of 2001, an advertisement that read, "How do you feel about paving over the amber waves of grain, the purple mountain majesties, and the fruited plain?" ran in Iowa media including newspapers, radio, and television. If you read the small print, you found not the anticipated environmental message but a proposal to reduce immigration to the United States to 200,000 people a year. The ad states: "Every year in America we pave an area equal to the state of Delaware. . . . Why? Because our nation's population is growing at an unprecedented rate, due primarily to an immigration policy that's changing the landscape of America."[3] This advertisement, part of a "public awareness campaign" sponsored by the anti-immigrant group Negative Population Growth, is a good example of the type of rhetoric being developed to link environmental degradation to immigration. The group has launched public awareness campaigns in Iowa, South Carolina, Maryland, and Virginia, in which they flood radio and television airways and print media with messages about immigration policy and its relationship to the environment. The Maryland and Virginia campaign asks the question "Population in 2050: Is Smart Growth Enough?" which refers to the exact year demographers predict people of color will outnumber whites in the United States.

The core of the environmental anti-immigration argument is this: Population growth in the United States is wreaking environmental havoc and causing declining quality of life both here and abroad. Since the fertility rate in the United States is low, near replacement level (one birth for each death), the primary source of U.S. population growth is immigration. In the words of NPG, "The U.S. is already the third largest country in the world. If present trends continue, we will add 117 million people by the year 2050, when our population could exceed 400 million. Our staggering population growth is a problem that must be addressed now, for the sake of our environment, our quality of life, and future generations of Americans."

It is generally agreed that immigration is a major contributor to population growth, but there is no consensus among demographers about how to measure the proportion of population growth caused by migration and the impact of immigration on future population growth. Nearly 100 percent of U.S. population growth since 1790 has resulted from immigration and the descendants of immigrants.[4] With the exception of Native American groups, immigrants and the descendants of immigrants make up almost the entire population of the country. Any measurement of the demographic impact of immigration depends on who you count as an immigrant, and what date you begin counting from.

For anti-immigrant environmentalists, however, immigration leads directly to "development-induced sprawl, congestion, and wanton destruction of the environment."[5] In this spirit, FAIR gives us the new equation: "$E = (I\downarrow)$" (presumably meaning a healthy environment equals lower immigration).[6] The logic here needs to be closely examined.

Critics point out that an anti-immigrant environmental platform manipulates real fears and concerns about environmental degradation and a decline in the quality of life, and scapegoats immigrants rather than addressing the actual roots of environmental problems in the United States.[7] In environmental anti-immigration rhetoric, immigration is often presented as either the primary source of environmental degradation or an impermeable barrier to environmental sustainability. A 1996 NPG advertisement states: "Immigration is the driving force behind the population growth that is devastating our environment and the quality of our lives. *Primarily because of immigration we are rushing at breakneck speed toward an environmental and economic disaster*" [emphasis in original].[8]

Yet there is insufficient evidence to support this theory. A recent U.S. Commission on Immigration Reform research paper titled *U.S. Immigration and the Environment: Scientific Research and Analytic Issues* reports that there is little evidence to support the theory that immigration to the United States has any effect on the environment. What little research has been done shows no connection between immigration and production, energy consumption, land use, or water conservation.[9]

The link between immigration and environmental degradation is *speculative,* not factual. That some environmentalists nonetheless call for severe measures to halt immigration demonstrates the anti-immigrant political agenda beneath their "green" message.

In the shadow of such speculation about immigration and environmental degradation, the root causes of human migration go unexamined. The economist Saskia Sassen has documented that American corporate expansion abroad plays a significant role in inducing migration to the United States. Emigration emerges as an option to people in the developing world partly because of the presence of foreign export goods manufacturers. The choice of where to migrate is directly correlated to the origins of direct foreign investment in export-oriented development. The United States accounts for almost half of all direct foreign investment worldwide, most of which is export-oriented. It is also perceived as a land of immigrants, especially since 1965, when its immigration policy was liberalized.[10] In the face of deepening economic impoverishment at home, many migrants come to view moving to the United States as their only viable alternative.

Scapegoating immigrants for environmental problems also diverts attention from the real agents of environmental degradation. One primary agent is the military. As of the mid-1980s, about 80 percent of military spending was in the developed world, with the U.S. military ranking as one of the dominant military powers. The U.S. military is the largest polluter in the nation, generating more toxic waste than the five largest U.S. chemical companies put together; it is also the largest sole consumer of energy in the nation, and possibly worldwide. Moreover, the Research Institute for Peace Policy in Starnberg, Germany, estimates that 20 percent of all global environmental degradation is due to military and related activities.[11]

Another primary cause of environmental degradation is overconsumption of natural resources and material goods in wealthy countries such as the United States. United Nations figures attest that the richest fifth of the world's people consume sixty-six times as much as the poorest fifth, including 45 percent of all meat and fish, 58 percent of total energy, and 84 percent of all paper.[12] This overconsuming lifestyle depends on commodities—especially energy, chemicals, metals, and paper—whose production itself degrades the environment. In the United States, these four industries are all in the top five of industry-by-industry rankings for energy intensity and toxic emissions, and they are major sources of air polluters such as sulfur and nitrogen oxides, particulates, and volatile organic compounds.[13]

Blaming immigrants for environmental problems is one way that people can ignore the disproportionate impact the United

States has on the environment and avoid criticizing industry and the U.S. military. The climate of blame fostered by anti-immigrant greens has roots in what's been termed "Malthusian" theory, based on the writings of Thomas Malthus, an English economist and clergyman. In 1798 Malthus published his *Essay on the Principle of Population,* best known for the theory that population would always increase faster than food supply. His theories about poverty, also included in *Essay on the Principle of Population,* though less widely discussed, have had a much greater impact on contemporary political thought.

He maintained that the poor are responsible for deepening their own poverty by overbreeding and that improving the quality of life for poor people would encourage them to have *more* children, placing an unnecessary burden on the wealthy. Just as Malthus shifted attention away from the social responsibilities of the industrial owning class and onto the fertility of the poor, anti-immigrant environmentalists shift the blame for environmental degradation from U.S. consumer, corporate, and military practices to one of the most politically vulnerable sectors of society. Shifting responsibility onto the "other" is exemplified in the concept of carrying capacity.

The Myth of "Carrying Capacity"

The term *carrying capacity* refers to the idea that any given region can support a definite and limited population, based on the amount and types of resources available in the region. Carrying Capacity Network (CCN), an anti-immigration organization that portrays itself as an environmental group, defines the

term this way: "the number of individuals who can be supported without degrading the natural, cultural, and social environment, i.e., without reducing the ability of the environment
to sustain the desired quality of life over the long term." [14] But
who decides what constitutes the limits of carrying capacity?
The network's definition itself is problematic: who determines
the "desired quality of life," and what is meant by degradation
of the "cultural and social environment"? These phrases could
easily be used to justify discriminatory decisions to restrict
immigration based on factors such as race, national origin,
political affiliations, religion, or sexual orientation.

The phrase "desired quality of life" must also be examined.
An *E-Magazine* article by the ecologist and educator Garrett
Hardin asks rhetorically, "Aren't luxuries for a few better than
luxuries for none?" [15] He asserts that limiting our consumption
is ultimately futile because eventually, even at the barest levels
of consumption, we would be forced to limit population for
the sake of survival. Hardin's claim illustrates how capitalist
and Malthusian ideologies can combine to legitimize conspicuous exploitation of the poor. Malthus's vision is convenient
for those who believe that resources are becoming so scarce
that their wealth and well-being are threatened by immigrants. [16]

The carrying capacity analysis does not adequately explain
the complex ways human societies interact with their natural
environments. As the California environmentalist Penn Loh
points out, "California is not a closed system like an ecosystem. Its boundaries are politically determined, and the resources
and goods used here come from all over the world." [17] Loh
articulates the central problem with the concept of carrying

capacity: people living in California and elsewhere in the United States rely heavily on resources from all over the world.

Ignoring this reality confuses the debates about immigration to the United States, as anti-immigration proponents urge us to think in isolationist terms, to protect what is "ours." Another Negative Population Growth ad proclaims: "As Americans, our first obligation, to ourselves and our children and grandchildren, is to restore and preserve the land we have inherited. In shaping our immigration policy, our top priority must be our own national interest, and the welfare of present and future Americans."[18]

Eugenic thinking often permeates anti-immigrant "environmental" rhetoric, casting immigrants' "higher fertility rates" and immigrant "offspring" as threats to the future "landscape of America." Both neo-Malthusian and eugenic ideology scapegoat immigrant women's reproduction. In fact, nativism, eugenics, and neo-Malthusianism have intertwined histories, often converging to control the reproduction of poor women, women of color, and immigrant women. This unsavory history provides a useful perspective on the contemporary environmental movement and its attack on immigrant populations.

Eugenics, Race Suicide, and the Politics of Exclusion

The English Darwinian scientist Sir Francis Galton developed the theory of eugenics at the turn of the twentieth century, asserting that the human race could be improved by selectively breeding individuals with the "best" traits and restricting the reproduction of individuals with "undesirable" traits. It took only a few years before the theory began to gain popularity in the United States. The idea of Anglo-Saxon "race suicide"— that the Anglo-Saxon race was being outbred by other "inferior" races—was gaining ground. Francis A. Walker claimed that immigration discouraged reproduction among the older (white) stock. Pioneer sociologist Edward A. Ross went so far as to suggest that unchecked Asiatic immigration might lead to the extinction of the American people. Even President Theodore Roosevelt criticized small families and called women who chose not to have children criminal. Given the widespread popularity of such theories, Roosevelt's injunction against birth control was probably targeted at individuals with Anglo-Saxon "stock."

Eugenics lent the credibility of modern science to beliefs about Anglo-Saxon superiority and, in turn, the perils of non-Anglo-Saxon immigration. As early as 1906, leaders of the Immigration Restriction League began to use eugenic arguments to support their cause.[19] In 1910 Prescott F. Hall, one of the league's leaders, wrote in a League publication: "The same arguments which induce us to segregate criminals and feebleminded and prevent their breeding, apply to excluding from our borders individuals whose multiplying here is likely to lower the average of our people." In 1917, when Congress enacted a literacy test for adult immigrants, excluding most Asians from immigration, Robert D. C. Ward, another leader of the Immigration Restriction League, was ecstatic. He declared that "the new law is, in its essentials, a eugenic measure, perhaps the most comprehensive and satisfactory ever passed by Congress."[20]

Eugenic arguments deeply impressed prominent lawmakers such as Albert Johnson, the chairman of the House Committee on Immigration and Naturalization, in 1919, and he was elected to the prestigious position of president of the Eugenics Research Association.[21] Johnson's influence on Congress undoubtedly aided enactment of the Immigration Restriction Act of 1924, which created a permanent quota system that favored immigrants from Northern Europe.

Meanwhile, the eugenics establishment, led by the Immigration Restriction League, was also forming a relationship with the movement for birth control in the United States. Anti-immigration eugenics and pro–birth control eugenics became complementary parts of a movement to control the racial "fitness" of America through exclusion and reproductive restraint.

Birth Control, Eugenics, and Neo-Malthusianism

The birth control movement in the beginning of the twentieth century was initially part of a radical socialist reform movement that offered resistance to patterns of social and economic exploitation. The career of Margaret Sanger, who coined the slogan "birth control" in 1915, was representative. A feminist who dedicated her life to the cause of contraception, Sanger with other activists demanded birth control as part of a larger movement for major societal change. They believed that extending birth control to poor and working-class women would result in a more equitable distribution of power. Yet later Sanger began to work with eugenicists and used eugenic rhetoric to promote birth control.

After the First World War, the socialist leadership in local birth control leagues lost momentum, while national organizations, especially Sanger's American Birth Control League, gained power. League membership was largely professionals, a wealthier, more conservative group than the working-class radicals of the previous movement. This shift changed the essential character of the effort, leaving the call for economic and social justice behind in favor of a heavily eugenic approach. Articles in the league's monthly publication, the *Birth Control Review,* reflect a deep engagement with eugenic ideas. The inaugural issue in February 1917 ran an article titled "Eugenics in Relation to Birth Control." Author Anna E. Blount wrote: "Exactly because birth control is here for the wise and provident we need it also for the isolated and ignorant; we need it, voluntary or enforced, if necessary by celibacy or segregation, for the seriously defective."

A later article by Blount, entitled "Large Families and Human Waste," stated plainly that those with "defective heredity . . . must be eliminated."[22]

In the review, eugenic beliefs emerge using terms such as *racial progress* or *degeneration* (for example, an article entitled "Birth Control or Racial Degeneration, Which?" appeared in the January 1921 edition). There were also more explicit appeals to racism. An article titled "Women and Children of the South" claimed that because the majority of blacks in the South were too poor and too exhausted from long working hours to seek entertainment in movies or the arts, "the sex relation is their amusement and enjoyment. The end of life is not education, not a broad or virtuous life, but the gratification of desire."[23] Thus, the *Birth Control Review* perpetuated stereotypical images of African-Americans as oversexed and driven by irrational desire.

Margaret Sanger's writing also engaged in racist alarmism. In *Woman and the New Race,* published in 1920, she invoked the racist fear of new immigrants. After citing illiteracy rates of the foreign-born, she asked rhetorically, "Do these elements give promise of a better race?"[24]

Sanger and the American Birth Control League called for extensive social action and public policy measures to assure eugenic results in the U.S. population. In her book *Pivot of Civilization,* she called for the segregation of "every feeble-minded girl or woman of the hereditary type" during her reproductive period, in addition to a policy of "immediate sterilization."[25] In 1924 the league wrote that it supported the sociologist Rev. Albert P. Van Dusen's call for "control of immigration by individual and genealogical examinations of the intending emigrant before he starts for America; uniform nation-wide marriage laws forbidding the marriage of the eugenically unfit; social and sexual segregation of the defective, extreme measures of asexualization or sterilization when needed; the extension of contraceptive knowledge to the inferior yet socially useful as a means of diminishing their numbers and at the same time giving their offspring better birth; the diffusion of eugenic sentiment."[26] The league's endorsement of these excessive measures for social control illustrate its dedication to eugenic political goals, even in the most extreme form.

Neo-Malthusian ideas also influenced the American Birth Control League during the 1920s and '30s, with the *Birth Control Review* regularly running articles with neo-Malthusian themes. In January 1920, Margaret Sanger called for a five-year "birth strike to avert world famine."[27] The First American Birth Control Conference, held in New York City in November 1921, asked participants to consider whether overpopulation was "a menace to the peace of the world" and the dissemination of birth control would "be the most logical method of checking the problem of over-population."[28]

The *Birth Control Review* sometimes published arguments using a combination of eugenic and neo-Malthusian doctrine. One example was a page in the August 1931 issue proclaiming "Birth Control Is an Economic Measure." It went on to explain:

> *BECAUSE* it enables parents to limit their children to those they can properly support. Over-large families lead to under-nourishment, overcrowding, child labor, low wages, unemployment; they are one of the most potent causes of poverty. *BECAUSE* it makes possible the elimination of the unfit, who place such a heavy burden upon the resources of the community. It is estimated that taxpayers spend close to two billion dollars per year for the care of dependency, much of which is preventable.

The first *because* draws on neo-Malthusian assumptions that "over-large families" are the root cause of poverty. The second *because* reflects the eugenic desire to eliminate the "unfit"— and the economic "burden" they place on society. The American Birth Control League often thus combined neo-Malthusian and eugenic ideology in its call for birth control as an economic measure.

Discussion about birth control, eugenics, and reproduction was implicitly gendered, with much emphasis on women's role in childbearing. As the legal scholar Dorothy Roberts has pointed out, the league's "Principles and Aims" declared, "Every mother must realize her basic position in human society. She must be conscious of her responsibility to the race in bringing children into the world."[29] Moreover, many eugenicists recognized the importance of the women's movement in fostering women's knowledge and acceptance of eugenic ideas. The British socialist Havelock Ellis asserted that "the realization of eugenics in our social life can only be attained with the realization of the woman movement in its latest and completest phase as an enlightened culture of motherhood."[30]

While the eugenics movement lent legitimacy and power to the activism of wealthy, white feminists, it certainly was not a liberating agent for poor women and women of color. This is not to say that only white women were involved in the struggle for birth control: Roberts has documented how black women were central agents in rallying support for birth control, education about methods, and clinics in black communities. But black supporters of birth control generally rejected eugenic ideology. As Roberts noted, "White eugenicists promoted birth control as a way of preserving an oppressive social structure; Blacks promoted birth control as a way of toppling it."[31]

Despite the rejection of the eugenics movement by the black community, eugenic ideology remained an integral part of the mainstream birth control movement. Eugenics provided more than legitimacy to the movement; it provided political and economic power. The widespread popularity of eugenics during the interwar period was maintained by the financial contributions of several wealthy individuals: Mrs. E. H. Harriman founded the Eugenics Record Office; Andrew Carnegie began the Station for Experimental Education; Henry Fairfield Osborn, founder of the American Museum of Natural History, also funded the eugenics societies; and later Frederick Osborn, Henry Fairfield's nephew, financed a research program for the Eugenics Research Association.[32] As this wealthy elite supported eugenic politics and ideology financially, it also subsidized a belief system that legitimized its own economic and political power.

The Ideology of Overpopulation

Though Western discourse about Third World overpopulation began before World War II, it wasn't until after the war that it gained political momentum in the United States.[33] Sentiment about eugenics had also radically changed after the Second World War. The American public was still reeling from the shock of the Nazi death camps, a eugenic "experiment" taken to awful extremes. Eugenicists in the United States found that they could not express their sentiments as frankly or openly as they had been able to before the war. However, eugenics soon found a new home in population control.

Key funders of eugenics began to support research on overpopulation in the Third World between 1930 and 1950. In the late 1940s the Milbank Memorial Fund, a key backer of eugenics research, began to support such research. Frederick Osborn organized the Population Council in 1952 and later set up the Population Association of America, while his cousin Fairfield Osborn eventually became a leader of Planned Parenthood–World Population. Well-known eugenicists also worked at

Princeton's Office of Population Research and on advisory boards for the Population Council.[34]

The Population Reference Bureau, known as a eugenics organization since 1929, also became invested in population control. The founder of the bureau, Guy Irving Burch, had been a member of the campaign for restricting immigration. He told the chairman of the Southern Baptist Convention in 1934 that he was active in Sanger's birth control movement because "my family on both sides were early colonial and pioneer stock, and I have long worked with the American Coalition of Patriotic Societies to prevent the American people from being replaced by alien or Negro stock, whether it be by immigration or by overly high birth rates among others in this country."[35] In its new role as a population control organization, Burch's Population Reference Bureau received funding from giants such as Rockefeller, Ford, Mellon, DuPont, Sloan, Standard Oil, and Shell.[36] These individuals and corporations had a vested interest in curbing overpopulation, which they believed to be the cause of a surge of movements for economic and political independence throughout Asia, Africa, and Latin America—movements that threatened to impinge upon U.S. industries' access to raw materials in these areas.[37]

The new population control approach imitated the American Birth Control League's tactic of combining eugenic arguments with neo-Malthusian ones. An advertisement created by the Committee to Check the Population Explosion in 1969 offers a vivid example: "How many people do you want in your country? Already the cities are packed with youngsters. Thousands of idle victims of discontent and drug addiction. You go out after dark at your peril. . . . Birth control is the answer. . . .

The evermounting tidal wave of humanity challenges us to control it, or be submerged with all of our civilized values."[38] This ad exemplifies the unique relationship between neo-Malthusian calls to end poverty, urban crime, and drug addiction through birth control (the term was used synonymously with population control during that time) and apocalyptic eugenic warnings to control the "tidal wave of humanity" or have "our civilized values" wiped out. The implication is obvious—the real population problem was not just too many people but too many of the wrong kind of people. And, as historian Linda Gordon has pointed out, although the correlation between urban crime and overcrowding is unsubstantiated, population controllers used such parallels because "urban crime was a *sotto voce* call upon racism."[39]

Population and the Environment

In the late 1960s, with the publication of Paul Ehrlich's *Population Bomb,* a bestselling book which warned that overpopulation would result in famine, the idea that population growth and environmental degradation were connected became popular.[40] Over the next decade Ehrlich's neo-Malthusian alarmism slowly spread into much of the mainstream environmental movement.

In 1970 Hugh Moore, population control activist and founder of the Dixie Cup corporation, initated a focus on population control at the Nationwide Enviromental Teach-In (a precursor to Earth Day). The historian Lawrence Lader described how Moore made sure population was addressed at the event:

First, a third of a million leaflets, folders and pamphlets [including a new pictorial edition of the venerable *Population Bomb*] were produced for campus and community distribution. Next, three efforts stressed the intimate relation between overpopulation and a degraded environment. One was the free distribution to three-hundred-odd college radio stations of a taped radio program featuring Paul Ehrlich and David Brower. The second was provision, for reproduction free by college newspapers, of a score of editorial cartoons highlighting the population crisis. The third was a contest, conducted on over two hundred campuses, that awarded prizes for slogans relating environmental problems to "popullution."[41]

Onslaughts of environmental population propaganda were not reserved for college campuses. In 1969 the Committee to Check the Population Explosion's advertising campaign included environmental messages. One ad carried a picture of a plump, smiling baby and underneath the words "We can't lick the environment problem without considering this little fellow."[42]

It wasn't long until the environmental mainstream began to embrace the population issue. Throughout the 1970s and the early 1980s, environmental groups such as the Sierra Club and the National Audubon Society devoted large portions of time and resources to the population issue. By the 1990s many other influential mainstream environmental organizations—including the National Wildlife Federation, the Natural Resources Defense Council, the Cousteau Society, the Worldwatch Institute, and the World Resources Institute—were devoting resources to population.[43]

Neo-Malthusian ideas about overpopulation are widely accepted in the mainstream environmental movement of today. Population organizations continue to portray overpopulation as an imminent threat to the environment, through campaigns such as "6 billion day" in October 1999, which marked the estimated date at which the world population reached 6 billion. Rarely do population alarmists acknowledge that population growth rates are dropping, faster than anticipated, in all areas of the world. The United Nations low, medium, and high projections for world human population estimate that it will reach 7.3, 8.9, or 10.7 billion in 2050 and then start to level off.

Although it could play a role in some instances of environmental degradation, population size is certainly not a major cause of such degradation. Indeed, few serious studies show a direct relationship between the two. Deforestation is a case in point. Serious literature does not support the claim that overpopulation is responsible for deforestation in developing countries. For example, an extensive study of the social dynamics of deforestation published by the UN Research Institute for Social Development noted that while many observers blame deforestation on forest clearing by poor migrants, they ignore the larger forces attracting or pushing these migrants into forest areas, such as the expansion of large-scale commercial farming, ranching, logging, and mining. The study finds no correspondence between deforestation rates and rates of either total or agricultural population growth.[44]

The neo-Malthusian (and eugenic) ideology within population environmentalism provided an essential foundation for the anti-immigrant "environmentalism" that surfaced in the 1990s. In fact, the threads of eugenics, neo-Malthusianism, and nativism that made their way through the early immigration restriction and birth control movements, the emergence of population ideology, and the eventual connection with the mainstream environmental movement are evident in the contemporary scapegoating of immigrants for environmental problems.

The Political Agenda of the Greening of Hate

The contemporary campaign to scapegoat immigrants for environmental problems does more than cultivate a climate of population panic and anti-immigrant hatred. The organizations and politicians involved in this campaign also share similar political and legislative goals. Central points on this nativist agenda include the number of immigrants granted legal entry to the country, the right to citizenship, access to public services, and reproductive control. Moreover, immigrant women are primary targets of the campaign.

The number of immigrants allowed to enter the United States has been a hot topic for anti-immigrant organizations for years. Those organizations that feature overpopulation as a primary issue are apt to focus on numbers as a way of igniting public alarm about population size. They cite the number of immigrants who arrive daily or how much the U.S. population will increase in our lifetimes. This tactic does little to educate the public about actual demographic trends in immigration but instead disseminate unsubstantiated and misleading information. Yet Project USA and groups like it use such claims to argue for restrictions on the number of immigrants allowed to enter the United States annually.[45]

"An immigration moratorium" is high on the agenda of many anti-immigrant groups. Carrying Capacity Network, for example, calls for "an immediate moratorium, and an eventual all-inclusive cap of 100,000 per year" as the key to stopping U.S. population growth.[46] A common theme in the call for lowering numbers is the idea that the current level of immigration is somehow "out of control" and that a number between 100,000 to 300,000 per year would be "more traditional." These assertions are based on myths. Currently, the foreign-born population makes up only about 10 percent of the total U.S. population,[47] whereas early in the century immigrants constituted 15 percent of the U.S. population.[48] Although the total population of immigrants in the United States, at 28 million in 2000, is higher than it has been in the past, it is actually a relatively small proportion of the total U.S. population of over 284 million.[49]

A basic problem of the numbers-only approach is that it dehumanizes the immigration process as well as immigrants themselves. It gives little attention to the complex economic, political, and social reasons that a person or a family would choose to leave their country of origin to come to the United States, and it is far too simple.

Citizenship: Regulating Who Belongs

Contemporary nativist groups are making every attempt to regulate the numbers of immigrants allowed to enter the United States; they also want to exclude recent immigrants from total membership in American society. The language they use to refer to immigrants and the U.S.-born reflects their intentions.

In the Federation for American Immigration Reform's report *The Environmentalist's Guide to a Sensible Immigration Policy,* immigrants and their children are consistently referred to as "natives of other lands and their offspring," while the U.S.-born are referred to as "Americans." Most anti-immigrant groups insist on using the term *illegal alien* to describe undocumented immigrants. This othering language suggests that immigrants are distinctly "un-American" and denies the possibility of their integration into U.S. society.

Citizenship for immigrants is also under attack. Many groups are pushing for a constitutional amendment that would deny citizenship to the children of undocumented immigrants. This proposal was first suggested in 1991 by California Representative Elton Gallegly, who argued that the amendment "would save taxpayers millions of dollars in welfare payments. He estimated that illegal immigrants receive $5.4 billion a year in social services nationwide, and cited Los Angeles County statistics that two-thirds of the babies born in county hospitals are children of illegal immigrants."[50] Although Gallegly's statistics were dubious at best, the proposal has made its way into the heart of the "green" nativist campaign. In one example, the Alliance to Stabilize America's Population campaign, organized by Population-Environment Balance, calls for "no citizenship for illegal aliens' offspring."[51] Not only is the language here particularly virulent, but the effects of such an amendment would be disastrous. The amendment would create an illegal "subclass" of people with virtually no civil rights. This attempt to deny citizenship to children of undocumented parents fundamentally denies undocumented women's right to motherhood. Excluding undocumented immigrant women from the right to give birth to citizen children would send a clear message that their lives and the lives of their children are seen as less valuable to U.S. society than those of the native born. Additionally, in a white supremacist society where most immigrants are Latino and Asian, the denial of this right would exacerbate and legitimize existing racial hierarchies.

Permission Denied: Restricting Access to Public Services

The belief that immigrant women's reproduction causes a social, economic, and environmental burden on U.S. society was central to the emergence of anti-immigrant "environmentalism." It is behind the effort to restrict immigrants' access to a variety of public services.

Many nativist organizations and conservative politicians have called for limits on welfare benefits and other forms of public assistance for legal immigrants, and on any state or federal funded program for so-called illegals. For example, the Diversity Alliance for a Sustainable America's platform states:

- Noncitizen legal immigrants should be denied all welfare benefits, cash and noncash, except emergency medical care.
- All illegal aliens should be denied all public services except emergency medical care.[52]

There is little evidence that reducing public services to immigrants will result in a decreased number of immigrants, or that immigrants receive more than their fair share of welfare benefits. Images of immigrants crossing the border to receive welfare benefits and free health care are commonplace; yet they are not based in reality. A 1996 report by the Urban Institute found that most immigrants do not use welfare as it is conventionally defined (to include Aid to Families with Dependent Children [AFDC], Supplemental Security Income, or General Assistance). Although immigrants have slightly higher welfare use rates than natives overall (6.6 versus 4.9 percent), welfare use among immigrants is concentrated among refugees and the elderly, who are on welfare rolls at rates disproportionate to their numbers. Nonrefugee working-age immigrants receive welfare at about the same rate as natives. Moreover, poor immigrants remain less likely than poor natives to use welfare (16 versus 25 percent).[53]

Policy proposals for restricting immigrant access to public benefits proliferated during the 1990s, especially in California's 1994 Proposition 187, and in the federal Personal Responsibility and Work Opportunity Reconciliation Act of 1996, commonly known as the Welfare Reform Act. Proposition 187 would have prohibited local and state agencies from providing publicly funded social services, education, welfare, and nonemergency health care to any person who cannot be verified as a U.S. citizen or lawfully admitted alien. Further, it would have required government agencies to report any applicant suspected of being an illegal immigrant to the Immigration and Naturalization Service.

Critics have noted that the proponents of Proposition 187 stressed the ban on public support for prenatal care for undocumented women. The "official estimate" that two out of three babies delivered at Los Angeles County hospitals were born to undocumented women, cited by Gallegly in 1991, became an oft-quoted statistic in the Prop 187 campaign. However, this figure is skewed; the legal scholar Dorothy Roberts contends that the number is probably inflated as a result of "county officials' unscientific survey methods and confusion of legal and illegal immigrants."[54] In any case, Prop 187 proponents clearly placed little value on undocumented women's reproductive health, or the health of their children.

Although Proposition 187 passed, it was declared unconstitutional and never made its way into law. However, the 1996 Welfare Reform Act would have a significant impact on the way both documented and undocumented immigrants are permitted access to public services. Before the act, services provided by the U.S. Department of Health and Human Services, with the exception of AFDC and Medicaid, were available to anyone residing in the United States, with eligibility based on need. The Welfare Reform Act barred *legal* immigrants from receiving food stamps and left it up to the states to determine whether legal immigrants are eligible for Temporary Assistance for Needy Families (TANF), the program which replaced AFDC. In addition, nonrefugee immigrants are banned from receiving "federal means-tested public benefits," including Medicaid, TANF, and the Children's Health Insurance Program, for the first five years of their residency. "Non-qualified aliens," including nonimmigrants (such as students, tourists, et cetera) and undocumented aliens, are also barred from receiving "federal public benefits." The act denies undocumented immigrants access to thirty-one Health and Human Services programs, including programs for alcohol and drug abuse and for the disabled.[55]

Immediately after the enactment of the Welfare Reform Act, former California Governor Pete Wilson made prenatal care the first target of his campaign to enact the federal law's ban on state and local assistance to illegal immigrants. His callous disregard for the health of undocumented women and their children cannot be written off simply as an attempt to cut California's expenditures. At its most basic level, the edict reflects assumptions about the value of immigrant mothers in American society.

Although Wilson's ban was later repealed by his successor, Governor Gray Davis, welfare reform has had a significant effect on immigrants' access to health and other public services. An Urban Insitute study of the effects of welfare reform on how immigrants use public benefits found that it discouraged some immigrants from using benefits for which they were still eligible and even confused providers about eligibility.[56]

The contemporary anti-immigrant movement has also fostered fear and suspicion of immigration, inhibiting immigrants from applying for benefits. Increasingly, women immigrants do not seek out medical care, a failure that is especially dangerous for pregnant women and young children.

Reproductive Control: Undermining Women's Choice

Frequently, calls to restrict immigration are paired with calls to restrict birth rates in the United States. For example, the Diversity Alliance for a Sustainable America, an organization focused on U.S. population stabilization, primarily through immigration reduction, also includes "replacement-level fertility (an average of two children per family)" in their platform.[57] Negative Population Growth advocates for a target population of "150 million, accomplished through voluntary incentives for smaller families and reducing immigration to 100,000 annually."[58]

Population-Environment Balance uses a facade of progressive environmentalism to mask its socially regressive political agenda. The organization claims to support "a woman's right to reproductive choice," yet calls for a U.S. population policy which would promote "a two child limit and incentives for small family size" including "tax credits for small family size and programs that pay teens not to get pregnant."[59] In this group's rhetoric, women have the right to choose—but only if they choose to have no more than two children. The demographic targets called for by these anti-immigrant environmental groups show their disregard for reproductive freedom. Clearly, these organizations are willing to sacrifice not only immigrant rights but also the reproductive rights of all women in the United States in the name of environmental protection.

Anti-immigrant environmental groups also clearly target the reproduction of immigrants. In addition to the policy platforms already discussed, many of these organizations foster the notion that first-generation immigrants have higher fertility rates than the native born.[60] The implication is clearly that immigrants' fertility rates are a threat to be tightly controlled.

The right to choose whether or not to have children is fundamental for all women. Contemporary anti-immigrant policies attempt to place governmental restrictions on immigrant women's ability to make their own safe and free reproductive choices. Furthermore, in the context of a nationalistic, anti-immigrant social and political climate, the assault on immigrant women's reproduction is fundamentally an assault on their right to contribute to the next generation of citizens. It is an attempt to control who may be considered "American" and to exclude undocumented immigrants, particularly Latinos and Asians, from the rights bestowed on citizens.

Erasing Green Hatred

The "green" platform of the anti-immigrant movement is characterized by the use of environmental language to justify right-wing policy demands. Just as the myth of overpopulation has been employed to justify increasing disparities between the developed and the developing world, it provides an explanation for growing disparity and falling quality of life within the nation. Elites in the United States can blame immigrants for driving population growth, providing an oversimplified explanation for a range of societal problems, including environmental degradation, urban poverty, job loss, declining income, inadequate education, and violence. Often, anti-immigrant environmentalists have more than numbers on their minds: discussion of who is overpopulating the nation is common in a movement with strong eugenic associations. Thus, immigrants are said to degrade "our" carrying capacity not only in terms of natural resources but also in terms of our so-called social and cultural environment.

The greening of hate masks the real sources of environmental degradation and fiscal crisis. Anti-immigrant environmental arguments take the blame off corporations, the military, and ·elite consumer practices for environmental degradation, while the economic scapegoating of immigrants does little to address the increase in income disparity that benefits the wealthy and hurts the middle and working classes.

The response of the mainstream environmental movement has been mixed. Population-Environment Balance has shown that there is approval in the movement for anti-immigrant organizing; their anti-immigrant ASAP! Alliance has drawn support from organizations such as Los Angeles Earth First!, the Gaia Institute, the Inland Empire Public Lands Council, Northwest Environmental Advocates, and many more. However, the struggle within the Sierra Club around the immigration issue shows that there is also resistance to the greening of hate within the environmental movement. The Sierra Club is one of the largest environmental organizations in the United States, traditionally associated with the environmentalism of mainstream liberals. The club views overpopulation as a primary source of environmental problems, exemplified by its use of a tree diagram which showed overpopulation as the root of all major environmental problems plaguing the planet.

In 1998 the Sierra Club faced a particularly dramatic stand-off between factions of its membership who believed the club should take a stance against immigration restriction and those who preferred that it maintain its neutral position on immigration. Members chose between two alternatives: "a reduction of net immigration" as a component of a "comprehensive population policy for the United States" or a countermeasure that reaffirmed the club's neutral position on immigration and committed it to work toward "addressing the root causes of global population problems . . . [through] the empowerment and equity of women, maternal and reproductive health care . . .

[and] to address the root causes of migration by encouraging sustainability, economic security, human rights, and environmentally responsible consumption."[61]

A coalition of environmental and immigrant rights groups formed to educate Sierra Club members about the significance of the vote and encourage them to support the second alternative. It passed with 60 percent of the votes. Environmentalists and immigrant rights advocates worked together to defeat the greening of hate.

The defeat of the first alternative has not, however, been the end of anti-immigrant activity in the Sierra Club. On September 6, 1999, the club's board of directors changed from a policy favoring population stabilization to one that advocates population "reductions" in the United States and worldwide. This seemingly slight change of language actually signifies a major capitulation to anti-immigrant forces, since reducing the U.S. population size would require blocking immigration. Although Director Carl Pope claimed that the club's policy had merely been "clarified—not changed" and that "any implication that it is retreating from its neutrality on immigration is false," this "clarification" suggests the dangerous possibility of anti-immigrant organizing within the Sierra Club.[62]

The contemporary anti-immigrant movement is attempting to unify a broad spectrum of political interests against immigrants. While some labor groups and many social conservatives have traditionally been anti-immigrant, the alliance with mainstream liberal environmentalists is new. Of course, alliances built on the pro-immigration side of politics are often equally unusual, with business interests seemingly working for the same goals as immigrant rights advocates and Latino and Asian organizations. At the same time, there is silence on the immigration issue from many women's rights, welfare, health, and education advocates, as well as many mainstream environmentalists.

As immigrant rights advocates, we need to get beyond the cost-benefit approach and challenge ourselves to do more than assert the economic benefits immigrants bring. This approach lends itself to a never-ending back-and-forth between studies with disparate conclusions; it also caters primarily to the needs of business and lacks a critical analysis of free-market capitalism.

Immigrant rights organizations have already begun to incorporate a critique of free-market capitalism into their political framework in order to build crucial alliances with the labor movement of the United States. Meanwhile, organized labor groups are rethinking their traditional anti-immigrant stance and beginning to move toward the view of immigrants as allies, not potential strikebreakers. The recent AFL-CIO policy recommending a general amnesty for undocumented workers and the elimination of employer sanctions or penalties for hiring undocumented workers is one positive step.

Mainstream environmentalists must add a societal analysis and an agenda for social justice to their work. The environmental justice movement has made great strides in formulating an agenda based on a commitment to social, economic, and racial justice, and there has been progress in the mainstream environmental movement as well. However, the greening of hate demonstrates that an environmental agenda does not necessarily prescribe a liberal or progressive political stance. It is imperative that environmental organizations formulate their political visions consciously and carefully.

Because anti-immigrant discourse and policy focus on reproduction, a broad-based movement for reproductive freedom and social justice could be built by the alliances among immigrant rights, reproductive rights, women's health, welfare, environmental justice, and youth advocates. Organizations such as Asian and Pacific Islanders for Reproductive Rights in Oakland, California and Communities Against Rape and Abuse in Seattle, Washington[63] are moving in this direction, as the need for strong alliances on multiple issues becomes more obvious.

The anti-immigrant movement's attempt to draw support from across the political spectrum presents a challenge for those of us on the other side. We need to deepen our political analysis in order to combat the simplistic scapegoating tactics of the nativists, bridge the gaps among our various movements, and create a strong political alliance for equality and social justice.

SHE WHO BELIEVES IN FREEDOM: YOUNG
WOMEN DEFY THE PRISON INDUSTRIAL COMPLEX

Robin Templeton

Robin Templeton is executive director of the National Campaign to Restore Voting Rights, a collaboration among eight national civil rights and public interest organizations. The campaign's mission is to secure the right to vote for the 4.65 million people in the United States denied access to the ballot because of felony conviction. It is piloting reenfranchisement efforts in Alabama, Florida, Maryland, New York, and Texas. Previously, she was communications director at the Ella Baker Center for Human Rights. She was a member of the founding organizing committee of Critical Resistance and worked with the acclaimed writing program for youth in detention, Pacific News Service's The Beat Within. She has a master's degree in education from Harvard University and has been widely published on juvenile and criminal justice issues.

> And if I know anything at all,
> it's that a wall is just a wall
> and nothing more at all.
> It can be broken down.
>
> —Assata Shakur

It is vague, and it is a possibility at best, but I know a place, a
refuge, where people love and live.

—George Jackson

In 2001 the prison population in the United States exceeded 2
million people, most of them illiterate, most under- or unem-
ployed, most in jail for nonviolent crimes, and a vast majority
people of color. The gargantuan total of 6.5 million people in the
United States are under some form of correctional supervision.[1]

Twenty-three-year-old Alicia Yang is trying to lower those
numbers by dedicating her life to fighting the prison industrial
complex. She says, "I know we need to build a fierce, strategic
movement to deal with the prison crisis, but I also know we need
to take care of people, to reach into people's hearts. We need to
heal communities. Ultimately, we need to create a society that's
based on redemption, a society that would refuse to allow 2 million people, most of them poor, to be locked up in cages."

Yang's cousin became one of the numbers when he got a life
sentence in a California penitentiary. Like many young women
who share her opposition to mass incarceration, Yang is driven
by more than political analysis. She says she was reborn as an
anti-incarceration activist because her cousin's imprisonment
is like having part of her soul locked away. Then, shifting in her
seat, she raises her voice and ebulliently describes visiting her
cousin behind bars and getting to know some of the men with
whom he's jailed: "They showed me the resiliency of the
human spirit and allowed me—for the first time in my life—to
really taste freedom."

How does freedom taste? "It's not like a flavor but a focus,"

Yang explains. "I examined my own life and started taking freedom very seriously. This fight against the prison industrial complex is a freedom struggle. Because prisons destroy and enslave life, the focus of our work against prisons has to be restoring life, liberating life."

Like slavery, that other "peculiar institution," prisons decimate life by stealing people from their communities, forcing families apart, and converting human beings into disposable parts that generate immense profit for private interests. The punishment sector has been one of the fastest-growing and most lucrative industries in the United States. Most prisoners do some form of work under repressive conditions and earn pennies per hour. Prisoners provide a pool of cheap labor that can be infinitely filled and exponentially enlarged. Eighteen private prison companies do business in the United States—Corrections Corporation of America and Wackenhut are the largest, operating eighty-one and fifty-two prisons respectively—and hundreds more corporations contract with publicly "owned" prisons to sell goods and services, usually at inflated, "captive market" prices. All the while, the institution perpetuates its legitimacy by criminalizing and bestializing the very lives it controls.

Yang's prison visits became for her an experience of restoring dignity and resurrecting hope in the face of a machine that dehumanizes life at a scale that is nearly—considering that African-American men have a greater than one in four chance of being incarcerated—genocidal. Visits with her cousin led Yang to teach in a prison-based adult education program. Subsequently, she started organizing on police and prison-related issues with an organization in Oakland called Asian American Youth Promoting Advocacy and Leadership. She explains, "We'd present workshops breaking down the prison industrial complex—using all the economic arguments about how much it costs to lock someone up and the terrible statistics about how many people of color are behind bars. But more and more, I just wanted to talk to people in my community about healing. I really wanted to stop and say: 'We won't be whole until we bring our sisters and brothers home from prison; until we learn to trust and forgive each other.'"

Sisters at the Center of the Prison Crisis

In the tenacity of her convictions as well as in her vacillation on what is to be done about the prison industrial complex, Alicia Yang is not alone. A new generation of young people is at the forefront of grassroots organizing against mass incarceration in the United States. They are demanding accountability from law enforcement and corrections agencies that are rife with abuse. And they are organizing toward investing prison funds in rebuilding eviscerated social programs, especially schools, instead.

According to data compiled by the Prison Activist Resource Center, over the past twenty years, at the local, state, and federal levels, spending on incarceration has increased 571 percent while spending on K–12 education has risen only 33 percent. The number of prison guards has increased 250 percent while the number of K–12 teachers has dropped by 8 percent. And over the past two decades, while the number of students graduating from high school has dropped by 2.7 percent, the number of people filling the nation's prisons and jails has increased by over 400 percent.[2]

Because the vast majority of these prisoners are incarcerated for nonviolent offenses, young antiprison activists say that prisons should not be a default public works program. People living in poverty and facing structural racism should have their basic human needs met, should have access to good schools and jobs, and should get treatment, not punishment, if they develop an addiction. But while the activists' goal is to create a society in which the prison industrial complex is unnecessary, they know that violent crime is a pernicious reality and that members of their communities need to be protected from it. In response to critics who say that violent criminals must be kept off the street, activists who want to shut down the prison industrial complex say that the priority should be changing the socioeconomic conditions which create violence. When asked about the child murderers, rapists, and serial killers, these activists do not readily contend that these few members of the population should not be kept away from the public. But, they underscore, people convicted of violent offenses are only a small fraction of those in prison and are illegitimately used to justify the buildup of a massive industry. And, they remind their critics, one of the most violent demographic groups in the United States is white men in their thirties, a segment of the population grossly underrepresented in the prison system.

Today women in general and young women in particular are the fastest-growing segments of the prison population in the United States. The prison crisis is for young women of color and poor women a double-edged sword: They have to take care of families, pick up the broken pieces, and earn income when men are removed from their communities. And they are increasingly entangled in the criminal justice system themselves. Dozens of criminal justice organizers have told me that the harder the system clamps down on young women, the harder they fight back. By founding grassroots organizations or taking control of preexisting ones in their communities, advocating that social services meet their and their children's needs so that they do not end up in the criminal justice system, and creating new forms of cultural expression that challenge criminalization, young women are disproportionately assuming leadership in the nascent movement against the prison industrial complex.

Largely as a result of their foremothers' work, young women are redefining grassroots leadership by ensuring that everyone is given credit for her work behind the scenes, building organizations from the bottom up, and constantly cultivating new leadership. But the scale of the prison crisis is also drawing on and pulling out something deeper. Young women are determined to fight prisons but also—at the risk of sounding biologically deterministic—to nurture human beings.

New Feminism: A First Line of Defense Against the Prison Industry

One, we are at war. Two, the natural response to oppression, ignorance, evil and mystification is wide-awake resistance. Three, the natural response to stress and crisis is not breakdown and capitulation, but transformation and renewal.

—Toni Cade Bambara

The young women coming to leadership in the twin struggles against police abuse and prison expansion are not only passionate activists; they're also interested in healing. They're strategizing the next campaign. They're working in their communities with the explicit intent of increasing trust and reciprocal respect as well as making their neighborhoods safer places in which to live. They're targeting prisons and police as enemies of the people. And young women are talking about how to render the state security apparatus irrelevant by meeting people's needs. This up-and-coming incarnation of the women's movement is still preaching liberation, but it's also cultivating a practice of redemption.

The feminist mantra "the personal is political" defines the relationship between women and prisons because "the political" has a profoundly personal impact. "For too long the women's movement didn't look inside the homes of women of color and low-income women whose experiences have pushed the envelope on the necessity of dealing with prisons," says Ellen Barry, founding director of Legal Services for Prisoners with Children and an organizer with the Critical Resistance, a national network of activists fighting the prison industrial complex. "I see the new leadership of the antiprison movement coming up from young women who are forming not women's organizations but youth organizations in response to the crisis of their generation. They're synergizing race and gender issues and moving forward."

Lateefah Simon, the twenty-six-year-old director of the Center for Young Women's Development, makes the point this way: "Poor women of color don't have a choice but to confront the prison industry because it so thoroughly impacts our daily lives." Simon learned about the stranglehold of the criminal justice system as well as how to wrestle with powerful institutions by watching women in her family organize to get family members out of jail. She recalls: "I saw the women in my community maintain pride and demand respect in the face of an irrational system determined to take away their loved ones. I learned about dignity and what it means to create a safe haven for someone to come home to."

As the criminal justice system wreaks havoc in poor communities of color, millions of families are struggling to maintain dignity and stability. "The women of these families," Simon says, "are the first line of defense against the prison industrial complex."

Meet the Incarceration Generation

Third wave feminists are the daughters of the "baby boomer" women's libbers of the 1960s and '70s. Those of us in the "third wave" are now in our twenties and thirties. The spike in prison construction in the United States began in our formative years, exactly coinciding with our maturation. The number of prison inmates in the United States quadrupled from 1980 to 2000, from 500,000 to 2 million.[3] During this time the U.S. population grew only 20 percent. California particularly dramatizes the prison boom of the last two decades of the twentieth century. In 1980 the state had twelve prisons. By 1998 it was home to thirty-three prisons but had constructed only one new state university.[4] In other words, young women have grown up with the biggest, most catastrophic prison boom in world history. Young women of color and low-income young women bring to the antiprison movement knowledge that they must respond not only to the social and economic conditions of those whose lives are torn apart by the powers that punish but also to their personal and spiritual needs.

America imprisons more human beings per capita than any country on the planet, with the exception of Rwanda. It costs about $41 billion a year for the United States to warehouse its 2 million prisoners.[5] Even adjusting for inflation, overall criminal justice spending has nearly doubled since the mid-1980s. And relative to population growth, per capita prison spending increased 69 percent, from $217 to $366, from 1983 to 1995.[6] These increases are irrational because exorbitant prison spending is throwing money at a problem that does not exist. The last time crime rates increased in the United States was between 1965 and 1973. Since then general crime trends have been stable or declined. From 1991 to 1998, violent crime in the United States fell by 25 percent.[7]

Most of these tough-on-crime dollars are spent incapacitating people for nonviolent offenses. Over the past twenty years, the growth of the nonviolent prison population has far outpaced the incarceration rate for violent offenders: 77 percent of those entering prisons and jails are sentenced for nonviolent offenses. From 1980 to 1997, the number of prisoners charged with violent offenses doubled while the number of nonviolent prisoners tripled, and the number of people convicted for drug offenses increased elevenfold. These numbers are steeper still for women. Eighty-five percent of women are imprisoned for nonviolent offenses.[8]

The drive to lock up nonviolent prisoners is all the more pernicious given that prisons constitute one of the United States' most well-endowed public works programs. The prison industrial complex—fueled by the War on Crime and the War on Drugs much as the Cold War drove its military predecessor—delivers big profits to private prison contractors and service providers, economic development for depressed rural areas, and jobs to blue-collar workers facing a deindustrialized economy. Working people from urban areas are increasingly removed from their communities to work in far-flung rural communities. The runaway growth of the U.S. prison system also corresponds—not coincidentally—with the structural decimation of public policy responses to poverty and other social problems.

The California Bay Area youth organizer Raquel Laviña offers this economic analysis: "For young women of color and poor women, it's not only that we're getting harassed by police and more and more often going to prison, but that the community is a different place when so many people get taken away. There are so many young women without their babies' fathers because over half of the men in their community are either dead or in jail. Women of color feel a responsibility for the men in our community. We have to hold the liberation of men and women at the same time."

Laviña explains that the prison industrial complex is a primary point of struggle for her generation and for those coming up after her: "It's a symbol of the freedom we don't have. There are so many things impacting young people of color and poor youth—poverty, homelessness, substandard education. But the police coming at you and taking people away from your community is immediate and direct. The others are more slow-burn ways of killing you. You know the police aren't there to protect you but the business across the street."

This generation's new movement has no choice but to take gender into account as it confronts the War on Crime and the War on Drugs, which frequently target young men of color. The rush to incarcerate nonviolent drug offenders began in the 1970s with New York's Rockefeller Drug Laws, which mandated fifteen-year prison sentences for nonviolent offenders guilty of small-time narcotics possession. By the end of the 1980s, nearly every state was enforcing mandatory minimum sentences for nonviolent drug offenders. From 1980 to 1990, the number of prisoners incarcerated for nonviolent drug offenses increased tenfold. Nonviolent offenders are overwhelmingly men of color, while most drug users are white. Decreased public funding for job training, education, and other social programs only increased the number of low-income young men of color who might be locked up for nonviolent offenses. Today young African-American and Latino men are more likely to get booked in prison or jail than to enroll in college.

Harmony Goldberg, cofounder and director of the youth political education center School of Unity and Liberation, says that the movement she's a part of is completely feminist in terms of its leaders, who are mostly young women, but not necessarily in terms of the issues it fights. "Traditional feminist issues"—reproductive rights, equal pay for equal work, how to transcend the glass ceiling—"have not been on the same level of priority for me as building a movement against racial and class oppression." Goldberg acknowledges that, in part, this is a reaction to the legacy of racism in the women's movement.

Women and Girls on Lockdown

Hermon Getachew, twenty-one-year-old director of the organization Sister Outsider in the Brownsville and East Flatbush
neighborhoods of Brooklyn, knows that many young women
are motivated by their own experiences to organize for a just
criminal justice system. "I've had a lot of encounters with the
police," Getachew says. "It really hits home, the women you
see in jail—they're just there on bench warrants, drug charges,
and for self-defense. Girls end up in the system when they're
just trying to support themselves. It just boils down to money.
I know women who have to support themselves and their families at the age of fourteen, and no one is trying to give those
women, especially those from immigrant communities, a job."

While prison spending siphons employment and education
resources out of needy communities, "prisons do not disappear
problems, they disappear human beings," charges the lifelong
antiprison activist Angela Y. Davis.[9] Increasingly, prisons are
disappearing "problematic" women. According to the National
Council on Crime and Delinquency, twenty-five years ago
women were virtually invisible in the criminal justice system.
Today more than 140,000 women are in U.S. prisons and jails,
nearly triple the number in 1985. The number of women
imprisoned in California alone is nearly twice that of women
incarcerated nationwide thirty years ago. African-American
women, the fastest-growing segment of the U.S. prison population, are incarcerated at a rate eight times that of white
women. Latina women are incarcerated at four times the rate
of white women.

Seventy percent of women in prison have been convicted of nonviolent offenses, and 80 percent of adult women prisoners have children—most are single mothers of children under eighteen. Half of all women imprisoned in the United States are African-American. As a result of War on Drugs legislation like mandatory minimums, women are twice as likely as men to be incarcerated for drug-related offenses. Men, however, are more likely than women to receive drug treatment.[10]

From 1930 to 1950, a total of five women's prisons were built in the United States. During the 1980s alone, thirty-four were constructed. According to a recent Amnesty International report: "Even this could not keep pace with the swelling numbers of women in prison. Women's prisons are understaffed, overcrowded, lack recreation facilities, serve poor quality food, suffer chronic shortages of family planning counselors and services, obstetrics and gynecological specialists, drug treatment and childcare facilities and transportation funds for family visits—which are necessary due to the remote locations of the women's prisons. A 2000 study by the General Accounting Office, commissioned by the Washington, D.C. congressional delegate Eleanor Holmes Norton, found that women in prison are more likely to suffer from HIV infection and mental illness than are incarcerated men.[11]

Like adult women, girls have become increasingly caught up in the criminal justice system in recent decades. Between 1993 and 1997, in almost every offense category, increases in arrests were greater—or decreases in arrests were smaller—for girls than for boys. Research on girls in detention consistently shows that girls rarely pose a threat to others' safety but that they are at the highest risk levels for becoming substance addicted and sexually active, and for failing out of school. "Tragically," says a report by the National Council on Crime and Delinquency, "these problems are almost always correlated with histories of violent victimization, poverty, and deeply fragmented families and public service systems."[12] According to the American Bar Association, between 1988 and 1997 delinquency cases involving girls jumped 83 percent. The spike was not in response to increased crime or violence by girls but rather "re-labeling of family conflicts as violent offenses, gender bias in the processing of minor offenses, changes in police practice . . . and a lack of services aimed at helping troubled girls."[13]

Further, the criminalization of poor people is a double-edged swipe at women, who are disproportionately poor. Two-thirds of adults living in poverty in the United States are women, and the poverty rate for children in female-headed households is over 50 percent. In fact, the wage gap between male and female workers is declining only because the real earnings of low-income men are falling. A female worker still earns seventy-two cents to a man's dollar.[14]

Suemyra Shah, a nineteen-year-old board member of the National Coalition to Abolish the Death Penalty, speaks to the prison system's dual attack on poor young women. "Young women are especially affected because we've always been the keepers of the family. Women have always played a central role, not only in leading political struggles but also in centering and preserving life. And it's escalating now, with the [criminal justice] system taking so many young people away from the community."

The Wars We Fight

A 1997 study by the Bureau of Justice Statistics reported that an African-American male born in that year had a 28 percent chance of serving a federal or state prison term at some point in his life.[15] If he grows up in a city, the setup gets even deeper: 76 percent of African-American males in urban areas who are currently eighteen years old will be arrested and jailed before age thirty-six, according to Jerome Miller, corrections expert and president of the National Institute on Institutions and Alternatives. "By the late 1990s," Miller has written, "federal statisticians were predicting that nearly one of every three adult black men in the nation could anticipate being sentenced to a federal or state prison at some point during his life."[16]

The racist myth of the "superpredator," a black or brown young man from the inner city who is genetically or culturally predisposed to violence, has been used to justify punitive measures such as "three strikes" laws, stiffer sentencing for juveniles, antigang laws, and "Weed and Seed" style guilty-until-proven-innocent policing.[17] Racism exacerbates the national crime neuroses much as the myth of the African-American "welfare queen" fueled the demolition of social welfare programs like Aid to Families with Dependent Children (AFDC). These correlative, gender-specific myths about low-income African-Americans mutually reinforced each other. From 1993 to 1996 government spending on AFDC shrank by almost $2 billion while public funding of corrections increased by $8 billion nationwide.[18] In 1993, the height of the demonization of the "welfare queen," $6 billion more was being spent on the failing

War on Drugs than on AFDC.[19] Professor David Courtwright of the University of North Florida depicts the War on Drugs "as a kind of giant vacuum cleaner, hovering over the nation's inner cities, sucking young black men off the street and into prison."[20]

The functional fallacy behind the prison-police system is that it keeps "good" neighborhoods "safe," incapacitates criminals, and deters crime. A recap of recent decades' most memorable crime coverage, however, presents another theme: that of white middle-class girls and women in need of protection from the nonwhite male "superpredator." Charles Stuart, a white man, murdered his pregnant white wife and attempted to pin the crime on an African-American man, triggering a police hunt for the "suspect" in Boston's African-American communities. The white female Central Park jogger who was raped in the mid-1980s signaled that none of "us" (read: white women and their men) is safe from young men of color. Willie Horton, an African-American man who after being granted furlough from prison by the Democratic presidential candidate Michael Dukakis raped an elderly white woman, was made symbolic of the hundreds of thousands of other black men "just like him."

State-sanctioned scapegoating, criminalization, and incarceration of young men of color have been particularly virulent over the past decade, forcing organizers to react, often in crisis mode. Jo Hirschmann, an organizer with the police accountability organization the Ella Baker Center for Human Rights, explains: "Proponents of draconian legislation use racist images of predators that are coded messages about young men of color. We've had to respond in a reactive, short time-frame." Hirschmann and her fellow antiprison and police accountability organizers look to integrate research and strategies on how the prison industrial complex affects people at society's margins: "We need to collectivize and systematize information, analysis, and tactics about how the criminal justice system impacts [not only young men of color but everyone including] girls [and] also queer youth and transgender youth."

In Our Hands

> All that is before us is in our hands. We have no right to assume otherwise.
>
> —James Baldwin

In response to the punitive zeal fueling the prison industrial complex, the leadership of the up-and-coming antiprison movement—with young women at the forefront—is decidedly interested in redemption. The inclusive style of leadership that young women bring to this seedling movement is rooted in a strong belief in community, passed down, perhaps, by grandmothers raising many of the 1.5 million children otherwise rendered parentless by prisons in this country. It is a method of leadership as determined to tackle adversaries as it is to build hope by reclaiming human beings from a system that irredeemably labels them "criminal." The processes of hope, restoration, and bringing people back into their communities are personal. But they are also political acts because they reverse the cultural and socioeconomic process of criminalization that vilifies people who are desperate for resources and isolated from others. This is not to say that "criminalized" people do not perform criminal acts. But young women who critique the criminal justice system are saying—at their peers' parole hearings, when they talk to the media, in hip-hop lyrics, and in conversation over the dinner table—that criminal mistakes should not define the sum total of one's humanity.

Feeding off of fear, criminalization distracts from social and economic problems by blaming those who bear the brunt of the injustices. Kate Rhee, the twenty-seven-year-old director of the New York–based Prison Moratorium Project explains: "The oppressor reinvents the oppressed for its purpose. This plays out in how we perceive criminals and crime and who deserves punishment."

Amanda Devecka-Rinear, a twenty-six-year-old organizer against police brutality with New York City PoliceWatch, is white and college-educated but empathizes with the experience of public vilification based on identity: "When I came out, I realized that millions of people hate me when they don't even know me. This gave me a sense of what it means to be feared, hated, and patrolled. More than anything else, this has committed me to the fight against the prison industrial complex, and it informs how I think about organizing and campaigning for police accountability."

Erin Hughes, an activist at the University of California at Santa Cruz, explains that her entry into antiprison work was also guided by a sense of personal accountability: "I grew up losing friends from my neighborhood to the criminal justice system." She reflects, "My commitment comes from my mother. She taught me to take care of the people I love fully. Women tend to be the ones on the outside, the mothers, wives, friends, and sisters, trying to bring a little love inside into a hateful system. Being there for people locked up means the entire schedule of your day changes to make sure you're there to get the collect phone call or make it to the post office on time." Hughes says she brings this same sense of personal commitment and urgency to her life as an organizer: "Being late for or missing a meeting takes on a whole other significance when you're working, ultimately, to make people safe from the prison machine."

Maintaining a relationship with a loved one or family member behind bars begins at the level of individual experience but extends into the realm of collective accountability. "You have no idea what it's like to love someone who is being tortured inside a prison. You never get used to living with so much horror," says asha bandele, an editor at *Essence* magazine and author of *The Prisoner's Wife*. Bandele describes how this experience stretches into the domain of collective responsibility: "Whenever I hear of police and prison abuses, it doesn't matter if I know the person or not because it could always be happening to anyone I love.

"I've often wondered," bandele says, "out of all the social justice work that could be my calling, why this work? Why immerse myself in a world where I know that someone I love may be kept from me and the rest of the community forever? I'm finally coming to understand that I do this work because I want to be free."

The work that young women are doing embodies an emphasis on freedom, liberation, and humanity. Recently the Center for Young Women's Development in San Francisco spearheaded a dialogue with young women in juvenile hall about what issues they felt were most pressing. As Lateefah Simon puts it, "We thought it was important to do something in the system where we usually have no power, and could show youth in the hall that things could indeed be changed." Working with the young women in the hall, the center was able to uncover harassment of queer women. Simon notes that, "even though none of our leadership was out and queer, we took on this issue because it came up so much as an issue that was important to the girls in the hall. We are developing their voices and their vision. Recognizing and supporting the fullness of everyone's humanity is embedded in the culture of the organization."

The center organized a group of legal experts to help draft a model policy for the city of San Francisco to address the concerns of queer youth in juvenile detention. As a result of the group's advocacy, and after a long struggle, the mayoral commission on juvenile justice and probation recently adopted the policy the center created—the first of its kind in the nation. The policy stipulates that juvenile hall staff be trained to work with queer youth and that monitoring and oversight be implemented to ensure that the concerns and complaints of queer youth are heard and tended to. Additionally, two center staffers (fifteen and seventeen years old, both former sex workers) were part of a mayoral committee to research and make recommendations to the city council on practical alternatives to incarceration for young women who have been arrested for prostitution. Formerly incarcerated girls (sixteen to nineteen years old) also developed workshops on "how to stay out of the system," which they present as an ongoing program in San Francisco's juvenile hall—a precedent for the facility.

Recognizing the power of the collective efforts of young

women, Simon notes, "Our power comes from the truth we speak. We are the first youth who have been through the system to serve on the juvenile probation commission. We told the commission real stories about real youth who have been in the hall. We could tell them which correction officers had been abusive, and we gave them testimony of the girls we work with. This issue is not sexy and it's not easy, but it's proof that we're really going to be doing this work on the inside for the long haul."

Visions of Freedom

The national attempt to deal with a wide array of economic, social, and personal problems through criminal justice processing has brought social disaster to our cities. If we are to make progress, we will need a new paradigm. It will be possible only when we begin handling most "criminalizable" situations outside the criminal justice system altogether.

—Jerome Miller

Young women are defining their work as a freedom struggle for all people; they are challenging racist assumptions and policies as well as the moral authority of law and order politics. They are countering dominant lies about crime with narratives of resistance and small acts of freedom. They speak of small victories, those momentary exchanges of humanity among people from divergent backgrounds. Amanda Devecka-Rinear, cofounder of Critical Resistance NYC, paraphrases the former Puerto Rican political prisoner Elizam Escobar in describing the importance of seeing change incrementally and focusing on the process of movement building: "We have to live every day like we are free."

"How can we become accountable to one another in our communities so people don't want to call the cops? How do we not legitimize the institution of police?" asks Hermon Getachew. In its educational work with youth, Sister Outsider explains the institutional racism of the criminal justice system and the fact that the police are an occupying force in communities of color. Given this analysis, Getachew says, "We want police out of our communities, but what do we do when someone rapes a sister?"

Getachew looks to history for an answer as well as a vision of what the new movement could create today. "Back in the day people would call the Black Panthers instead of the police. Now we have 'copwatch' programs to monitor the police, but we also have to have accountability to one another. We have to feel responsible for one another."

Raquel Laviña agrees: "Women of color need to seize the opportunity to say that the solution to feeling threatened is not to have more police in our community. We need to make sure we don't pathologize men of color—violence against women is sanctioned [by societal norms], and so is state violence against men of color. Women need to stand up and work to protect our own communities, and we can also argue that no community needs a bigger police force."

Joy Enomoto, a thirty-year-old economic justice organizer who works with the women's organization Just Economics, describes her vision of freedom from the prison industrial complex in bottom-line, practical terms: "We can fight all we want against the state. But unless we're putting alternatives to punishment in place and focusing on sustaining life, there's really no point in tearing down prisons. Slavery never ended, it just shifted its form because abolition did not change the fundamentally racist social and economic system."

Is any part of Enomoto's critique feminist? "I don't care what you call it," she responds. "I just know we need an alternative system, one that is structurally different. My system would definitely have women in leadership; it would not blame women for anything and everything, and it would definitely not allow violence against women."

"I don't fight the prison industry because I am a feminist," Suemyra Shah echoes, "but because I am a human being."

Epilogue

There is so much ground this essay does not cover: the murderous medical neglect and sexual abuse of women prisoners; the children left behind when mothers and fathers are locked away; the rising numbers of girls landing in the juvenile justice system for the illegalities of just trying to survive in the street economy, where labor market opportunities to sell drugs or themselves abound, whereas the "aboveground" economy is a continuum of slammed doors; and the tens of thousands of aging and ill prisoners who are denied compassionate release despite their families' appeals.

I began writing about young women's leadership in the nascent movement against the prison industrial complex by asking organizers why they thought so many young women were leading the work. No one really knew how to answer. Neither did I. Then I asked why they themselves did the work and if their motivation had anything to do with feminism. There was consensus among all the women I talked to that, though they consider themselves feminists, this self-definition was not the basis for their commitment. Rather, they tended to say, they do this work because they are human beings, they love freedom, and they want all human beings to be free.

They also wanted to raise a consideration that mainstream society considers ridiculous: What would it take to make mass incarceration obsolete and police abuse unthinkable? Beyond the obvious answers of economic justice and ending racism, there are more nuanced responses that involve the difficult work of transformation, redemption, and renewal.

LOOKING AHEAD: BUILDING A FEMINIST FUTURE

Vivien Labaton and
Dawn Lundy Martin

Instead of looking for the real work that young feminists are doing, the media would often rather cast feminists as a dying breed or pose questions such as Do young feminists exist? To us, the question that is more compelling than Where are all the young feminists? is How are young feminists—women and men—building a progressive feminist movement for social change? Does all the work described in this book exist in discrete pockets around the country (and around the world), or is it part of a burgeoning movement for social change that has serious potential to alter the political and economic landscape? What would unify a progressive feminist movement for change? In the past, unifying goals have included the quest for legal change (abortion rights, the Equal Rights Amendment) and the right to vote. But what are today's catalysts?

To consider this question, we also need to think about what defines our moment in history. We live in a time that academics would describe as postmodern, post-gender, post-colonial, post-this and post-that. We live in a time far removed from the dire racial and religious consequences of slavery and the Holocaust, seemingly far removed from the Vietnam War and the civil rights struggle. Ours is a time of huge technological advances that both liberate and imprison us. It is one in which political activism for social justice is not really on the mainstream radar screen. And, as Michael Hardt and Antonio Negri pointed out in their book *Empire*, "Some celebrate this new era as the liberation of the capitalist economy from the restrictions and distortions that political forces have imposed on it; others lament it as the closing of the institutional channels through which workers and citizens can influence or contest the cold logic of capitalist profit."[1] Today economic globalization is one prime catalyst for social change activists, young feminists among them. Increasingly over the past several years we have witnessed the impact of underregulated free trade and corporate corruption, as well as popular uprisings that have arisen in response to these problems. This collection illustrates the alternative avenues young feminists have forged to gain access to limited spaces in which repressed populations— including women, people of color, young people, and queer people—can act on their own behalf. Feminists are paying close attention to the ways in which power is manifested differently now than it was thirty years ago and are developing appropriate new frameworks for social justice work. The young feminists in this collection demonstrate a keen understanding of the multiple occupations necessary to envision and create a feminist world.

The work of Young Women United in Albuquerque, New Mexico, epitomizes this multi-issue approach to grassroots organizing. An organization led by and for young women of color, Young Women United focuses on sexual violence, reproductive rights, and racial and economic justice. By addressing issues of race, class, and gender in all of its programs, Young

Women United seeks to infuse its work with a multi-issue analysis. Most recently the group spearheaded a campaign against the sexual education curriculum currently taught in local public schools. Disappointed with its overwhelming emphasis on abstinence, Young Women United is advocating an educational program that will be more supportive of young women and their sexual choices. Though this campaign appears to address only gender empowerment, it is, like all the work being done by the group, infused with an analysis that addresses how race and economic class might affect sex education.

North Carolina Lambda Youth Network also employs a strong multi-issue agenda. As they put it, "NCLYN recognizes how our struggles as young people, people of color, and people of different abilities, sexualities, genders, and class backgrounds, are intimately connected. Our commitment to end homophobia includes a commitment to fighting for social justice and equality for all."[2] In addition to offering support groups and a meeting space for queer youth, lobbying the state legislature on lesbian and gay issues, and providing support services within the school system, NCLYN is a central participant in the Anti-Prison Action Coalition. The coalition provides trainings on how to combat local incidents of police brutality. It also led a successful yearlong campaign against a proposed private juvenile detention facility. By drawing connections among the experiences of various marginalized groups, NCLYN recognizes that parallel organizing efforts on many fronts will bring them closer to the world they wish to create.

Sisters in Action for Power, based in Portland, Oregon, is a multiracial organization that seeks to strengthen low-income communities and communities of color by waging campaigns on issues that affect them and encouraging young people to organize. Their campaign on transportation equity won the creation of a pilot program that will provide students who are eligible for free and reduced lunch with a free bus pass to travel to and from school. The campaign grew out of the frustration many low-income girls experienced in seeking money to get to and from school every day. In addition to targeted campaigns, Sisters in Action for Power conducts leadership training programs that include political education. By linking discussions of history and colonialism to modern-day challenges presented by globalization, Sisters in Action for Power attempts to provide a context in which participants can place their own struggles and organizing efforts.

A shared understanding of the fact that seemingly disparate issues are indeed all feminist does not mean, however, that there is consensus on how to address them. Whether all this progressive feminist motion has the capacity to turn into a social movement remains to be seen. For this to happen, there needs to be a certain amount of strategy and infrastructure (membership and advocacy organizations, networks, think tanks, media outlets, and funders) in place. In these areas, the conservative right is far ahead of the left. As Jean Hardisty noted in *Mobilizing Resentment,* the right has "exceptionally strong movement infrastructure. . . . While a movement cannot succeed without substantial mass sentiment to support it, the strength and effectiveness of its infrastructure shape its precise level of success." Communication in this context plays a pivotal role. Again, the leadership of the right provides a cue: it "is in constant discussion: working to coordinate political campaigns, recruit and mobilize new followers, and plan long-

term strategy. The right's ability to capitalize on economic inse-
curity . . . reflects in large part its leadership's ability to work col-
laboratively to build a coordinated political movement."[3]

Right now there is no shortage of progressive networks that
are either youth-centered or include large numbers of young
people; they speak to different communities and at times over-
lap. Some are local, some are regional, some are national, some
are even international.[4] These structures need to be put to good
use. Networks need to be in communication with one another,
utilized strategically, and analyzed in terms of how they relate to
major centers of power. Some have begun to do this extraordi-
narily well. In 2000 a number of progressive youth organizations
in California created a strategic coalition to fight the punitive
juvenile crime bill Proposition 21. They generated large amounts
of publicity, educated voters of all ages, mobilized youth in
unprecedented numbers, and got out the vote. Though the
proposition passed, the number of votes against it in areas where
the coalition organized were substantially higher. Perhaps more
important, this fight laid the groundwork for future campaigns
on long-term strategy issues that concern young feminists.

Diversity or Division?

One failure of progressive activism thus far has been that what
began as a call for diversity has often devolved into division. The
queer movement is over here with this agenda, and the racial justice activists are over there with that agenda. One of the reasons
the right has been so successful in this regard is that, as Hardisty
says, "by combining forces through its networks and coalitions,

each sector of the right has dramatically increased its impact. United, the secular and religious right has seized power. Separately, that would have been unlikely."[5] As feminists, and as part of a progressive movement for social change, we need to be able to deal with the tensions of a movement that is made up of many different identity and interest groups. Identity politics have been instrumental in developing a progressive movement for social change, but they have also hindered its fruition. Legal scholar Kimberlé Williams Crenshaw notes, "Feminist efforts to politicize experiences of women and antiracist efforts to politicize experiences of people of color have frequently proceeded as though the issues and experiences they detail occur on mutually exclusive terrains. Although racism and sexism readily intersect in the lives of real people, they seldom do in feminist and antiracist practices."[6] If we get stuck in the politics of identity claims, we will lose the battle for justice and equality because it will be far from our internal squabbles.

The dichotomy that Crenshaw describes has prevented a progressive movement from developing the cohesion necessary for it to endure. Because of a failure to recognize the intersections that various identity groups share, and the differences that they don't, long-term coalition-building has remained elusive. As this collection illustrates, though, young feminists readily reject the dichotomy Crenshaw describes. We hope that this new willingness to work across identity categories signals a turning point in the development of the progressive movement and will provide the staying power needed for such a movement to survive and flourish.

The work of the Audre Lorde Project illustrates this tendency to move beyond identity claims and participate in broad multi-issue coalitions. The organization provides a center for community organizing for queer people of color in New York City. But it also participates in multiracial coalition-building on issues not specific to queer people of color. It was one of the founding organizations of a coalition against police brutality and has taken public positions on issues such as the war in Iraq.

In its statement against the war, the Audre Lorde Project articulated the connection between homophobia and militarism: "We know that militarism and war rely on and promote many forms of oppression—including homophobia, transphobia, sexism, and racism. As LGBTST people, we know what it means to be targets of hate and violence. We understand what it means to be scapegoated. We believe that the ever-changing targets of the U.S. government's 'War on Terrorism' simply provide a permanent and unending list of scapegoats—distracting all of us from the challenging and necessary task of building communities and a world based on principles of peace, justice, self-determination and human dignity." Articulating the logic behind this multi-issue approach to activism is an an Audre Lorde quotation that precedes the statement: "There is no such thing as a single-issue struggle because we do not live single-issue lives."[7]

Putting Our Money Where Our Mouths Are

Money or, more accurately, access to money, plays a central role in activist work. The right has been enormously successful in building large bases of financial support among groups across the socioeconomic spectrum, as well as using foundation support in strategic and coordinated ways. In 1997 the National Committee for Responsive Philanthropy issued a report tracking the grantmaking of twelve conservative foundations. It found that "in just a three year period, the twelve foundations awarded $210 million to support a wide array of conservative projects and institutions. It is not simply the volume of money being invested that merits serious attention, but the way in which these investments have helped to build the power and influence of the conservative policy movement."[8]

Bridging the class divide has remained a challenge for progressive young activists. Being a person of wealth is often seen by middle-class and low-income activists as being in conflict with the values of left activism. Conversely, not enough young people of wealth have committed themselves to working in the trenches of social justice. This divide not only hinders our ability to build cross-class organizations but also impedes our efforts to establish diversified bases of financial support for our organizations. While the right—specifically organizations such as Focus on the Family—has been successful in creating mass-based organizations with broad-based memberships as well as incorporating the interests of the economic elite, progressives have not been as successful in reaching out to upper-class constituencies for support. Granted, doing so is considerably easier when fighting for economic justice and a more equitable redistribution of wealth are not the major underpinnings of struggle, as they are for progressives. Nonetheless, a progressive feminist movement must be cross-class if it is to succeed.

The women's funding movement, which began in the early

seventies and grew out of the women's liberation movement, has been at the forefront of social change philanthropy and provides a useful road map for young feminist activists. In many ways, it is a model of hope. Galvanized by women whose lives were transformed by the feminist movement—lower- and middle-income women as well as women of wealth—feminist philanthropists recognized that philanthropy, when done in alignment with one's values, is itself a form of activism.

In 1973, when the Ms. Foundation for Women—the first national fund devoted exclusively to funding women's projects—was created, "women's issues" wasn't even a category in the funding world. Today there are almost a hundred women's funds around the country committed to supporting social change work. Contributors include a cross-class group of people, all of whom are committed to progressive social change. As Chris Grumm, the executive director of the Women's Funding Network, a network of women's funds all over the world, says, "The women's funding movement is one of the few examples of how very diverse groups—across age, race, income level, sexuality, nationality—can come together around a single goal and achieve success. It has raised millions of dollars for women. It has gathered large amounts of money and funded important work. The women's funding movement is potentially one of the keys to the regeneration of the women's movement in this country."[9] The women's funding movement serves as a reminder of the critical role that philanthropy plays in building a social change movement.

A small group of organizations is attempting to surmount class divisions by linking progressive young people from financially privileged backgrounds with social justice organizations. Programs such as Making Money Make Change, an annual national gathering, offer wealthy young women and men an opportunity to share resources and information about activist groups and to gain skills in creating a giving plan and investing in socially responsible companies.

Given that we will soon witness the largest-ever intergenerational transfer of wealth—$41 trillion in the next fifty years—this kind of philanthropic education is more important than ever. In building feminist communities, young activists need to seek allies in both the most likely and the most unlikely of places. As Billy Wimsatt, author of *No More Prisons,* put it,

> There are 5 million millionaires in this country, and some of their kids are really down for the movement. With the unprecedented affluence of our generation, we have an unprecedented opportunity to fund movement-building on a much greater scale than has ever been imagined. And if we don't organize those rich kids, Harvard's endowment is going to get them. Harvard is the number one charity in the country and they have 400 people to raise money for them. The movement needs a fund-raising office that size. There have always been rich revolutionaries who have used their privilege as part of their strategy. If it's about power for the people, then people need to start out using the power they have.[10]

In other words, we need to recognize the full range of talents and resources—financial and otherwise—that everyone can bring to this work, regardless of socioeconomic background. In fact, we can't afford not to.

Making It Happen

We decided to put this collection together because we were looking for literature that reflected what we were doing at Third Wave and what we knew was happening all over the country. We wanted to make visible the ways young women are enacting feminism beyond the traditional models of "feminist activism." We wanted to highlight young feminist experts who are doing cutting-edge work and who are some of the leaders of our generation. And we wanted to identify the multiple endeavors that young activists understand to be inherently feminist, to broaden the public discourse about what feminist work is and who is doing it. We hope that in some small measure this book succeeds in these goals. There are many other issues and forms of activism not represented here. We have not provided a definitive map of what young feminist activism looks like today, but we hope we've offered a good sense of its broad scope.

When Third Wave was created, many people expressed surprise that four young women were starting a foundation. But, as many of the essays in this book attest, young women are doing such things and much, much more. Young feminists are not only creating new organizations, new models of organizing, and new forms of cultural work but reenvisioning the world in which we live, and placing a renewed feminism at its center.

CODA

Wilma Mankiller

The compelling essays in *The Fire This Time* dispel the popular myth that young women are apolitical, self-absorbed, and no longer interested in feminism. Young women have not lost interest in feminism. They have no interest in a singular, narrow definition of what it means to be a feminist in the twenty-first century. They want to broaden the definition of what it means to a feminist, and to reinvent feminism for their generation. They create an expanded and more interconnected definition of feminism, which includes a range of social justice and human rights issues. They make it clear they are not advocating an abandonment of core women's issues but want to view those issues within a larger context, such as global economic policies. Nowhere is the line between second wave and third wave feminists clearer than in the editors' desire to make feminism "hot, sexy, and newly revolutionary." While those of us in the second wave like to believe we were once hot, sexy, and newly revolutionary, that has never been a widely held perception of feminism.

One of the most valuable discussions in *The Fire This Time* centers on the issue of fully including women of color in third wave feminism. Few would argue that women of color have been excluded from second wave feminism. The concern is that mere inclusion of women of color did not materially change the definition of core feminist issues in second wave feminism. Third wave feminism's goal is to embrace a wide range of issues facing women of color, particularly low-income women. The editors again draw a thin but significant line between second wave feminism and third wave feminism by stating, "We see a new movement evolving from one in which there is a dialogue *about* feminism and race to a feminist movement whose conversation *is* race, gender, and globalization."

While reading these essays, I repeatedly murmured, "I didn't know that." I learned about the growing trend toward independent media, about hip-hop theater, about the contemporary version of Emma Goldman's brand of anarchism. I was fascinated by girl zines, and inspired by the courage of the young women working for a more equitable criminal justice system. I like a young justice organizer's quotation: "I don't fight the prison industry because I am a feminist, but because I am a human being." And I love the rap poem with the opening line "Your revolution will not happen between these thighs," a takeoff on Gil-Scott Heron's "The Revolution Will Not Be Televised." The essay on how women could use new technology to advance gender equity is full of intriguing data. I was angered to learn about the U.S. Navy's forced removal of Vieques families from their communities and homes in order to occupy their land for military purposes. The story is strikingly similar to that of the U.S. government's military removal of indigenous people from their homelands.

The thoughtful discussion of the anti-immigration movement helps describe the senselessness of anti-immigration laws in a country settled by immigrants. Several nations of indigenous people in the American Southwest have traveled back and forth across what is now a restrictive border between the United States and Mexico. The United States has long exploited any marketable natural resource of Mexico and Central and South America, displacing indigenous people and disrupting local economies. As people from these countries have sought jobs and residency in the United States, they have been met with the range of nonsensical anti-immigration arguments described here.

One cannot possibly read this book without feeling very confident that younger feminists will help move us closer to gender equity as they work on a wide range of social justice issues. This revised feminist movement has replaced the goal of having white women in power reach out to women of color with the goal of having women of color as full partners in leading the movement and framing its issues. Younger feminists have many challenges ahead of them. With the creativity, intellect, and compassion expressed in *The Fire This Time*, they are more than ready to face those challenges.

RECOMMENDED ORGANIZATIONS

Get Involved!
Here are some of the organizations, publications, and other media doing new feminist work. The list begins with a group of feminist foundations that provide general information and can direct you to technical and financial resources. The rest of the list is grouped by topic to correspond with the order of the chapters in this book. If there's not an organization in your area, start your own.

FEMINIST FOUNDATIONS

The Global Fund for Women
1375 Sutter Street, Suite 400
San Francisco, CA 94109
(415) 202-7640
(415) 202-8604 (fax)
www.globalfundforwomen.org
gfw@globalfundforwomen.org

The Global Fund is a grantmaking organization that supports women's human rights organizations around the world that address critical issues such as economic independence for women, girls' access to education, and violence against women.

Ms. Foundation for Women
120 Wall Street, 33rd floor
New York, NY 10005
(212) 742-2300
(212) 742-1653 (fax)
www.ms.foundation.org
info@ms.foundation.org

The Ms. Foundation for Women supports the efforts of women and girls to govern their own lives and influence the world around them. Through its leadership, expertise, and financial support, the Foundation champions an equitable society by effecting change in public consciousness, law, philanthropy, and social policy.

The Sister Fund
116 East 16th Street, 7th Floor
New York, NY 10003
(212) 260-4446
(212) 260-4633 (fax)
www.sisterfund.org
info@sisterfund.org

The Sister Fund is a private fund that supports programs promoting women's social, economic, political, and spiritual growth. Through their grantmaking, The Sister Fund responds to problems of racial and gender discrimination, AIDS, violence against women, growing inequality, and widespread poverty. They give primary consideration to organizations that are led by women most affected by oppression, especially women of color, lesbians, and economically disadvantaged older or disabled women.

Third Wave Foundation
511 West 25th Street, Suite 301
New York, NY 10001
(212) 675-0700
(212) 255-6653 (fax)
www.thirdwavefoundation.org
info@thirdwavefoundation.org

The only national young feminist organization in the country, the Third Wave Foundation operates on the premise that young women are at the forefront of many social justice movements. Their inspired visions and innovative strategies have continuously pushed boundaries in society and opened new doors of equality and justice, yet their work has often been ignored by society. The Third Wave Foundation helps support the leadership of young women fifteen to thirty by providing technical and financial resources, public education, and relationship-building opportunities.

The Women's Funding Network
1375 Sutter Street, Suite 406
San Francisco, CA 94109
(415) 441-0706
www.wfnet.org

The Women's Funding Network is an international partnership of women's and girls' foundations, donors, and allies that works to increase available funds for feminist and other social justice work. There are member organizations, foundations, and women's funds located throughout the U.S. and in several other countries.

HIP-HOP AND SOCIAL JUSTICE

The Active Element Foundation
532 LaGuardia Place #510
New York, NY 10012
(212) 283-5622
(212) 694-9573 (fax)
www.activeelement.org
info@activeelement.org

The Active Element Foundation provides grants and philanthropic education to support arts, media, and youth organizing for social and economic justice. Active Element refers to the original four elements of hip-hop identified by Afrika Bambaataa in the 1970s (Rap, Breakdancing, Graffiti, and DJing). The foundation conducts extensive grassroots research to identify emerging leaders. It currently has the largest database of young activists in the United States.

Critical Breakdown
American Friends Service Committee
2161 Massachusetts Avenue
Cambridge, MA 02140
(617) 661-6130
(617) 354-2832 (fax)
www.afsc.org/newengland/critbrk.htm
afscnero@afsc.org

Critical Breakdown is a monthly free, nonalcoholic event that brings people together with hip-hop, spoken word, and other forms of socially conscious performance art.

FreeStyle Union
Founder: Toni Blackman
Washington, DC
www.freestyleunion.org
freestyleunion-subscribe@lists.riseup.net

FreeStyle Union provides a forum for creating community and developing awareness of the global cultural movement through people who create ritual environments in music, art, movement, crafts, and the sustainability of subculture.

Urban Think Tank Institute
P.O. Box 1476
New York, NY 10185-1476
(718) 670-3739
www.UrbanThinkTank.org
UrbanThinkTank@usa.net

Urban Think Tank Institute is a nonpartisan, community-based home for a body of thinkers in the hip-hop generation. It examines political, economic, and cultural issues, particularly those of concern to people of color, and it uses a multimedia strategy to encourage an open dialogue and to influence public policy. The institute publishes the quarterly magazine *Doula: The Journal of Rap Music and Hip Hop Culture.*

INDEPENDENT MEDIA

Allied Media Projects
P.O. Box 20128
Toledo, OH 43610
(419) 243-4688
www.alliedmediaprojects.org
info@alliedmediaprojects.org

Allied Media Projects is building a network of participatory media producers and organizations so the world can know what people—not corporations or political parties—are saying, singing, rapping, writing, painting, sculpting, scratching, and filming. Launched by the editors of *Clamor Magazine,* AMP also organizes the annual Allied Media Conference in Bowling Green, Ohio.

Center for International Media Action

1276 Bergen Street #4
Brooklyn, NY 11213
(646) 249-3027
(815) 642-0801 (fax)
www.mediaactioncenter.org
cima@mediaactioncenter.org

The Center for International Media Action is a not-for-profit organization that offers strategic services and tools to strengthen cooperation among media advocacy, education, and reform groups. CIMA develops and distributes publications, curricula, workshops, and online information-sharing tools to help diversify participants in media policy debates.

FAIR
(Fairness and Accuracy in Reporting)

112 West 27th Street
New York, NY 10001
(212) 633-6700
(212) 727-7668 (fax)
www.fair.org
fair@fair.org

FAIR, the national media watch group, has been offering well-documented criticism of media bias and censorship since 1986. FAIR works to invigorate the First Amendment by advocating for greater diversity in the press and by scrutinizing media practices that marginalize public interest, minority, and dissenting viewpoints. As an anticensorship organization, it exposes neglected news stories and defends journalists when their work is restricted or suppressed. FAIR believes that structural reform is ultimately needed to break up dominant media conglomerates, establish independent public broadcasting, and promote strong nonprofit sources of information.

Indymedia
www.indymedia.org

Indymedia is a network of collectively run media outlets, called Independent Media Centers (IMCs), that encourage communities to report their own news. The first IMC was a single newsroom that independent media at the Seattle WTO protests in November, 1999 shared; there are now over 125 IMCs around the world, publishing in more than twenty languages.

W.E.R.I.S.E.
(Women Empowered through Revolutionary Ideas Supporting Enterprise)
111 East 14th Street #392
New York, NY
(212) 561-9746
www.werise.org
werise@hotmail.com

W.E.R.I.S.E. provides forums, workshops, events, and venues where women can share information, educate one another, realize their artistic potential, and benefit financially from their efforts. The community encourages women to use their skills as artists and organizers to empower themselves by creating their own spaces, venues, collectives, organizations, and businesses in the arts. W.E.R.I.S.E. also organizes the annual International Women Artists Conference in New York City.

ZINES

Bamboo Girl
Sabrina Margarita Alcantara-Tan
P.O. Box 507
New York, NY 10159-0507
www.bamboogirl.com

Bamboo Girl is an independent print publication, printed as often as financially possible—either annually or biannually—and funded in part by yearly Bamboo Girl Zine Benefit Parties. Bamboo Girl challenges racism, sexism, and homophobia from the Filipina/Asian Pacific Islander (API)/ Asian mutt feminist point of view.

Fierce
595 Piedmont Avenue
Suites 320–321
Atlanta, GA 30308
(404) 412-8000
www.fiercemag.com

Fierce is a revolutionary print and online magazine with an urban and multicultural spin for all women over twenty-one (and young, smart, edgy chicks over eighteen). The editors believe women are smart, curious, and opinionated about more than the usual glossy magazine topics and seek to provide a place for them—especially women of color—to express their individuality.

Hip Mama
Print:
Ariel Gore
P.O. Box 12525
Portland, OR 97212
Online:
Bee Lavender
P.O. Box 28870
Seattle, WA 98118
www.hipmama.com

Hip Mama is a magazine bursting with political commentary and ribald tales from the front lines of motherhood. Published in print and online, the zine started as a forum for young mothers, single parents, and marginalized voices, but has grown to represent progressive families of all varieties. *Hip Mama*'s editorial vision qualified it for the title "conservative America's worst nightmare."

Nervy Girl
Nervy Girl Magazine
P.O. Box 33100

Portland, OR 97292-3100
(503) 256-3789
(503) 257-3091 (fax)
www.nervygirlzine.com
editors@nervygirlzine.com

Nervy Girl is a challenging, engaging, and edgy Portland-based e-zine for women. It publishes news, features, poetry, first-person essays, and reviews, keeping women informed about politics, business, and technology as well as popular culture.

Zine World

P.O. Box 330156
Murfreesboro, TN 37133-0156
www.undergroundpress.org
jerianne@undergroundpress.org

Zine World features news, small-press reviews, letters, and other information you can't find anywhere else. The guide's staff is excited about the potential of the free press, and they want to tell you everything they know about it—which zines are terrific (and which aren't); how you can find underground books, papers, videos, and websites on exactly the topics you're interested in; and news about people who are threatened, sued, expelled from school, or jailed for what they've said or written. *Zine World* is an excellent resource for publishers, writers, artists, videomakers, and anyone who's up to anything interesting.

HIP-HOP THEATER

BLACKOUT Arts Collective

1576 Tomlinson Avenue
Bronx, NY 10461
(917) 548-5116
www.blackoutartscollective.com
bacdatabase@hotmail.com

The BLACKOUT Arts Collective is a nonprofit organization with chapters in eight U.S. cities. It brings together artists and activists to address social, political, and economic issues, and to develop solutions for critical concerns facing communities of color. Their work focuses on the expanding prison industrial complex, police brutality, domestic violence, the arts in public schools, and voter registration.

NYC Hip-Hop Theater Festival
532 LaGuardia Place #409
New York, NY 10012
(718) 782-2621
(718) 782-1246 (fax)
www.hiphoptheaterfest.com
info@hiphoptheaterfest.com

The NYC Hip-Hop Theater Festival is committed to the creation and production of theater that addresses the sociopolitical issues of its target audience: underserved youth and young urbanites. The Festival presents and supports live events created by artists who stretch, invent, and combine a variety of theatrical forms, including theater, dance, spoken word, and live music sampling.

Youth Speaks
Youth Speaks @ The Box Factory
A New Literary Arts Center for the Bay Area
2169 Folsom Street
San Francisco, CA 94110
(415) 255-9035
(415) 255-9065 (fax)
www.youthspeaks.org
info@youthspeaks.org

Youth Speaks, founded in San Francisco in 1996, now has bases in New York City, San Francisco, and Seattle. It is the premiere youth poetry, spoken word, and creative writing program in the country. It provides free after-school workshops and organizes and produces poetry slams, literary arts festivals, documentaries, and videos. Combining public performance and publication opportunities with educational workshops, mentoring, and cooperative learning, Youth Speaks is committed to creating spaces that celebrate the youth voice.

WOMEN AND TECHNOLOGY

Institute for Women and Technology
1501 Page Mill Road, ms 1105
Palo Alto, CA 94304
(650) 236-4756
(650) 852-8172 (fax)
www.iwt.org
info@iwt.org

The Institute for Women and Technology works to create a world in which technology serves everyone in a positive way. It supports women's active involvement in all aspects of technology, and also seeks to assure both that women's needs are considered in the development of every technology, and that government, industry, and academic technology policies fully account for women.

Society of Women Engineers
230 East Ohio Street, Suite 400
Chicago, IL 60611-3265
(312) 596-5223
(312) 596-5252 (fax)
www.societyofwomenengineers.org

The Society of Women Engineers is the largest nonprofit educational and service organization that represents student and professional women in engineering and technical fields. Its mission is to stimulate women to achieve their full potential in careers as engineers and leaders, expand the image of the engineering profession as a positive force for improving the quality of life, and demonstrate the value of diversity in the field.

CLOSE THE SCHOOL OF THE AMERICAS AND STOP PLAN COLOMBIA

Colombia Support Network
P.O. Box 1505
Madison, WI 53701
(608) 257-8753
(608) 255-6621 (fax)

www.colombiasupport.net
csn@igc.org

Colombia Support Network is a grassroots organization that offers solidarity with the Colombian people through sister city projects and a variety of initiatives to educate members of the U.S. government and the general public. It also has an Urgent Action service to mobilize action in emergency situations.

Latin American Working Group
110 Maryland Avenue NE
Washington, DC 20002
(202) 546-7010
www.lawg.org
lawg@lawg.org

The Latin America Working Group is one of the nation's longest-standing coalitions dedicated to influencing foreign policy. Along with its sister organization, the Latin America Working Group Education Fund, LAWG encourages U.S. policies toward Latin America that promote human rights, justice, peace, and sustainable development. As a coalition, LAWG represents the interests of over sixty major religious, humanitarian, grassroots, and policy organizations to Washington, D.C. decision makers. Well-respected by Congress, the group provides reliable guidance to policy makers who want their decisions to be grounded in human rights.

The North American Congress on Latin America (NACLA)
38 Greene Street, 4th Floor
New York, NY 10013
(646) 613-1440
(646) 613-1443 (fax)
www.nacla.org

The North American Congress on Latin America is an independent nonprofit organization founded in 1966. Policy makers, analysts, academics, organizers, journalists, and religious and community groups turn to it for information on major trends in Latin America and its relations with the United States. The core of the NACLA's work is its bimonthly magazine

Nacla Report on the Americas, the most widely read English language publication on Latin America.

School of the Americas Watch
P.O. Box 4566
Washington, DC 20017
(202) 234-3440
(202) 636-4505 (fax)
www.soaw.org
info@soaw.org

School of the Americas Watch is an independent organization that seeks to close the U.S. Army School of the Americas, under whatever name it is called, through vigils and fasts, demonstrations and nonviolent protest, as well as media and legislative work.

SOA Watch/Northeast
(215) 477-5892
(215) 473-2162
www.soawne.org
info@soawne.org

SOA Watch/NE is a grassroots organization committed to working in solidarity with the poor. It educates the public and Congress about atrocities committed by graduates of the School of the Americas. The website offers many resources for potential organizers and activists, including a media guide, internships at its headquarters, and online links to organizations working on related issues.

DOMESTIC WORKERS' RIGHTS

Andolan: Organizing South Asian Workers
P.O. Box 2087
Long Island City, NY 11102
(718) 350-7264
(718) 728-1768 (fax)
andolan_organizing@yahoo.com

Founded in 1998 by low-wage South Asian immigrant workers, Andolan is a nongovernmental, membership-based group that organizes and advocates on behalf of immigrant South Asian workers. It helps working-class communities with language barriers, discrimination, and immigration status, and supports their self-empowerment. Most of Andolan's members are employed as babysitters, housekeepers, and restaurant workers.

DAMAYAN Migrant Workers Association
c/o Metro Baptist Church
406 West 40th Street, Second Floor
New York, NY 10018
(212) 564-6057
www.damayanmigrants.org
contact@damayanmigrants.org

Damayan is a Filipino word that means helping each other. DAMAYAN Migrant Workers Association is an independent nonprofit grassroots organization for migrant workers in New York, New Jersey, and Connecticut. It aims to educate, mobilize, and organize migrant workers to promote and uphold their rights and welfare, to work for social justice for all working people, and to understand the root cause of migration.

Women of Color Resource Center
1611 Telegraph Avenue #303
Oakland, CA 94612
(510) 444-2700
(510) 444-2711 (fax)
www.coloredgirls.org
info@coloredgirls.org

Founded in 1990, the Women of Color Resource Center is headquartered in the San Francisco Bay Area and promotes the political, economic, social, and cultural well-being of women and girls of color in the United States. It is committed to organizing and educating women of color across lines of race, ethnicity, religion, nationality, class, sexual orientation, physical ability, and age.

Women Workers Project of CAAAV
(Committee Against Anti-Asian Violence)
2473 Valentine Avenue
Bronx, NY 10458
www.caaav.org
justice@caaav.org

Women Workers Project organizes Asian immigrant women working in the growing New York City service sectors of domestic work, nail salons, and laundries, among others. It also mobilizes Asian women workers to oppose racist immigration practices and promotes policies that support human rights and dignity for all.

UNITED STATES MILITARY OUT OF VIEQUES

ProLibertad
P.O. Box 477
New York, NY 10159-0477
(718) 601-4751
(718) 601-3909 (fax)
http://prolibertadweb.tripod.com
prolibertad@hotmail.com

The ProLibertad Freedom Campaign is a New York–based anti-imperialist and anticolonialist organization that supports the release of all United States political prisoners and opposes the United States' colonial control of Puerto Rico and its military presence in Vieques. It publishes a newsletter called *El Coqui Libre,* organizes fund-raisers, coordinates campaign donations, promotes lobbying, and helps youth organizations and student groups organize.

Red Betances
100 Gran Bulevar Paseos
Suite 112–293
San Juan, Puerto Rico 00926
www.redbetances.com
editores@redbetances.com

Red Betances is a comprehensive Spanish language website devoted to public awareness of Puerto Rico and the Puerto Rican independence movement.

Vieques Libre
www.viequeslibre.org

Vieques Libre is a website and newsletter dedicated to the liberation of Vieques. It contains articles in both Spanish and English, and includes news updates, historical information, articles, information on activist campaigns, and relevant links.

Vieques Support Campaign
402 West 145th Street
New York, NY 10031
www.viequessupport.org
contactus@viequessupport.org

The Vieques Support Campaign works to build support for the people's struggle on the island municipality of Vieques, Puerto Rico. The VSC was created after the April 19, 1999 target practice "accident" that claimed the life of David Sanes Rodrigues and injured four others. It seeks to get the U.S. Navy out of Vieques and opposes U.S. military intervention anywhere in the world.

TRANSGENDERS, FEMINISM, AND THE LAW

Survivor Project
P.O. Box 40664
Portland, OR 97240
(503) 288-3191
www.survivorproject.org
info@survivorproject.org

Survivor Project is a nonprofit organization dedicated to addressing the needs of intersex and trans survivors of domestic and sexual violence by offering workshops, consultations, access to resources, and opportunities for action. It also helps shelters and other agencies better serve intersex and trans survivors.

Transgender Law and Policy Institute
(917) 686-7663 or (415) 595-2125
www.transgenderlaw.org
info@transgenderlaw.org

The Transgender Law and Policy Institute is a nonprofit organization that brings experts and advocates together to work on law and policy initiatives designed to advance transgender equality. The TLPI tracks developments in legal and public policy issues that affect transgender people and their families, and provides summaries of these trends for activists, policy makers, and the media; offers legal, medical, and social science resources to attorneys and others who advocate on behalf of transgender individuals; and makes litigation, legislative, and education advocacy materials available for advocates of transgender people.

The Transgender Law Project
1800 Market Street, Suite 408
San Francisco, CA 94102
(415) 865-5619 or (415) 865-0176
(415) 865-5601 (fax)
www.transgenderlawcenter.org
info@transgenderlawcenter.org

The Transgender Law Center is a civil rights organization for transgender communities. The Center connects transgender people and their families to technically sound and culturally competent legal services. It also works to increase acceptance and enforcement of laws and policies that support California's transgender communities, and to change laws and systems that fail to incorporate the needs and experiences of transgender people.

GENDER, IMMIGRATION, REPRODUCTION, AND THE ENVIRONMENT

Committee on Women, Population and the Environment
P.O. Box 16178
Baltimore, MD 21218
www.cwpe.org
info@cwpe.org

The Committee on Women, Population and the Environment is a multi-racial alliance of feminist activists, health practitioners, and scholars that advocate the social and economic empowerment of women in a context of global peace and justice. CWPE supports women's rights to safe, voluntary birth control and abortion, while strongly opposing demographically driven population policies; challenges the belief that population growth is the primary cause of environmental degradation, conflict, and growing poverty; and works to provide a broader analysis that reflects the complexity of these issues and locates the true causes in a global economic system based on exploitation, profit, and consumerism, the structures of patriarchy and racism that underlie it, and the militarism that enforces and perpetuates it.

National Network for Immigrant and Refugee Rights
310 Eighth Street, Suite 303
Oakland, CA 94607
(510) 465-1984
(510) 465-1885 (fax)
www.nnirr.org
nnirr@nnirr.org

The National Network for Immigrant and Refugee Rights is comprised of local coalitions and immigrant, refugee, community, religious, civil rights, and labor organizations and activists. It serves as a forum for sharing information and analysis, educating the public, and developing and coordinating action on important immigrant and refugee issues. It works to promote a just immigration and refugee policy in the United States and to defend and expand the rights of all immigrants and refugees, regardless of immigration status.

Political Research Associates
1310 Broadway, Suite 201
Somerville, MA 02144
(617) 666-5300
(617) 666-6622 (fax)
www.publiceye.org
pra@igc.org

Political Research Associates is an independent, nonprofit research center that studies antidemocratic, authoritarian, and other oppressive movements, institutions, and trends. PRA is based on progressive values, and is committed to advancing an open, democratic, and pluralistic society. PRA provides accurate, reliable research and analysis, as well as extensive directories and resource information, to activists, journalists, educators, policy makers, and the public at large.

THE PRISON INDUSTRIAL COMPLEX

Bay Area PoliceWatch
Ella Baker Center for Human Rights
1230 Market Street
PMB #409
San Francisco, CA 94102
(415) 951-4844
(415) 951-4813 (fax)
www.ellabakercenter.org/pages/police.html

Low-income communities and communities of color are routinely policed by heavily armed officers subject to little or no civilian oversight. Transgressions of civil rights have occurred with greater frequency and Bay Area PoliceWatch is addressing them by documenting, exposing, and challenging police violence in the San Francisco Bay Area. PoliceWatch operates a misconduct hotline, documentation center, and lawyer referral service for survivors of police abuse, and offers a lawyer training program to help attorneys take on and win police misconduct cases.

Center for Young Women's Development
1550 Bryant Street, Suite 700
San Francisco, CA 94103
(415) 703-8800
(415) 703-8818 (fax)
www.cywd.org
cywd@cywd.org

The Center for Young Women's Development is a nonprofit organization in San Francisco whose mission is to provide gender-specific, peer-based opportunities for high-risk low- and no-income young women to build healthier lives and healthier communities. It provides referrals and "street law" training, and offers employment training programs to ensure that young women who have been homeless, incarcerated, involved in the juvenile justice system, or severely limited by poverty are able to achieve self-sufficiency and become positively engaged in their communities.

Critical Resistance

National Office
1904 Franklin Street, Suite 504
Oakland, CA 94612
(510) 444-0484
(510) 444-2177 (fax)
www.criticalresistance.org
crnational@criticalresistance.org

Critical Resistance seeks to build an international movement to end the prison industrial complex by challenging the belief that caging and controlling people makes us safe. It believes that basic necessities such as food, shelter, and freedom are what make communities secure. CR's local organizing across the country ranges from providing services for prisoners' children, to developing political education curricula and trainings, to producing publications, videos, and film festivals, to grassroots organizing with local communities. There are Critical Resistance chapters in Los Angeles, Oakland, Western Massachusetts, New Haven, Washington, D.C., and Kentucky.

Prison Activist Resource Center

P.O. Box 339
Berkeley, CA 94701
(510) 893-4648
(510) 893-4607 (fax)
www.prisonactivist.org
parc@prisonactivist.org

The Prison Activist Resource Center exposes and challenges the institutionalized racism of the criminal justice system. The Center provides support for educators, activists, prisoners, and prisoners' families. It also builds networks for action and produces materials that expose human rights violations.

Prison Moratorium Project
388 Atlantic Avenue, 3rd Floor
Brooklyn, NY 11217
(718) 260-8805
(718) 260-0070 (fax)
www.nomoreprisons.org
info@nomoreprisons.org

The Prison Moratorium Project seeks to build a future beyond prisons. PMP was formed in 1995 to end prison expansion and promote a youth voice in the criminal justice policy debate. PMP has mobilized opposition to prison development, built ties between rural and urban youth, and helped achieve change in New York State budget spending patterns.

NOTES

INTRODUCTION

1 Sister Outsider, Sista II Sista, Sisters in Action for Power, Third Wave Foundation, Center for Young Women's Development, Young Women United, and the Audre Lorde Project are just a few young-women-led organizations. Many more such projects exist around the country.

2 Rebecca Walker, *To Be Real: Telling the Truth and Changing the Face of Feminism* (New York: Anchor Books, 1995), xxxvi.

3 Jennifer Drake and Leslie Heywood, eds., *Third Wave Agenda: Being Feminist, Doing Feminism* (Minneapolis: University of Minnesota Press, 1997), 2.

4 Angela P. Harris, "Race and Essentialism in Feminist Legal Theory," *Stanford Law Review* 42 (February 1990), 581.

5 Kum-Kum Bhavnani, ed., *Feminism and "Race"* (Oxford and New York: Oxford University Press, 2001), 5.

6 Quoted in ibid., 89.

7 Alice Walker, *In Search of Our Mothers' Gardens* (New York: Harcourt Brace, 1984), xii.

8 Ann J. Tickner, *Gendering World Politics* (New York: Columbia University Press, 2001), 66.

CLAIMING JEZEBEL

1 Officially titled "The Negro Family: The Case for National Action" and written in 1965.

2 In 1987 Tawana Brawley was found in upstate New York covered with racial slurs and charcoal. She alleged that a gang of six white police officers

had "abducted and held her for four days in the woods, raping her repeatedly, writing KKK and NIGGER on her belly, smearing her with dog feces and leaving her in a plastic garbage bag outside an apartment complex where her family had once lived," but a grand jury found her story to lack credibility. See http://www.time.com/time/magazine/1998/dom/980727/file.stories_sacred_lies18.html.

3 bell hooks, *Black Looks: Race and Representation* (Boston: South End Press, 1992), 127.

4 Ibid., 64.

5 Tricia Rose, *Black Noise: Rap Music and Black Culture in Contemporary America* (Middletown, Conn.: Wesleyan University Press, 1994), 2.

6 Ibid., 9.

7 The stereotypical depiction of the black female body as licentious during the nineteenth century was one of two primary stereotypes.

8 Jan Nederveen Pieterse, *White on Black: Images of Africa and Blacks in Western Popular Culture* (New Haven: Yale University Press, 1992), 181.

9 Roseann M. Mandzuik, "Feminist Politics and Postmodern Seductions: Madonna and the Struggle," in *The Madonna Connection: Representational Politics, Subcultural Identities, and Cultural Theory,* ed. Cathy Schwichtenberg (Boulder, Colo.: Westview Press, 1993), 183–84.

10 Quoted in Charisse Nikole, "Invisible Women," *Blaze,* April 1999, 68.

11 Michelle Buford and Christopher John Farley, "Foxy's Dilemma," *Essence,* August 1999, 72.

AN INDEPENDENT MEDIA CENTER OF ONE'S OWN

Our notes are extensive because we usually write in hypertext, where additional information can be placed a mere click away. We have included references to Internet sites wherever possible, often because that is where we found our information and always because that is where we hope you will find more. If you have any comments, questions, suggestions, or responses, you can contact us at ana@indymedia.org and breitbart@indymedia.org.

1 Rebecca Farmer, "National Organization for Women to Protest Inauguration on January 20" (press release), 5 January 2001, http://www.now.org/press/12-00/01-05-00.html.

2 Jim Naureckas, "Protesters Rain on ABC's Parade," *Extra!* March–April 2001, http://www.fair.org/extra/0103/abc-parade.html.

3 For a compilation of IMC coverage of George W. Bush's Inauguration Day, see http://dc.indymedia.org/j20.php3.

4 L.A. Kauffman, "Militants and Moderates," *Free Radical* 15 (January 2001), http://www.free-radical.org/issue15.shtml.

5 The Black Bloc is a loose international affiliation of autonomous groups and individuals who use similar protest tactics, most notably but not always or exclusively wearing black clothing and masks, destroying property, and fighting back against violent police forces. It is also one of the more inscrutable elements of the antiglobalization movement; any brief definition of this often maligned group is necessarily inadequate. For a more in-depth perspective, see "Letter from Inside the Black Bloc," published on Alternet.org in the aftermath of the G8 protests in Genoa, Italy, July 25, 2001, http://alternet.org/story.html?StoryID=11230.

6 Kauffman, "Militants and Moderates."

7 Katherine Ainger, "Empires of the Senseless," *New Internationalist* 333 (April 2001).

8 Quoted in ibid.

9 Reed Hundt, quoted in "Speaking with One Voice: Does Media Cross-Ownership Stifle Diversity?" *Freedom Forum,* December 2000, http://www.freedomforum.org/templates/document.asp?documentID=3183.

10 "News Corporation 1999 Annual Report," cited in "Ultra-Concentrated Media: The Media Ownership Chart," ed. Granville Williams, MediaChannel.org, http://www.mediachannel.org/ownership/chart.shtml.

11 Quoted in *New Internationalist* 333 (April 2001), http://www.newint.org/issue333/facts.htm, and "Ultra-Concentrated Media: The Media Ownership Chart," ed. Granville Williams, MediaChannel.org, http://www.mediachannel.org/ownership/chart.shtml.

12 Consolidation of media ownership is happening at such a fast pace that we dare not list the current information czars. By the time this book comes out, the media landscape will look significantly different than it does right now—we hope for the better but probably for the worse. We suggest the latest edition of Ben Bagdikian's *The Media Monopoly* (Boston: Beacon Press, first published in 1983). You can also visit the Project on Media Ownership at http://www.promo.org or the *Columbia Journalism Review*'s "Who Owns What" at http://www.cjr.org/owners/index.asp.

13 Quoted in "What Women Want: AOL Takes a Cue from Female Subscribers," July 2001, http://www.timewarner.com/focuson/aolwomen.html (link inactive).

14 Gloria Steinem, "Sex, Lies and Advertising," in *Moving Beyond Words* (New York: Simon & Schuster, 1994), 147.

15 The decline in circulation, though not cheerful news, should not be taken as a barometer of feminism, or even of the magazine exactly. Early on, the print run was greatly inflated as part of the fruitless attempt to attract advertisers.

16 G. Spears, K. Seydegart, and Margaret Gallagher, "Global Media Monitoring Project 2000: The Results," *Media and Gender Monitor* 7 (2000) July 2000, http://www.wacc.org.uk/publications/mgm/07/gmmp_results.html.

17 Ibid.

18 Ibid.

19 Jennifer Pozner, interview with the authors, 1 June 2001. Thanks also to Ms. Pozner for her suggestions for further research.

20 Greg Ruggiero, "Re: Draft of a Proposal for an IMC Encuentro in 2000," e-mail to Joshua Breitbart, 29 October 2000.

21 Tom Regan, "The Mosquitos and the Elephants," *Christian Science Monitor,* 9 December 1999, http://www.csmonitor.com/atcsmonitor/cybercoverage/bandwidth/p-120799mosquito.html.

22 Those IMCs without websites organize their independent media movements using face-to-face strategies, including video making, newspaper printing and distribution, and other means of information distribution.

23 Sheri Herndon, e-mail discussions, Seattle IMC, 2000, http://lists.indymedia.org.

24 The proposed Free Trade Area of the Americas would combine all the countries of the Western Hemisphere except Cuba into the largest free trade zone in the world, with a population of 800 million and a combined gross domestic product of $11 trillion (USD). The Organization of American States met April 20–22, 2001, in Quebec City to negotiate the agreement. Despite restricted access through the U.S.–Canada border and the construction of a ten-foot-high fence around the section of the city where the meetings were being held, an estimated eighty thousand people were there to protest the proposal and the secretive process of negotiations. For an index of further readings, see the FTAA Educational Materials page of the Stop the FTAA website, http://www.stopftaa.org/info/index.html, especially Maude Barlow, "The Free Trade Area of the Americas and the Threat to Social Programs, Environmental Sustainability and Social Justice in Canada and the Americas" (also available on the Council of Canadians website, http://www.canadians.org/campaigns/campaigns-tradepub-ftaa2.html).

25 The Group of Eight, or G8, is a meeting of the leaders of some of the world's most economically influential nations—the United States, France, the United Kingdom, Germany, Russia, Japan, Italy, and Canada—to discuss and coordinate their nations' policies. For more information, start with Patrick Beckett, "Seeking Change in Genoa," http://la.indymedia.org/display.php3?article_id=8772. For IMC coverage of the 2001 G8 protests in Genoa, see http://italy.indymedia.org.

26 Regan, "Mosquitos and the Elephants." He adds, "But even on the issue of covering the protests, the mosquitos [alternative media] were often ahead of the elephants [corporate media], providing edgy, fresh, dramatic video of the events, compared to repeated footage of a couple of incidents and interviews with establishment talking heads that the network and cable news operations favored."

27 Image URL: http://nyc.indymedia.org/front.php3?article_id=6920.

28 For their mission statement and self-description, see http://chiapas.indymedia.org/about.php3.

29 Reynalda Pablo Cruz, "Women's Denouncement of Violence in San Jose, Marques de Comillas: Chronicle of the Police Action in Marques de Comillas on July 27th and Its Impact on the Women of the Community," *Chiapas IMC*, 30 July 2001, http://chiapas.indymedia.org/display.php3?article_id=101385.

30 Donna Allen, "Women News," *Quill,* May 1991, 36–37.

31 Ibid. (Also see www.reporttowomen.com.)

32 Madhava, "Reclaim the Streets, Reclaim the Code," *Punk Planet* 43 (May–June 2001), 102.

33 Norman Solomon, "The Media Battle of Seattle," in *Censored 2000: The Year's Top 25 Censored Stories,* eds. Peter Phillips et al. (New York: Seven Stories Press, 2000), 212–13.

34 Michael Eisenmenger, "Re: Strategies, TV Programming Alert," Strategies Listserv, strategies@lists.myspinach.org (closed subscribership), 1 March 2001. For information on the Paper Tiger TV collective, see http://www.papertiger.org.

35 Governments and corporations have taken steps to limit Indymedia's reach by attempting to suppress their capacity to report the news, distribute information, and have office space. A Seattle IMC press release about a subpoena delivered to them during the Quebec City protests can be found at http://seattle.indymedia.org/display.php3?article_id=3013. For coverage of the raid on the Italy IMC during the G8 protests, see http://sf.indymedia.org/display.php?id=102064.

36 *Zapatista Encuentro: Documents from the Encounter for Humanity and Against Neoliberalism* (New York: Seven Stories Press, 1998), 53–54.

37 Naomi Klein, "The Unknown Icon," *The Guardian,* 3 March 2001, http://www.guardian.co.uk/weekend/story/0,3605,445513,00.html.

CUT-AND-PASTE REVOLUTION

1 Elizabeth Snead, "Feminist Riot Girls Don't Just Wanna Have Fun," *USA Today,* 7 August 1992, 5D.

2 Margot Mifflin, "Girlzines Attract New Feminist Breed," *Dallas Morning News,* 26 November 1995, 5F.

3 Naomi Klein, *No Logo* (New York: Picador, 1999), 72–73.

4 Michelle Goldberg, "Feminism for Sale," *Alternet,* 8 January 2001, http://www.alternet.org/story.html?StoryID=10306.

5 Tanja's last name was unavailable.

6 U.S. Department of Commerce, *Falling Through the Net: Toward Digital Inclusion* (Washington, D.C., 2000).

7 National Telecommunications and Information Administration, *A Nation Online: How Americans Are Expanding Their Use of the Internet,* 5 February 2002 (Washington, D.C.), http://www.ntia.doc.gov/ntiahome/dn/html/toc.htm.

8 See http://www.thirdwavefoundation.org/programs/summer00.pdf for more information about Black Grrrl Revolution.

CAN YOU ROCK IT LIKE THIS?

1 Performances include Theater Artaud in San Francisco, the American Dance Festival in Durham, North Carolina, the Joyce Theater in New York, and Dance Umbrella and the Lyceum in the United Kingdom.

2 Suzanne Carbonneau, "Verona as Philadelphia, Shakespeare as an M.C.," *New York Times,* 24 September 2000, late ed., 2.

3 Deborah Jowitt, "Homeboy Shakespeare," *Village Voice,* 13–19 September 2000, http://www.villagevoice.com/issues/0037/jowitt.php.

4 Reference to Mike Ipiotis and the Tortuga Project's live performance "Roots of Hip Hop Culture," and conversation with the artists.

5 West African slaves brought to Brazil disguised their martial arts practices as dance in order to avoid reprisals from the slave masters. The warrior martial arts survive today as *capoeria angola*.

6 However, when he presented his complete solo show earlier that year, he received a rave review from the same newspaper.

7 "The Revolutionary Worker Interview: Danny Hoch's People," *Revolutionary Worker,* #909, 1 June 1997, http://rwor.org/a/v19/905-09/909/dhoch.htm.

8 Danny Hoch is a founding board member of the Active Element Foundation, which builds relationships among grassroots youth activists, professionals, donors, and artists through grantmaking, technical assistance, and hip-hop culture. In 2000, Active Element Foundation funded a thirteen-state Environmental Justice Youth Initiative, the Rap-The-Vote Campaign,

and ten youth-led, hip-hop-related organizations that campaigned against Proposition 21, a juvenile crime referendum approved by California voters in 2000. Also see www.dannyhoch.com.

9 In the Matter of the KBOO Foundation, 16 FCC Rcd 10741 (2001), the FCC fined KBOO radio of Portland, Oregon, $7,000 for "willfully broadcasting indecent language." After this happened, radio stations across the country refused to play Jones's song out of fear of getting fined by the FCC. After Jones brought a case against the FCC, which was dismissed by a New York federal court, the FCC vacated its earlier decision in In the Matter of the KBOO Foundation, 18 FCC Rcd 2472 (2003), and rescinded the fine because KBOO did not violate the statute.

10 Sarah Jones, interview with the author, 2 July 2001.

THE NEW GIRLS NETWORK

1 Anita Borg, *Technology, Democracy, and the Future* (Palo Alto, Calif.: Institute for Women and Technology, 2001), http://www.iwt.org/newsletter/nlarticles/techanddemocracy.html.

2 U.S. Department of Labor, Bureau of Labor Statistics, "BLS Releases 2000–2010 Employment Projections," 3 December 2001, http://www.bls.gov/news.release/ecopro.nr0.htm.

3 Mary Thom, *Balancing the Equation: Where Are Women and Girls in Science, Engineering, and Technology?* (New York: National Council for Research on Women, 2001) http://www.ncrw.org/research/iqsci.htm.

4 Patricia B. Campbell and Lesli Hoey, *Saving Babies and the Future of SMET in America* (Washington, D.C.: Congressional Commission on the Advancement of Women and Minorities in Science, Engineering and Technology Development [CAWMSET], 1999).

5 Advocates for Women in Science, Engineering and Mathematics, "AWSEM Gender Equity Facts in Brief," 25 May 2000, http://www.ogi.edu/satacad/awsem.html.

6 Congressional Commission on the Advancement of Women and Minorities in Science, Engineering and Technology Development (CAWMSET), *Land of Plenty: Diversity as America's Competitive Edge in Science, Engineering and Technology* (Arlington, Va.: 2000), 50.

7 American Association of University Women (AAUW) Educational Foundation, *The AAUW Report: How Schools Shortchange Girls* (Washington, D.C. 1992).

8 Patricia Campbell, interview with the author, 12 December 2000.

9 Patricia B. Campbell and Beatriz Chu Clewell, "Science, Math, and Girls . . . Still a Long Way to Go," *Education Week,* 15 September 1999, 50, 53.

10 Patricia Campbell, interview with the author, 12 December 2000.

11 Katie Wheeler, interview with the author, 26 April 2001.

12 CAWMSET, *Land of Plenty,* 59.

13 Ibid, 18.

14 Lisa Vaas, "Minorities Are Crossing the Digital Divide—Industry, Government Work to Close the Gap," *PC Week,* 31 January 2000, 65.

15 Anemona Hartocollis, "Ideas and Trends: Women Lawyers; Justice Is Blind. Also, a Lady," *New York Times,* 1 April 2001, late ed., 3.

16 National Science Foundation, "Table 26: Engineering Degrees Awarded by Degree Level and Sex of Recipient: 1966–2000" (Washington, D.C.), http://www.nsf.gov/sbe/srs/nsf02327/pdf/tab26.pdf.

17 Patricia Campbell, interview with the author, 12 December 2000.

18 Karen A. Calo, "Why Women Aren't Becoming Engineers," *San Francisco Chronicle,* 11 April 2001, 23.

19 Sokunthear Sy, interview with the author, 14 December 2000.

20 Laurie J. Flynn, "Compressed Data: Survey on Women's Role in Silicon Valley," *New York Times,* 23 April 2001, C3.

21 Sokunthear Sy, interview with the author, 14 December 2000.

22 Michael D. Haydock, "The GI Bill," *American History* 2, no. 17 (September–October 1996), 31.

23 CAWMSET, *Land of Plenty,* 11.

24 "Internet Is Great Equalizer for Women," *Employment Review,* February 2001, http://www.employmentreview.com/2001-02/departments/CNjobhunt.asp.

25 Ibid.

26 Center for Women's Business Research, "Key Facts," October 2001, http://www.nfwbo.org/key.html.

27 Ibid.

28 Ta'chelle Herron, interview with the author, 10 April 2001.

29 Flynn, "Women's Role in Silicon Valley."

30 Small Business Administration, Office of Women's Business Ownership, "Introduction," 18 April 2001, http://www.sbaonline.sba.gov/womeninbusiness/welcome.html.

31 Rebecca Tadikonda, interview with the author, 19 April 2001.

32 James N. Baron, Michael T. Hannan, Greta Hsu, and Ozgecan Kocak, "Gender and the Organization-Building Process in Young, High-Tech Firms," *The New Economic Sociology,* eds. Mauro F. Guillén, Randall Collins, Paula England, and Marshall Meyer (New York: Russell Sage Foundation).

33 David Brooks, *Bobos in Paradise* (New York: Touchstone, 2000), 10–11.

34 D. M. Osborne, "A Network of Her Own," *Inc. Magazine,* September 2000, http://www.inc.com/articles/details/0,3532,CID20125_REG3,00.html.

35 Ibid.

36 Springboard Enterprises, "About Springboard," 2001, http://www.springboard 2000.org.

37 Lakshmi Chaudhry, "Springboard for Women's Biz," *Wired Online,* 27 January 2000, http://www.wired.com/news/print/0,1294,33846,00.html.

38 Ibid.

39 Willa Seldon, interview with the author, 13 July 2001.

40 Robin Stern and Melissa Bradley, "Women and Money," *New Capitalist.*

41 Women all over the United States protested the appointment of John Ashcroft as attorney general because of his dismal record on women's issues. Rebecca Tadikonda, interview with the author, 19 April 2001.

42 Robin Clewley, "Women Power Web of Protests," *Wired Online,* 16 April 2001, http://www.wired.com/news/politics/0,1283,43063,00.html.

43 Institute for Women and Technology, http://www.iwt.org/home.html.

44 AAUW Educational Foundation, *Tech-Savvy: Educating Girls in the New Computer Age* (Washington, D.C., 2000), http://www.aauw.org/research/girls_education/techsavvy.cfm.

EXPORTING VIOLENCE

1 Spanish for "Hope, Light, Memory, Singer, Teacher."

2 Mark Danner, "The Truth About El Mozote," *New Yorker,* 6 December 1993, 50–74.

3 *School of Assassins,* directed by Robert Richter (New York: Richter Videos, 1994).

4 Ibid.

5 Danner, "The Truth About El Mozote," 50–74.

6 Jack Nelson-Pallmeyer, *School of Assassins: The Case for Closing the School of the Americas and for Fundamentally Changing U.S. Foreign Policy* (New York: Orbis Books, 1997), xi, xii.

7 "Accountability and Human Rights: The Report of the United Nations Commission on the Truth for El Salvador," *Human Rights Watch,* August 1993, http://www.hrw.org/americas/elsalvador.pdf.

8 *Vietnam Veterans Against the War Anti-Imperialists,* http://www.oz.net/~vvawai/.

9 "Reuters AlterNet—El Salvador," Reuters Foundation, http://www.alertnet.org/thefacts/countryprofiles/215623.htm?v=details.

10 "The Army's 'New' School Is the Same Old SOA," *School of the Americas Watch,* http://www.soaw.org/new/article.php?id=109.

11 "School of the Americas: U.S. Military Training for Latin American Countries," Letter Report, 22 August 1996, http://www.globalsecurity.org/intell/library/reports/gao/nsi96178.htm.

12 *School of Assassins,* directed by Richter.

13 For more information see the School of the Americas Watch homepage, http://www.soaw.org/new/faq.php?typeid=2, and School of the Americas Watch Northeast, http://www.soawne.org/colombia.html.

14 Gerry Gilmore, "School of the Americas: Spreading the Spirit of Democracy," *Soldiers*, September 1999, 2–7.

15 Joseph Blair, "SOA Isn't Teaching Democracy," *Columbus Ledger-Enquirer*, 20 July 1993, opinion page.

16 *School of Assassins*, directed by Robert Richter.

17 Office of Representative Joseph Kennedy, *Report on the School of the Americas*, 6 March 1997, http://www.fas.org/irp/congress/1997_rpt/soarpt.htm.

18 Ibid.

19 Nelson-Pallmeyer, *School of Assassins*, 65.

20 Ibid.

21 See mission statement from the official website of the Western Hemisphere Institute for Security Cooperation, http://www.benning.army.mil/whinsec/index.htm.

22 Nelson-Pallmeyer, *School of the Assassins*, 63.

23 "School of the Americas: U.S. Military Training for Latin American Countries."

24 Domestic Abuse Intervention Project, "Domestic Violence Handbook: Power and Control Wheel," 1999, http://www.domesticviolence.org/wheel.html.

25 Carol J. Adams, "I Just Raped My Wife! What Are You Going to Do About It, Pastor?" in *Transforming a Rape Culture*, eds. Emilie Buchwald, Pamela R. Fletcher, and Martha Roth (Minneapolis: Milkweed Editions, 1993), 67.

26 Susan George, *A Fate Worse Than Debt* (New York: Grove Weidenfeld, 1990), 22.

27 Ibid., 3, 49.

28 Feminist Majority Foundation, *Feminists Against Sweatshops*. Copyright 2001, http://www.feminist.org/other/sweatshops/sweatshops.html.

29 "WEDO Primer: Women and Trade: A Gender Agenda for the World Trade Organization, Women's Environment and Development Organization," November 1999, http://www.wedo.org/global/wedo_primer.htm. This

primer was researched by Riva Krut, Benchmark Environmental Consulting, with Naomi Gabarones.

30 Ibid.

31 Ibid.

32 Marceline White, *Women's Edge Factsheet: The World Trade Organization's Rulings and Women,* December 1999.

33 "WEDO Primer: Women and Trade."

34 Joseph G. Stiglitz, *Globalization and Its Discontents* (New York: W. W. Norton, 2002) 18.

35 "Statistics About Domestic Abuse," Women's Rural Advocacy Programs, http://www.letswrap.com/dvinfo/stats.htm.

36 Teresa Wiltz, "The Survivor: Sister Dianna Ortiz's Torturers Almost Took Her Life, and Her Faith," *Washington Post,* 26 May 2003, C01.

37 Dianna Ortiz, "The Vigil Begins," *Sojourners,* July–August 1996, 18.

38 Ibid.

39 Ibid.

40 Lisa Haugaard, "Colombia: 10,000 SOA Graduates," *State Terrorism in Colombia* (1993) was issued by a cluster of nongovernmental organizations (NGOs) including, most prominently, the Belgium-based Pax Christi International.

41 United States General Accounting Office, *School of the Americas: U.S. Military Training for Latin American Countries GAO/NSIAD-96-178,* 14 August 1996 (Washington, D.C.), http://www.gao.gov/archive/1996/ns96178.pdf.

42 Winifred Tate, "Repeating Past Mistakes: Aiding Counterinsurgency in Colombia," *NACLA Report on the Americas* 34, no. 2 (September–October 2000), 16–20.

43 Lisa Haugaard, "Colombia: 10,000 SOA Graduates," http://www.soawne.org/colombia.html.

44 "Plan Colombia, Fact Sheet, Bureau of Western Hemisphere Affairs," U.S. Department of State, (Washington, D.C.), http://www.state.gov/p/wha/rls/fs/2001/1042.htm; "U.S. Aid to Colombia: The Contents of the Colombia Aid Package," *Center for International Policy,* 26 January 2001.

45 Robert E. White, "Shades of Vietnam: Heading for Trouble in Colombia," *Washington Post,* 8 February 2000, A23.

46 Haugaard, "Colombia: 10,000 SOA Graduates."

47 Ricardo Vargas Meza, "Biowarfare in Colombia? A Controversial Fumigation Scheme," *NACLA Report on the Americas* 34, no. 2 (September–October 2000), 20, 23.

48 Karen Lyden Cox, "Questions Gerry Adams Could Have Asked the U.S. Congress About the Andean Regional Initiative," *The Blanket: A Journal of Protest and Dissent,* 4 May 2002, http://lark.phoblacht.net/questionsga.html.

49 Tate, "Repeating Past Mistakes," 16–20

50 Marjon van Royen, "Colombian Children Poisoned by U.S. Drug War Herbicide," *Asheville Global Report Online,* 28 December 2000, http://www.agrnews.org/issues/104/.

51 "Statement from the U'wa People," 10 August 1998, reprinted in *In Defense of Sacred Lands: The U'wa People's Struggle Against Big Oil,* Rainforest Action Network, http://www.ran.org/ran_campaigns/beyond_oil/oxy/uwa_facts.html.

52 Ibid.

53 *In Defense of Sacred Lands.*

54 Rod Amis, "Blood, Drugs and Oil," *G21 News,* Special Report, 10 March 1999, http://www.g21.net/news8.html.

55 Ann Schottman Knol, "Menominee Leader Blames U.S. for Deaths," *Milwaukee Journal Sentinel,* 7 March 1999, 1. Liz Hill, "U.S. Accused of Destabilizing Hostage Talks, Leading to Colombia Deaths," *Indian Country Today* (Rapid City, S.D.), 29 March 1999, A1.

56 In May 2002 Occidental announced it was withdrawing from its exploratory drilling sites on U'wa territory. Their first exploratory drilling effort turned up dry. They cited economic and public relations issues for the decision.

57 Garry Leech, *Colombia Report: The Case of the U'wa* (New York: Information Network of the Americas, 9 July 2000).

58 Lisa Haugaard, "Declassified Army and CIA Manuals Used in Latin America: An Analysis of Their Content," Latin America Working Group, 18

February 1997; an excerpt from the Human Resource Exploitation Manual. Washington, DC.

DOMESTIC WORKERS ORGANIZE IN THE GLOBAL CITY

1 On June 3, 2003, CAAAV's Women Workers Project joined other members of the Domestic Workers United coalition for Mayor Bloomberg's signing of Intro. No. 96 and Resolution No. 135 in support of rights and dignity for domestic workers. The new law follows powerful organizing on the part of hundreds of Domestic Workers United members and compels domestic employment placement agencies in New York City to take critical measures to ensure the protection of workers' rights. Several New York legislators including Council Members Christine Quinn, John Liu, and Charles Barron have pledged their allegiance to domestic workers, vowing to lend their support to policies that further protect their rights.

2 Grace Chang, *Disposable Domestics: Immigrant Women Workers in the Global Economy* (Boston: South End Press, 2000), 1–17.

3 Officially called the Illegal Immigration Reform and Immigrant Responsibility Act. This act also allows legal immigrants to be penalized.

4 For a good discussion on forced migration, see Saskia Sassen, *The Mobility of Labor and Capital: A Study in International Investment and Labor Flow* (Cambridge and New York: Cambridge University Press, 1988).

5 See "Dignity and the Domestic Sweatshop," *CAAAV Voice* 10, no. 4 (Fall 2000), 4–7.

A BAPTISM BY FIRE

1 Twenty-three years later Lébron was released from prison under the clemency of the Carter administration.

2 This denial of statehood followed Lébron's attack on the House of Representatives.

3 Orishas are deities in the Yoroba and Santería religious traditions.

4 Mayor Santiago Collazo of Vieques, interview with the author, 1995.

5 Luis Muñoz Marin was governor of Puerto Rico from 1948 to 1964.

6 Ernest Renan, *What Is a Nation? Qu'est qu'une nation?*, trans. Ida Mae Snyder (Paris: Calmann-Levy, 1882), 26–29.

7 The halting of military exercises on Vieques was originally a George W. Bush administration promise, but since the 9/11 attacks on the World Trade Center and the Pentagon, American resistance to the military's occupation of the island has lessened.

8 Stephen Trombley, "Exploring Sterilization," in *The Right to Reproduce: A History of Coercive Sterilization* (London: Weidenfeld and Nicolson, 1988), 214–34.

9 Harriet B. Presser, "Puerto Rico: Recent Trends in Fertility and Sterilization," *Family Planning Perspectives* 12, no. 2 (March–April 1980).

10 *La Operación,* directed and produced by Ana Maria García (New York: Cinema Guild, 1982, videocassette).

11 Robert Rabin, *Compendio de lecturas sobre la historia de Vieques* (Vieques, Puerto Rico: Museo Fuerte Conde Mirasol, 1994).

12 Toby Eglund, "Vieques: Puerto Rico Under Fire," *The Gully,* 3 May 2000, http://www.thegully.com/essays/puertorico/000503vieques.html.

13 Committee for the Rescue and Development of Vieques (CRDV), Press Release, 14 February 2002. Dr. Porto is the environmental adviser to the CRDV. For more information about CRDV, e-mail bieke@prdigital.com.

14 Betita Martinez, *De Colores Means All of Us* (Boston: South End Press, 1998), xvii.

WHEN TRANSGENDERED PEOPLE SUE AND WIN

1 The website http://www.transgender.org is a comprehensive gathering of transsexual-transgender support organizations on the Internet. Another significant Internet presence is the Ingersoll Gender Center at www.ingersolcenter.org. The Ingersoll Center is a nonprofit agency that provides services to the transsexual, transvestite, and transgender community. Its website is a wealth of contacts, support groups, publications, mailing lists, and information. For a general perspective on the transsexual civil rights struggle, see Kristine W. Holt, "Reevaluating Holloway: Title VII, Equal Protection, and the Evolution of a Transgender Jurisprudence," *Temple Law Review* 70 (1997),

283–319; and Hasan Shafiqullah, "Shape-Shifters, Masqueraders, and Subversives: An Argument for the Liberation of Transgendered Individuals," *Hastings Women's Law Journal* 8 (1997), 195.

2 Janice G. Raymond, *The Transsexual Empire: The Making of the She-Male* (London: Women's Press, 1980). For a detailed account of a conflict between feminist organizers of a "womyn-born womyn only" music festival in Michigan and transsexual activists, see Riki Anne Wilchins, *Read My Lips: Sexual Subversion and the End of Gender* (Ithaca, N.Y.: Firebrand Books, 1997), 112–14; and Pat Califia, *Sex Changes: The Politics of Transgenderism* (San Francisco: Cleis Press, 1997), 227–29. The activists set up "Camp Trans" outside the festival after being turned away for not being "real women," and they offered workshops on female to male (FTM) and transsexual issues for the festival goers. At one point a debate broke out between preoperative and postoperative male to female (MTF) transsexuals, with one postoperative woman arguing that she should be admitted but those who still had some form of male genitalia should not. See Califia, *Sex Changes,* 229.

3 D. Travers Scott, "Le Freak, C'est Chic! Le Fag, Quelle Drag! Celebrating the Collapse of Homosexual Identity," in *PoMoSexuals: Challenging Assumptions About Gender and Sexuality,* eds. Carol Queen and Lawrence Schimel (San Francisco: Cleis Press, 1997), 67.

4 Ibid., 65.

5 Califia, *Sex Changes,* 273, discussing Kate Bornstein, *Gender Outlaw: On Men, Women, and the Rest of Us* (New York and London: Routledge, 1994).

6 *Rentos v. Oce Office Systems,* 1996 U.S. Dist. LEXIS 19060 (S.D.N.Y. 1996), 18. This federal trial court, noting the arguments over how to identify Ms. Corrine Rento's sex, was nonetheless able to say that "this question of categorization is, of course, critical to the application of the federal, state, and local anti-discrimination laws," 19.

7 Federal Rule of Civil Procedure 12(b)(6) allows the defendant to move to dismiss the lawsuit because no legal claim has been properly stated. One of the elements of a sex discrimination suit, for example, is to plead that the event (firing, not hiring) happened on account of the plaintiff's sex. If a transsexual really wants to plead that it happened because her boss was disgusted at her plans to take hormones and have her penis removed and could not bear to look at her every day, then the lawsuit may not really be about

"sex," as in "because I'm a woman." Thus the choice is to fit erroneously into the category meant for nontranssexual women or to face dismissal of one's claim.

8 David Gelman et al., "Born or Bred?" *Newsweek,* 24 February 1992, 46; Kim Painter, "Is There a Gay Gene?" *USA Today,* 16 July 1993, 1A.

9 Several U.S. cities, including San Francisco, Pittsburgh, and Boulder, have added clauses to their civil rights ordinances to protect transsexuals and transgendered people. See http://www.transgenderlaw.org for a collection of civil rights policies from across the country.

10 Wendy Brown, *States of Injury: Power and Freedom in Late Modernity* (Princeton, N.J.: Princeton University Press, 1995), 99. For additional discussion, see Vicki Schultz, "Women 'Before' the Law: Judicial Stories About Women, Work, and Sex Segregation on the Job," in *Feminists Theorize the Political,* eds. Judith Butler and Joan W. Scott (New York: Routledge, 1992), 297–338.

11 The Supreme Court has since overruled Bowers, overturning a similar Texas law that criminalized homosexual sex. See *Lawrence v. Texas,* 123 S. Ct. 2472 (2003). The reasoning of the majority opinion focused on the privacy interests of the two men (who had been arrested in a private home) rather than on whether gays and lesbians should be a legally protected class.

12 Janet Halley, "The Politics of the Closet: Towards Equal Protection for Gay, Lesbian, and Bisexual Identity," *University of California, Los Angeles, Law Review* 36, no. 5 (June 1989), 915–16, 920–21.

13 Ibid., 97.

14 Janet Halley, "'Like Race' Arguments," in *What's Left of Theory? New Work on the Politics of Literary Theory,* eds. Judith Butler, John Guillory, and Kendall Thomas (New York: Routledge, 2000), 51.

15 Janet Halley, "Sexuality, Cultural Tradition, and the Law," *Yale Journal of Law and Humanities* 8, no. 1 (1996), 103.

16 Shannon Minter, "Do Transsexuals Dream of Gay Rights? Getting Real About Transgender Inclusion in the Gay Rights Movement," *New York Law School Journal of Human Rights* 17 (2000), 592.

17 See, for example, books written from therapists' perspectives, such as Mildred L. Brown, *True Selves: Understanding Transsexualism—For Families, Friends, Coworkers, and Helping Professionals* (San Francisco: Jossey-Bass Press, 1996); and Kim Elizabeth Stuart, *The Unvited Dilemma: A Question of Gender* (Portland, Ore.: Metamorphous Press, 1991).

18 Of course, law has not created single-handedly the hope to unify body and soul—many people spend their lives in the same pursuit as the transsexuals described here. As Ronald Garet, professor of law and religion at the University of Southern California Law Center, argues in his article on self-transformation and the ethics of sex change, "Transsexuals hold out the same hopes for their bodies that other people do. . . . They want to let go of what is false and unimportant and cling to the truth about themselves. In this, again, they are like all of us, even to the point of not being able to prove which is the truth and which the falsity." "Self-Transformability," *Southern California Law Review* 65, no. 1 (November 1991), 121–203, 203.

19 Jan Morris, *Conundrum* (New York: Harcourt Brace Jovanovich, 1974), 104.

20 Riki Anne Wilchins, *Read My Lips: Sexual Subversion and the End of Gender* (Ann Arbor, Mich.: Firebrand Books, 1997), 67.

21 See Leslie Feinberg, *Transgender Warriors: Making History from Joan of Arc to RuPaul* (Boston: Beacon Press, 1996), 21–29.

22 Wilchins, *Read My Lips,* 67.

23 *B v. Lackner,* 80 Cal. App. 3d 64 (1978). The plaintiffs I discuss in this section are male-to-female transsexuals, so I use the feminine pronouns. In *Davidson v. Aetna Life & Casualty Insurance Company,* 101 Misc. 2d 1, 420 N.Y.S. 2d 450 (1979), a private insurance company was not permitted to exclude sex reassignment surgery from reimbursement under its policy. The company argued likewise that the surgery was essentially cosmetic, but the court followed the same reasoning discussed in *Lackner* to classify sex-change surgery as a cure for medical illness.

24 *B v. Lackner,* 66.

25 Ibid., 70.

26 Ibid., 71.

27 "Gender identity disorder" is the working medical definition applied to anyone seeking sex reassignment surgery, characterized by "a strong and persistent cross-gender identification (not merely a desire for any perceived cultural advantages of being the other sex)" and "persistent discomfort about one's assigned sex or a sense of inappropriateness in the gender role of that sex." *Diagnostic and Statistical Manual of Mental Disorders (DSM-IV-TR),* (Washington, D.C.: American Psychiatric Association, 2000), 532–33, 537.

28 *Pinneke v. Preisser,* 623 F.2d 546 (1980).

29 Americans with Disabilities Act, sec. 3(2), 42 U.S.C.A. sec. 12102(2) (1990).

30 *Smith v. Rasmussen,* 249 F.3d 755, 761, 760 (2001).

31 *Doe v. Yunits,* 2001 Mass. Super. LEXIS 327 (2001). See also a New Jersey Supreme Court case, *Enriquez v. West Jersey Health Systems,* 777 A.2d 365 (2001), holding that gender dysphoria–transsexualism could indeed be a disability under that state's laws and summarizing the position of many other states on that question.

32 Ibid., 17.

33 Ibid.

34 *Diagnostic and Statistical Manual of Mental Disorders (DSM-IV-TR),* (Washington, D.C.: American Psychiatric Association, 2000), 532–33, 537.

35 Harry Benjamin International Gender Dysphoria Association, Inc., *Standards of Care,* 7 June 1999, http://www.hbigda.org/soc/html (visited February 11, 2004).

36 Ibid.

37 *In the Matter of Richard Clark Maloney,* 2001 Ohio App. LEXIS 3550 (13 August 2001), 9.

38 Ibid.

39 James Green, Introduction to *Transgender Equality: A Handbook for Activists and Policymakers,* eds. Paisley Currah and Shannon Minter (Policy Institute of the National Gay and Lesbian Task Force, 2000), 7. The handbook is available on the NGLTF website: http://www.ngltf.org/library.

40 Wilchins, *Read My Lips,* 47.

41 Kim Elizabeth Stuart, *The Uninvited Dilemma: A Question of Gender* (Portland, OR: Metamorphous Press, 1991).

42 Ibid., 118–20.

43 *Christian v. Randall,* 33 Colo. App. 129 (1973).

44 *Frances M. Coulter v. David F. Coulter,* 141 Colo. 237 (1959).

45 *Christian,* 131.

46 Ibid., 133, 132.

47 *Daly v. Daly,* 715 P.2d 56, 59, 57n (1986).

48 Ibid., 59, emphasis mine.

49 An article in a *New York Times Magazine* symposium on love in the twenty-first century tells about a lesbian couple turned man and woman when one partner underwent a sex transformation, focusing particularly upon the lesbian woman's reactions to finding herself now in love with a man. The article is unique as a mainstream, sympathetic portrait of a relationship that takes note of the transgendered person's partner, who is often invisible in other accounts. Sara Corbett, "When Debbie Met Christina, Who Then Became Chris: Does a Sex Change Mean the End of a Relationship?" *New York Times Magazine,* 14 October 2001, 84–87.

50 Riki Anne Wilchins, "Lines in the Sand, Cries of Desire," in *PoMoSexuals,* 141–42.

51 *J.L.S. v. D.K.S./S.K.S.,* 943 S.W.2d 766, 775, 769, 775 (1997).

52 *Daly v. Daly,* 62.

53 Kevin R. Johnson, "Race, the Immigration Laws, and Domestic Race Relations: A 'Magic Mirror' into the Heart of Darkness," *Indiana Law Journal* 73 (1998), 1111–59.

54 *Ulane v. Eastern Airlines,* 581 F. Supp. 821 (1983); overruled in *Ulane v. Eastern Airlines,* 742 F.2d 1081 (7th Cir.,1984); Lisa C. Bower, "Queer Acts and the Politics of 'Direct Address': Rethinking Law, Culture, and Community," *Law and Society Review* 28 (1994), 1009–38, 1023.

55 Testimony of Jack Berger before the Eastern Airlines Pilots System Board of Adjustment, Miami, Fla. (18 November 1982), doc. 977-1155, 1017–19, box 193001. See also Transcript of Proceedings, vol. 15 (16 December 1983), 1030–1127, box 193005.

56 *Price Waterhouse v. Hopkins,* 490 U.S. 228, 235, 288 (1989).

57 Mary Anne C. Case, "Disaggregating Gender from Sex and Sexual Orientation: The Effeminate Man in the Law and Feminist Jurisprudence," *Yale Law Journal* 105, no. 1 (October 1995), 4.

58 *Rosa v. Park West Bank & Trust Co.,* 214 F.3d 213, 214 (1st Cir. 2000).

59 See *Schwenk v. Hartford,* 204 F.3d 1187, 1201–2 (9th Cir. 2000), a prisoner's rights case involving a transsexual woman sexually assaulted by a guard, in which the Ninth Circuit concluded that "the initial judicial approach taken in cases such as *Holloway* [which denied transsexuals rights under Title VII] has been overruled by the logic and language of *Price Waterhouse,*" at 1201. Both the Gender Motivated Violence Act and Title VII were found to protect people based upon "sex" as well as "gender," with the latter category extending to transsexuals and transgendered people.

60 *Broadus v. State Farm Insurance,* U.S. Dist. LEXIS 19919 (2000), 11, 14.

61 *Doe v. Yunits,* Mass. Super. LEXIS 491 (2000), 4, 14.

62 Case, "Disaggregating Gender from Sex and Sexual Orientation"; and Francisco Valdes, "Unpacking Hetero-Patriarchy: Tracing the Conflation of Sex, Gender, and Sexual Orientation to its Origins," *Yale Journal of Law & Humanities* 8 (1996), 163, n.7–8.

63 Judith Butler's answer to the contradictions of antidiscrimination law is to argue for "unsettling the social conditions by which persons become intelligible at all" though a reflexive process of encounter. Butler, "Appearances Aside," *California Law Review* 88 (2000), 63. For her process to work, "it must be possible for a person whose appearance calls the category of the person into question to enter the field of appearance precisely as a person."

64 Judith Butler urges feminists to bear in mind that these words are not produced innocently but rather are forged and put to use by power: "It is not enough to inquire into how women might become more fully represented in language and politics. Feminist critique ought also to understand how the

category of 'women,' the subject of feminism, is produced and restrained by the very structures of power through which emancipation is sought. Indeed, the question of women as the subject of feminism raises the possibility that there may not be a subject who stands 'before' the law, awaiting representation in or by the law. Perhaps the subject . . . is constituted by the law as the fictive foundation of its own claim to legitimacy." Butler, *Gender Trouble: Feminism and the Subversion of Identity* (New York: Routledge, 1990), 2–3.

65 Case, "Disaggregating Gender from Sex and Sexual Orientation."

66 Califia, *Sex Changes,* 277.

BEARING THE BLAME

1 Tim McGirk, "Border Clash," *Time,* 26 June 2000, 26, 27.

2 Jim Motavalli, "Balancing Act: Can America Sustain a Population of 500 Million—or Even a Billion by 2100?" *E-Magazine,* VIII no. 3, Nov–Dec 2000, 26–33.

3 Negative Population Growth, "Iowa Public Awareness Campaign Print Ad," http://www.npg.org.

4 Ellen Percy Kraly, *U.S. Immigration and the Environment: Scientific Research and Analytic Issues* (Washington, D.C.: U.S. Commission on Immigration Reform, February 1995), iv.

5 Scipio Garling and Ira Mehlman, *The Environmentalist's Guide to a Sensible Immigration Policy* (Washington, D.C.: Federation for American Immigration Reform, 1999), Chapter 2, http://www.fairus.org/Research

6 See www.fairus.org.

7 Brad Erickson and China Brotsky, "Blunting the Wedge," *Political Environments* 6 (1998).

8 Negative Population Growth, "Why Does Our Government Allow Over One Million New Immigrants to Come Here Every Year?" Advertisement (1996).

9 Kraly, *U.S. Immigration and the Environment,* i.

10 Saskia Sassen, *The Mobility of Labor and Capital: A Study in International Investment and Labor Flow* (Cambridge and New York: Cambridge University Press, 1988).

11 Patricia Hynes, "Taking Population out of the Equation: Reformulating I = PAT" (North Amherst, Mass.: Institute on Women and Technology, 1993), 49.

12 United Nations Development Programme, *Human Development Report 1998* (New York: Oxford University Press, 1998), 49–50.

13 Cited in Alan Thein Durning, "The Conundrum of Consumption," in *Beyond the Numbers: A Reader on Population, Consumption and the Environment,* ed. L.A. Mazur (Washington, D.C.: Island Press, 1994), 44.

14 Carrying Capacity Network, Member Mailing Letterhead (1997).

15 Garrett Hardin, "Sheer Numbers: Can Environmentalists Grasp the Nettle of Population?" *E-Magazine,* I no. 6, (1990), 40–47.

16 Eric B. Ross, *The Malthus Factor: Poverty, Politics and Population in Capitalist Development* (New York: Zed Books, 1998), 204.

17 Penn Loh, "Border-Patrol Ecology," *San Francisco Bay Guardian,* 1 December 1993, 6.

18 Negative Population Growth, "Immigration Fuels U.S. Population Growth," Advertisement (1996).

19 John Higham, *Strangers in the Land: Patterns of American Nativism, 1860–1925* (New York: Atheneum Press, 1963), 152.

20 Mark H. Haller, *Eugenics: Hereditarian Attitudes in American Thought* (New Brunswick, N.J.: Rutgers University Press, 1963), 146, 154.

21 Ibid., 155.

22 Anna E. Blount, "Large Families and Human Waste," *Birth Control Review,* September 1918.

23 Chandler Owen, "Women and Children of the South," *Birth Control Review,* January 1919.

24 Margaret Sanger, *Women and the New Race* (New York: Blue Ribbon Books, 1920), 33.

25 Margaret Sanger, *Pivot of Civilization* (New York: Brentano's, 1922), 101–2.

26 Albert P. Van Dusen, "Birth Control as Viewed by a Sociologist," *Birth Control Review,* May 1924, 134.

27 See, for example, articles in these issues: September 1918, May 1919, March 1920, January 1921, and March 1923. This listing is by no means extensive; it merely provides examples of *Birth Control Review* articles with neo-Malthusian content. Margaret Sanger, "Birth Strike to Avert World Famine," *Birth Control Review,* January 1920.

28 Sanger, *Pivot of Civilization,* 19.

29 Dorothy Roberts, *Killing the Black Body* (New York: Vintage Books, 1997), 76.

30 Quoted in ibid.

31 Ibid., 86.

32 Linda Gordon, *Woman's Body, Woman's Right: Birth Control in America* (New York: Penguin Books, 1990), 276.

33 See, for example, Margaret Sanger, "The World We Live In," *Birth Control Review,* March 1923. This editorial blames India's distress not on British oppression but on India's high birth and death rates.

34 Gordon, *Woman's Body, Woman's Right,* 393–94.

35 Cited in Allan Chase, *The Legacy of Malthus: The Social Costs of the New Scientific Racism* (New York: Alfred A. Knopf, 1977), 367.

36 Gordon, *Woman's Body, Woman's Right,* 394.

37 Betsy Hartmann, *Reproductive Rights and Wrongs: The Global Politics of Population Control* (Boston: South End Press, 1995), 101–5.

38 Committee to Check the Population Explosion, Advertisement, *New York Times,* May 11, 1969.

39 Gordon, *Woman's Body, Woman's Right,* 395.

40 Paul Ehrlich, *The Population Bomb* (New York: Ballantine Books, 1968).

41 Lawrence Lader, *Breeding Ourselves to Death* (New York: Ballantine Books, 1971), 6.

42 Cited in Chase, *Legacy of Malthus*, 384.

43 Hartmann, *Reproductive Rights and Wrongs*, 141–42.

44 Cited in ibid., 27.

45 Project USA, "Our Billboards," available at http://www.projectusa.org/pics.html.

46 Carrying Capacity Network, "Mission Statement," http://www.carryingcapacity.org.

47 Lisa Lollock, "The Foreign Born Population in the United States: Population Characteristics, March 2000," U.S. Census Bureau, January 2001 http://www.census.gov/prod/2000pubs/p20-534.pdf

48 Political Ecology Group, *Immigration and the U.S.: Myths and Facts*, http://www.igc.org/peg.

49 U.S. Census Bureau, *DP-2. Social Characteristics: 1990, Data Set: 1990 Summary Tape File 3, Geographic Area*, http://factfinder.census.gov.

50 Cited in Santiago O'Donnell, "Angry Latino Leaders Decry Gallegly Proposal," *Los Angeles Times*, Ventura County ed., 26 October 1991, B5.

51 Population-Environment Balance, "ASAP! Immigration Moratorium Action Plan," http://www.balance.org/asap/asapplan.html.

52 *Diversity Alliance for a Sustainable America*, "DASA's Mission Statement and Platform," http://www.diversityalliance.org.

53 Michael Fix, Jeffrey S. Passel, and Wendy Zimmermann, *Summary of Facts About Immigrants' Use of Welfare*, http://urban.org/url.cfm?ID=410345.

54 Dorothy Roberts, "Who May Give Birth to Citizens," in *Immigrants Out!* ed. Juan Perea (New York and London: New York University Press: 1997), 205.

55 U.S. Department of Justice, Immigration and Naturalization Service, and U.S. Department of Labor, Bureau of International Labor Affairs, *The Triennial Comprehensive Report on Immigration* (Washington, D.C.: 1999), 153.

56 Michael Fix and Jeffery S. Passel, *Trends in Noncitizens' and Citizens' Use of Public Benefits Following Welfare Reform: 1994–97* (Washington, D.C.: Urban Institute, 1999), 7–8.

57 Diversity Alliance for a Sustainable America, "DASA's Mission Statement."

58 "NPG Special Report; Our Demographic Future: Why Population Matters to America," http://www.npg.org/specialreports/demofuture/demofuture _section3.htm.

59 Population-Environment Balance, *Balance Newsletter,* 1993, http://www. balance.org.

60 See, for example, Mark W. Novak, *Immigration and U.S. Population Growth: An Environmental Perspective* (Washington, D.C.: Negative Population Growth, 1997).

61 Quoted in Erickson and Brotsky, "Blunting the Wedge."

62 Hartmann, *Reproductive Rights and Wrongs,* 200.

63 Other organizations that bring a multi-issue analysis to environmental justice and reproductive health activism are Sistas on the Rise in Bronx, NY; Khmer Girls in Action in Los Angeles, CA; and the Los Angeles Indigenous People's Alliance.

SHE WHO BELIEVES IN FREEDOM

1 Jerome Miller, "American Gulag," *YES! Magazine* 15 (February 2000), http://www.futurenet.org/15prisons/miller.htm.

2 Prison Activist Resource Center, "Education vs. Incarceration: A Stacked Deck," http://www.prisonactivist.org/factsheets/ed-vs-inc.pdf.

3 Fox Butterfield, "Study Finds Big Increase in Black Men as Inmates Since 1980," *New York Times,* 28 August 2002, late ed., A1.

4 "Class Dismissed: Higher Education vs. Corrections During the Wilson Years," Press Release, Center for Juvenile and Criminal Justice (2002), http://www.cjcj.org/pubs/classdis/classdis.html.

5 Alan Elsner, "U.S. Prison Population Social Costs Mount," Reuters, 23 January 2001.

6 Tracy L. Huling, "Prisons as a Growth Industry in Rural America: An Exploratory Discussion of the Effects on Young African American Men in

the Inner Cities," paper presented at Consultation of the U.S. Commission on Civil Rights, April 15, 1999; also in "The Crisis of the Young African Male in the Inner Cities," U.S. Commission on Civil Rights, Washington, D.C., July 2000.

7 Elsner, "U.S. Prison Population Social Costs Mount."

8 John Irwin and Jason Ziedenberg, "America's One Million Nonviolent Prisoners," Press Release, Justice Policy Institute (March 1999).

9 Angela Y. Davis, "Masked Racism: Reflections on the Prison Industrial Complex," *Colorlines* 1, no. 2 (Fall 1998), 12.

10 Mandatory minimum laws remove judges' discretion to determine sentences according to the crime committed, and according to its context. For example, a drug addict who is charged with drug possession may be best served by an effective treatment program; however, as a result of mandatory minimum laws, the judge is forced to sentence the addict to twenty years of hard time. Mandatory minimum sentences mostly and most unfairly apply to drug offenses. Organizations like Families Against Mandatory Minimums point out that both drug addicts and the partners of drug dealers—mostly women—are caught in the net of mandatory minimums.

11 Arthur Santana, "Female Prison Ranks Double; Citing Study, Norton Plans to Improve Conditions, *Washington Post,* 1 February 2000, A08.

12 Ibid.

13 Karen Gullo, "Report Decries Jailing Girls," *Chicago Tribune,* 16 May 2001, 8.

14 Real earnings are the real value of a dollar earned. Low-income male workers may make more in dollars today than they did ten years ago, but the value of that money is falling. This explains why a factory worker in 1965 might have been able to buy a new car or a house, but his twenty-first-century equivalent is taking the bus and renting. Women made so much less than men in 1965 that their wages have risen relative to low-income men's but only because they were starting at such a deficit; the wage floor was very low. David Moberg, "Bridging the Gap: Why Women Still Don't Get Equal Pay," *In These Times,* 8 January 2001, 24.

15 Cited in Huling, "Prisons as a Growth Industry."

16 Miller, "American Gulag."

17 Punitive legislation like three strikes laws has meted out life sentences to people whose third and final "strike" could have been theft in which no one was injured and whose first two "strikes" could have been relatively minor drug possession. The first President Bush, a militant drug warrior, inaugurated Operation Weed and Seed militarized sweeps, allegedly to seize drugs, in communities of color that were already embattled by Ronald Reagan's war on social and human services.

18 Gregory Winters, "Trading Places: When Prisons Substitute for Social Programs," *Colorlines* 1, no. 2 (Fall 1998), 21.

19 Jerome Miller, *Search and Destroy: African-American Males in the Criminal Justice System* (New York: Cambridge University Press, 1996), 1.

20 David Courtwright, "Drug War's Hidden Toll," *Issues in Science and Technology* 13, no. 2 (1996–97), 71–77.

AFTERWORD

1 Michael Hardt and Antonio Negri, *Empire* (Cambridge, Mass.: Harvard University Press, 2000), xi.

2 See the North Carolina Lambda Youth Network's website: http://www.nclambdayouth.org/whoweare.htm.

3 Movement infrastructure is laid out in great detail in Jean Hardisty's *Mobilizing Resentment* (Boston: Beacon Press, 1999), in which she provides a map of the movement infrastructure of the right and recommendations for what the left needs. Hardisty, *Mobilizing Resentment,* 13.

4 Some such networks are the Third Wave Foundation, the Active Element Foundation, Listen Inc., Youth Action, W.E.R.I.S.E., Direct Action Network, Food Not Bombs, Southerners on New Ground, Black Radical Congress, Youth Force Coalition, Just Act, 21st Century Youth Leadership Movement, National Youth Advocacy Coalition, National Gay and Lesbian Task Force, Student Environmental Action Coalition, United Students Against Sweatshops, Student Alliance to Reform Corporations, Students for a Free Tibet, and Indymedia.

5 Hardisty, *Mobilizing Resentment*, 14.

6 Kimberlé Crenshaw ed., *Critical Race Theory: The Key Writings That Formed the Movement* (New York: New Press, 1995), 357.

7 See the Audre Lorde Project's website, http://www.alp.org/alerts.html.

8 Sally Covington, *Moving a Public Policy Agenda: The Strategic Philanthropy of Conservative Foundations* (Washington, D.C.: National Committee for Responsive Philanthropy, July 1997).

9 Chris Grumm, interview with Vivien Labaton, August 10, 2001.

10 Billy Wimsatt, interview with Vivien Labaton, August 10, 2001.

ACKNOWLEDGMENTS

Many friends, allies, and supporters have helped us to bring this book from an idea to a reality. Without them, *The Fire This Time* would not exist, and neither would the new feminist activism of which we write.

A huge thank-you to Jill Grinberg, our literary agent, who supported the book from the beginning. She acted as a sounding board for ideas, allayed our fears, gave us pep talks, offered important insights as the book developed, answered many questions, and gave us invaluable advice. Jill has been a superwoman of a literary agent, and we feel blessed to be working with her. And many thanks to our editors at Anchor Books, Alice van Straalen and Amber Hoover, whose careful guidance and precise feedback helped us to be better writers.

Thank you to the board and staff—past and present—of the Third Wave Foundation for providing the space from which we were able to see, and participate in, the emergence of a broader, more inclusive feminism. To all the people with whom we have worked at Third Wave and other progressive feminist organizations, you have opened up our worlds and our imaginations in ways we never thought possible.

This book has come to fruition because of the hard work and patience of the contributors to this anthology. We thank all of you from the deepest place in our hearts. If not for your vigilant pursuit of a feminist future, the movement would want for the fresh energies you have brought to it. Those who took the time to read parts of the manuscript along the way and provide critical feedback also have our most sincere gratitude: Nicholas Arons, Rosanna Barbero, Charles Barley, Lara Bazelon, Joshua Breitbart, Todd Chandler, Peter DiCola, R. Erica Doyle, Gita Drury, Victoria Eby, Alexis Gannon, Megan Hustad, Leila Kazemi, Margherita Maffii, Catita Perron, Cathy Schlund-Vials, Jamie Schweser, Shauna Seliy, and Hannah Sholl. A special thanks to Melissa Fendell, whose research efficiency provided the help we needed to meet deadlines while simultaneously living our lives, and to Nicholas Arons, whose eleventh hour editorial support was invaluable. Thanks, too, to Dawn Davis, who initially acquired this collection for Anchor and had faith in this project in its early stages.

Thanks to the following organizations for providing inspiration and moral support: Active Element Foundation, the Black Took Collective, New WORLD Theater, Political Research Associates, Third Wave Foundation, W.E.R.I.S.E., Women's Funding Network, and Womyn's Agenda for Change.

We are extremely grateful to family and friends, particularly Arnold Labaton, Doris Martin, and Kathy Martell, who helped guide us through this process with love. There are several women in particular who have inspired us as we paved our own path in the feminist movement. As we work and encourage other young women to believe that they can accomplish change in the world, Regina Barreca, Angela Davis, Amy Richards, and Gloria Steinem still inspire us. We will always be grateful to them.

Last, we want to thank those who came before us, the women who laid the groundwork for the expanded nature of our current social and political feminist pursuits, those countless women who motivate us to do activist work. We also want to thank those who could not participate in previous feminist movements because they were too poor, or too isolated, or too beaten down, or too otherwise burdened to care about much more than daily survival. We thank all of these women for the example of their courage.